An Introduction to the Theory of Macro-Economic Policy

An Introduction to the Theory of Macro-Economic Policy

THIRD EDITION

G.K. Shaw
READER IN ECONOMICS, UNIVERSITY OF ST. ANDREWS

Martin Robertson

First edition published 1971
Second edition published 1973 by
Martin Robertson & Company Ltd
17 Quick Street London N1 8HL

ISBN 0 85520 024 3 (paperback)
ISBN 0 85520 023 5 (case)

Printed by The Pitman Press Bath

Contents

For Nobbins

Preface

The present volume is directed towards the student who has followed a fairly basic course in macro-economic theory but who has not progressed far into the more esoteric branches of the subject and who has not yet mastered the more refined quantitative techniques which necessarily accompany them. It seeks to introduce some controversial issues in macro-economic policy which derive from the more advanced treatment of the underlying theory. To this end, it inevitably simplifies and glosses over the refinements and sophistications of the protagonists in the debate. It is hoped, nonetheless, that these respective viewpoints are presented without undue distortion of their basic positions.

The book avoids mathematical technique and for the most part discussion of empirical findings. The latter decision stems partly from the conflicting nature of the conclusions suggested by the available evidence and also from the belief that a thorough assessment of the econometric evidence presupposes a degree of sophistication beyond that reasonably expected of the reader to whom this volume is directed. It should also be noted that, whilst the concern is with policy formation, the approach is essentially theoretical and institutional matter is generally avoided. As far as is possible, the book adopts an impartial stance; it seeks to clarify and describe the main areas of controversy whilst in no way attempting the resolution of conflict.

The present work makes no great claim to originality. Indeed, it is decidedly eclectic and I have drawn upon numerous sources both published and unpublished. With regard to the former, it is hoped that full acknowledgement is contained in the text and I apologise if through oversight on my part this is not the case. With regard to the latter I must express my indebtedness to those who have helped me most. To Professor Kilpatrick of Cornell University and to Professor Rousseas of Vassar College I express my thanks for first introducing me to the fields of fiscal policy and monetary policy respectively. To

Professor Shoup of Columbia University I owe an even greater debt for showing me that economic problems are never so simple as they may appear at first sight. I must also acknowledge my indebtedness to past and current colleagues at the Universities of York and St. Andrews. To Professor Peacock of the University of York I am especially grateful not only for many helpful insights into policy issues generally but also for allowing me to draw generously upon works which we have co-authored. To Professor Robson of St. Andrews University I am grateful for help with the development section and to Dr. Jones-Lee of the same institution I express my appreciation for showing me that pure intuition is seldom sufficient. I also acknowledge my debt to countless students, both past and present, who by their questions and occasionally by the lack of them have sharpened my awareness of the basic issues. My wife is responsible for considerable improvements in style and also undertook the laborious task of compiling the index.

Needless to say, the aforementioned are in no way responsible for the errors which remain but deserve full credit for banishing many others out of sight and, hopefully, out of mind.

Preface to the Second Edition

I am grateful to my publishers for allowing me to revise the present work especially since it enables me to take account of the many suggestions and comments for improvement which I have received from students and colleagues in the field. In particular, I must express my indebtedness to Professor J. Black of the University of Exeter for a most detailed and constructive criticism of the former volume.

In between the appearance of the first and second editions I have had the enjoyable and stimulating experience of working with the Harvard University Development Advisory Service in Indonesia, and members of that team will certainly perceive their influence in Part II. In this connection, I am especially indebted to Professor Schydlowsky for many useful insights into the applicability of the Keynesian analysis to developing economies.

Apart from changes to the development section, extension of the fiscal policy chapter, additional appendices, numerous corrections and the updating of references, the major alteration to the original work lies in the addition of a separate chapter dealing with the micro-economic underpinnings of macro-economic policy. Under the persuasive influence of the work of Clower and Leijonhufvud, it is becoming increasingly clear – regardless of how one may interpret the work of Keynes – that macro-economic policy conclusions depend for their validity, if only implicitly, upon a micro-economic framework. This additional chapter attempts to indicate the micro-economic building blocks required in the construction of macro-economic policies as well as outlining the essence of the 'new' view of Keynes and the classics.

Preface to the Third Edition

In many respects, the changes to the present edition are more fundamental than those contained in the second. In particular, Part Two of the former edition, dealing with macro-economic policy in developing economies, has been eliminated entirely and some explanation is called for – at least to those readers who expressed their interest in that section. When I first came to write the book in 1969, I was impressed by the comparative unawareness of the employment problem in the less advanced economies. Attention was pivoted firmly upon the need to raise *per capita* income and it was assumed that the way to achieve this was through a policy of economic growth. The employment consequences of such growth, particularly in the case of growth through capital intensive investment, was accorded comparatively little attention and the existence of a trade-off between the growth objective and the employment objective was scarcely perceived. Part Two of the original volume, therefore, attempted to correct this deficiency by focussing specifically upon the employment issue. Today, this need no longer exists. An extensive literature, in part springing from empirical and theoretical OECD studies, now deals with the employment problem in developing countries and it has rapidly become a priority objective in the formation of development policies. Whilst one could hardly claim that governments and international agencies have been successful to any marked degree in alleviating the extent of third world unemployment, there can be no question that the problem is now fully recognised.

Secondly, more attention in the present edition is given to the issues raised by monetarism and in particular a new chapter is included dealing with the economics of the budget constraint – a concept of increasing importance in the professional literature and one which contains the essence of the policy dispute between the monetarists and the neo-Keynesians. There is also an additional chapter dealing with economic growth, which many critics felt had been accorded inadequate attention in former editions. There are several new appendices and some of the former ones have disappeared in the attempt to bring the volume up to date. As before, the objective has remained that of introducing the areas of policy controversy and not the resolution of conflict.

Between the appearance of the second and third editions I have had the enjoyable experience of spending a visiting year at the University of Guelph, Ontario, and I would like to express my thanks to colleagues there who, unconsciously or otherwise, influenced the contents of the new edition. I have a particular debt to Professors Auld, Christofides, Forster and Vanderkamp.

My colleague R. B. Cross is responsible for sharpening my perception of some of the more controversial areas, whilst in no way responsible for any confusion which remains. To Mrs Joan Reed and Mrs Elizabeth Usher I owe thanks for considerable secretarial and typing services and finally, I would like to express my appreciation to my publishers for the opportunity to revise *Macro-Economic Policy* once again.

'It is astonishing what foolish things one can temporarily believe if one thinks too long alone, particularly in economics (along with the other moral sciences), where it is often impossible to bring one's ideas to a conclusive test either formal or experimental.'

J.M. Keynes

Part One

Macro-Economic Policy

Chapter I The Nature of Macro-Economic Policy

Introductory

Macro-economics is conventionally looked upon as the study of the relationships between broad economic aggregates seeking to explain the changes in those aggregates through time. In contrast to micro-economics, which is concerned primarily with the rationalistic decision-making processes of individual units, macro-economics attempts to understand and relate the key variables which govern the performance of the economy as a whole. The formulation of functional relationships of aggregate economic behaviour and the specification of such relationships in a manner which lends itself to empirical verification or rejection constitutes the primary purpose of macro-economic theory.

Macro-economic policy may be looked upon as the normative counterpart to macro-economic theory. Whereas the latter is concerned solely with the formulation of aggregative models which explain the functioning of the economy, macro-economic policy attempts to assess the behaviour of the economy as a whole and to seek ways in which its aggregate performance might be improved. As soon as we depart from the realm of mere explanation to suggest measures to alter the existing state of affairs, we enter the policy framework and implicitly we are making value judgements about the desirability of differing situations. Inevitably, questions of welfare are involved. The issue may be immediately raised: "with whose welfare is macro-economic policy concerned?". In a democratic society, it is generally assumed that the elected representatives of the people seek in some way to fulfil the pledges contained in their mandate. The political process, then, may be regarded as providing a substitute, admittedly imperfect, for the social welfare function which the policy-maker is attempting to maximize.* Whilst there are enormous difficulties with this concept, especially when it is realized that the decisions of economic policy-makers today may profoundly influence the welfare of generations as yet unborn (who presumably are entitled to a place in the social welfare function even if denied the opportunity of voting), we shall nonetheless accept this proposition. We are not concerned, then, to enquire into the manner in which policy objectives are formulated and related to each other. We shall simply assume that a consensus exists with respect to the objectives enumerated below, and our primary concern will be to indicate the policy measures which may be combined for their attainment and the nature of the constraints and conflicts which may prevent their realization.

Even though there may be complete agreement upon the nature of policy objectives, the task of the decision-taker involved in the formulation of macro-economic policy is by no means a simple one. In practice, the decision-taker will not be a professional economist but a politician or administrator, yet he has to choose between competing policy recommendations offering alternative means of achieving stated goals. Essentially this task is threefold. Confronted with a policy recommendation implicit in a given theory, he must first decide whether the theory is valid. That is to say, he must first decide whether the theory underlying the policy recommendation is internally consistent given its assumptions. If this is the case then the policy recommendations follow logically from the model analysis. The validity of a theory, however, implies nothing about its usefulness. The usefulness of economic theory depends largely upon the extent to which the simplifying assumptions necessary and essential to the process of model-building approximate the actual conditions of the real world. The adoption of a different, and possibly more realistic, set of assumptions may be sufficient to change the qualitative conclusions of the model. An illustrative example of a useful and mathematically convenient assumption often invoked is that of perfect competition. While few economists would wish to assert that the perfect competition

* A social welfare function is a concept frequently invoked by economists to summarise that state of affairs (including for example the 'correct' distribution of income) which maximises well-being. It is a convenient simplifying step in economic analysis. Theoretical work by Kenneth Arrow (1) has argued the impossibility of society ever being able to derive the social welfare function given certain reasonable restrictions. For a useful introduction to the "Impossibility Theorem" see especially Vickrey (2).

model approximates reality, it is nonetheless the case that many conclusions of the analysis hold even when considering alternative market structures. Finally, even if the decision-taker decides that the underlying theory is valid, and that the assumptions invoked correspond sufficiently to reality to leave the qualitative nature of the conclusions unaffected, he must still decide whether the quantitative impact of the policy is sufficient to warrant its inception, since certain costs adhere to almost any policy action.

In order to resolve this latter question, the policy-maker will require access to accurate estimates of the key economic magnitudes and their rate of change through time. Without such information, it is not possible to attach meaningful values to target variables or to assess the potential contribution of a given policy measure towards their attainment. In turn, information of this nature will require a complex system of social accounts, supplemented, where possible, by financial accounts detailing money flows and the structure and composition of financial assets. In order to interpret this information optimally, a knowledge of the difficulties inherent in collecting and collating the data is invaluable; it is highly desirable, therefore, that the policy-maker be conversant with the conventions of national income accounting.

In order to assess the impact of a policy measure upon the aggregate economy it is also necessary to have some knowledge of the relevant coefficients applicable to the macro-economic model which implicitly or explicitly underlies the policy recommendation. Since estimation of these coefficients invariably encounters the pitfalls and dangers of spurious correlation, suggesting conclusions which may not be justified in practice, it is extremely desirable that the policy-making authorities be acquainted with the relevant econometric techniques. In particular, some knowledge of the limitations associated with the use of simple regression techniques is an invaluable aid in the formation of concrete policy proposals. Also, in deciding whether or not to adopt a particular policy recommendation, the policy-maker will need to take account of its chances of obtaining legislative approval – if such sanction is needed – and also whether the administrative machinery for its enactment is readily available. Particularly, in the less advanced economies, recommendations stemming from outside 'experts', which pass all the relevant economic objective criteria, are frequently ruled out because they demand an administrative capacity in excess of that currently available. Finally, domestic stabilization measures will often exert international repercussions – as for example the decision to float sterling – and to the extent that such repercussions may imply future costs they must be fully allowed for in the adoption of the policy proposal.

Consensus with regard to policy objectives, therefore, is just the beginning of macro-economic policy-making, and even so it is unlikely that consensus would ever prevail. Whilst the majority of economists would be willing to endorse in general terms the policy objectives which constitute the declared aims of macro-economic policy, differences would inevitably arise over the precise way in which any one objective should be defined, and in particular, considerable disagreements would emerge as to the extent to which any one objective should be accorded priority over another.

The Policy Objectives

1. Full Employment of the Labour Force

Ever since the Keynesian revolution full employment has ranked highly amongst the goals of government policy. However, it is not always clear exactly what this objective implies. An economic interpretation commonly used defines full employment as a situation where no-one is unemployed who wishes to work at the existing wage rate. This definition may be modified by specifying a time dimension to take account of unemployment in the case of people transferring from one occupation to another and who find themselves temporarily out of work. Difficulties arise, however, when it is appreciated that this definition is perfectly consistent with almost any amount of under-employment, i.e. a situation where one seeks employment but obtains work for a limited number of hours only – decidedly less than the socially accepted norm. Moreover, this definition is also compatible with a situation which Joan Robinson (3) originally termed disguised unemployment* where labour may be employed but in occupations with an average productivity vastly below that of which it is capable. A further difficulty arises when this definition is used in measuring the extent of any existing unemployment. This occurs because the number of people wishing to enter the labour force at any given wage rate may itself be a function of the extent of unemployment. On the one hand,

* Today, the term disguised unemployment is almost invariably used with reference to the less advanced economies to denote a situation where labour has zero, or near zero marginal product.

more women members of the household may enter the labour force when their husbands are unemployed in an attempt to maintain family earnings. On the other, more people may enter the labour force when employment rates are high, since they rate their chances of actually obtaining work distinctly higher. Thus the "participation" rate may vary with the state of the economy. It follows that what constitutes full employment in one situation may not in another, and further, that policies to attain full employment may not completely succeed even if they are successful in raising the employment level by the amount originally intended.

In practice, in the United Kingdom the extent of unemployment is measured (and hence the level of full employment implicitly defined) by reference to the number of people who are formally registered as unemployed. For the most part, these will be individuals who are entitled to unemployment benefit. British figures are admittedly deficient and violate the economic definition given above by ignoring those people out of work who seek employment but do not register since they are not entitled to unemployment benefit. This omission is of particular importance with respect to school leavers and new entrants to the labour force. In contrast, the United States estimates do attempt to allow for this factor by using sampling techniques, and thus approximate closer to the economic meaning of unemployment. It is for this reason that great care should be used when comparing British and American employment data; the American figures as reported will almost invariably be proportionately higher, even when the state of the two economies is basically similar.

In a dynamic society, it is unlikely that full employment could ever be achieved. Imperfections in the adjustment process are inevitable and there will doubtless always be those members of society who, through no fault of their own, find their specialized skills suddenly becoming obsolete and who cannot be reabsorbed into the labour force without prior re-training. It is for this reason that full employment is conventionally regarded as something less than one hundred per cent. In the United Kingdom, a two per cent unemployment level is conventionally generally accepted as indicating a full employment economy; in the United States the comparable figure is nearer four per cent. There are, of course, economists who disagree with these estimates and argue that with the appropriate policies the figures could be reduced. Regardless of the definition ultimately decided upon, it is clear that no government or policy-maker could ignore the employment objective for long; the interesting question which then arises is: to what extent does meeting the full employment objective constrain the attainment of other policy goals?

2. Price Stability

A second policy objective which most people, economists and laymen alike, seem anxious and willing to endorse but which is even more difficult to define precisely, is that of price stability. How should price stability be defined? Clearly, we would not expect prices to remain unchanged indefinitely; comparative prices will change as fluctuating tastes alter the composition of demand, as new products are developed and as cost-reducing technologies are introduced. Differential price changes are essential to the allocative function performed by the market economy. Moreover, since modern economies tend to exhibit fairly rigid downward price inflexibility, differential price changes will only be attained by gradual increases in the aggregate price level over time. In addition, prices may change as a direct consequence of government policy as for example in the case of devaluation which increases the cost of imports, or owing to a fundamental change in the structure of taxation. Consider for example British entry into the European Common Market and the necessary adoption of a value added tax raising the prices of most goods and services. Is such a once and for all price rise to be regarded as conflicting with the objective of price stability and to be classified in the same category as inflation which is normally looked upon as a condition in which there is a persistent tendency for prices to rise? How then is price stability to be defined? What most people appear to mean by price stability is simply the avoidance of inflation which they equate with the *rate* of increase in an aggregate price index, usually the consumer price index, being held within some "tolerable" limit.* Opinions of what is tolerable differ widely. Fixed income groups generally exhibit a lower tolerance level than the average wage-earner, who may reasonably expect his rate of remuneration to keep pace. It is not always readily appreciated by the latter, however, that even if his annual earnings and savings are maintained in real terms the accumulated value of his total savings may

* A further difficulty arises in the choice of index to assess or to measure inflation. The consumer price index may rise whilst the wholesale index displays comparative stability. This is likely to be the case if the cost of personal services is substantially increased independently of changes in the cost of manufactured output – for example owing to taxation policy.

shrink over the course of his working life if the nominal interest rate does not adjust to the pace of inflation. The real charge against inflation lies in its inequitable treatment of different individuals with differing bargaining potential: inevitably it is the very poor who are least able to rectify their disadvantaged position.

Whilst few economists would wish to deny that reasonable price stability ought to be included amongst the goals of macro-economic policy, it is perhaps of interest to note that cost of living indices generally overstate the degree of inflation if we think primarily in welfare terms. For example, if we consider the income needed to maintain a fixed degree of consumer satisfaction at some given level of the consumer price index, and after some interval we notice that the price index has doubled, it will not normally require a doubling of the income level to leave welfare unchanged. This is because the consumer price index measures a fixed bundle of goods and does not allow for the consumer responding to differing price changes by substituting one good for another, and secondly it ignores any improvement in the quality of the product. Considerations of this nature make it extremely difficult to specify the objective of price stability in precise terms and inevitably opinions as to the permissible extent of inflation will differ. Indeed it may be argued that it is easier to adapt to inflation and learn to live with its consequences rather than to risk substantial unemployment or the imposition of resource-distorting controls (4).

3. Economic Growth

In recent years, the objective of advanced economic growth has been accorded more and more attention by economists, laymen and statesmen alike. A variety of reasons have combined to ensure the growth objective a primary place in the objective function of the policy-maker. On the one hand, it reflects a growing concern with the military and strategic implications of differential growth rates between eastern and western blocs. Especially in the nineteen-fifties, concern was expressed that the sluggish growth performance of the western nations, particularly in the United States and Britain, was being outstripped by phenomenal growth rates in the Soviet and communist territories. One consequence of superior communist growth performance was the demand that a greater proportion of resources should be devoted to the military preparedness of the West. The rationale for this position lay in the far greater size of the United States *vis-á-vis* Soviet GNP. Accordingly, it was argued that for the Soviet

Union to maintain the same degree of military preparedness would require a greater percentage of national resources being devoted to military needs. A raising of defence expenditures in the West, therefore, would divert a larger percentage of national resources away from alternative investments in the communist bloc and would impose a more deleterious impact upon the latter's growth rate. It is difficult to assess the extent to which such arguments actually influenced policy decisions but there can be no doubt that the growth objective was coveted both for its strategic as well as its welfare implications. There are inevitably innumerable difficulties in making comparisons of international growth rates; in particular, much depends upon the selection of the initial base year to compute the index. Moreover, since changes in the size of recorded GNP are composed of both output and price changes, it is necessary to deflate the resultant figures by a quantity index keeping prices constant. For this purpose, a common form of the Laspèyres index is often used which weights quantities by the constant price of the base year. Such an index is commonly employed because it avoids the need to reassess prices from year to year. However, the great difficulty with this type of index is that it tends to contain an inherent upward bias if products still in their development stages, and hence highly priced, are included in the base year. The rapid development of such "infant" industries as, for example, the plastics and electronics industries of the nineteen-fifties with the accompanying reductions in cost, would seriously distort the index. Considerations of this nature have led many economists to question the extent of the gap between western and eastern growth rates.

The success achieved by Japan in reaching and maintaining a high rate of growth and the apparent correlation between economic integration and enhanced growth within the EEC countries also contributed to the interest in the growth objective and to the belief that the overall growth rate was amenable to appropriate policy action. The increasing concern with the need for economic growth has also stemmed from the conviction that it is the only possible solution to poverty in many of the developing countries with rapid rates of population growth, and further, that it is only by raising the growth rate in the advanced economies that adequate development aid will be forthcoming. Moreover, economic growth is desired for its own sake since it permits an increase in *per capita* income levels raising consumer choice and well-being. It should be noted that this latter view has been brought into question, in particular by E.J. Mishan (5). Stressing the social costs of economic growth, associated with pollution, congestion and the like, Mishan argues also that the concept of consumer sovereignty is a myth and that the range of choice facing the consumer may actually decrease as a consequence of economic growth.* Certainly, one may question whether the quality of life has been significantly improved by many of the innovations associated with the technological revolution of the post-war years. But all that is implied in adopting this position is that economic growth should be controlled more strictly; the true cost of economic growth may be the necessary extension of the public sector which one may, or may not, be willing to accept. Considerations raised by Mishan may justifiably limit the enthusiasm for economic growth; it is unlikely, however, that the growth objective will cease to occupy a primary rôle in the mapping of macro-economic policy.

4. The International Balance of Payments

The attainment of a satisfactory balance of payments equilibrium has become one of the most sought-after objectives of government policy in the post-war world. The concern with the balance of payments has intensified as world trade has expanded at a pace far in excess of the growth of world liquidity, and as it has become increasingly recognised that the existence of a deficit will seriously curtail the ability of the economy to attain other policy goals. In addition, many developing economies have faced the alarming situation of witnessing the export promotion of their primary products being accompanied by ever-worsening terms of trade – with the development effort suffering in consequence as imports of essential capital equipment are prohibited. Just as with the other policy goals, however, it is not clear what constitutes a satisfactory balance of payments position. Clearly a country with a net debt must aim at a surplus to repay the debt over a reasonably short period of time. Once any debt has been repaid and an adequate reserve attained a zero balance maintained over time would

* An illustrative example afforded by Mishan is the case of a commuter who makes a 10-minute bus journey to work in the absence of private traffic. He decides to purchase a car which allows him to make the journey in half the time. However, the impact of economic growth is universal, others follow his example. The resulting congestion means his journey now takes 15 minutes and he recognises that he was better off in the initial situation. But that alternative is no longer open to him; the bus now takes 25 minutes and in addition bus fares have risen!

meet the policy objective. But how is this satisfactory balance to be achieved, on the trading account or on the capital account? Would a country which maintained balance of payments equilibrium by inducing an inflow of speculative capital be judged to have reached a satisfactory payments position? If we interpret the payments objective as the need to maintain international competitiveness then it seems clear that the onus of satisfactory performance must fall principally on the trading account. The capital account must be looked upon as fulfilling merely a short-term emergency rôle in times of crisis.

5. Regional Policy

A macro-economic policy objective which has come into prominence in recent times is the desire to maintain a balanced regional development. It is recognised that labour is still relatively immobile and that failure to maintain regional balance amounts to changes in the spatial distribution of income and wealth. Moreover, there are intangible benefits claimed for preventing the decline of a traditionally specialized region by the promotion of more diversified economic activities, and there are also social costs to be avoided by maintaining a relatively dispersed population. All these issues render regional policy a fitting objective of macro-policy. It must, of course, be recognised that within the context of a dynamic economy changes will inevitably occur; the difficulty faced by policy-makers lies in combining regional development with policies which will not impede necessary and desired economic change.

Conflicts and Constraints

If all objective functions were monolithic, macro-economic policy-making would be a relatively simple task. Alternatively, if policy objectives were positively correlated, in response to any given measure, so that the attainment of any one goal necessarily implied progress toward achieving the remainder, little difficulty would be encountered in the formation of policy. It is the fact that macro-economic objective functions are multi-dimensional and that for the most part the objectives are negatively related with respect to a given policy change, which means the decision-maker's lot is not a happy one.

A common example, which is currently enjoying a wide vogue, is that afforded by the Phillips curve which postulates a trade-off between the level of employment and the degree of price stability. Raising the level of employment increases the level of inflation and *vice versa*. We will return to consideration of the Phillips curve later when illustrating the possible approaches to macro-economic policy; for the moment we may note that the existence of trade-off between conflicting policy objectives may demand the partial abandonment of all declared policy objectives simultaneously – the 'second best' solution may be one in which no declared target value is achieved. *A priori*, there is no reason to assume that attainment of one stated policy objective (with the remainder being passively determined in consequence), is preferable to the attainment of none. The difficulty confronting the decision-taker when faced with a situation of objectives in conflict is two-fold. First, the purely technical one of determining the trade-off boundary; here past experience may not provide a helpful guide if the boundary is itself subject to shifts in response to policy changes – and secondly, the almost impossible task of determining societies preference function when objectives conflict. It is no simple task to derive value free decision rules to resolve these problems (6).

The issue of trade-off between competing policy objectives has taken on renewed significance in the policy statements emanating from the less advanced economies. Hitherto, it has all too often been assumed that increased growth was the key to the solution of all outstanding economic problems. More recently, the wisdom of attracting foreign investment of a highly productive but highly capital intensive nature has been questioned in the light of growing unemployment in many developing countries, and the inability to exercise effective macro-economic control over foreign owned enterprises. This issue is closely linked to the force of economic nationalism. For the moment, we may note that there is no simple solution to the question of establishing priorities when policy objectives conflict and for all practical purposes the issue must be resolved by the political process in the light of the value judgements held by the policy-maker. Moreover, the nature of the trade-off will itself depend upon the time period under consideration and in all probability the latter will be arbitrarily determined by reference to political realities and not by reference to any objective economic criteria.

It is not solely the existence of conflict between competing macro-economic objectives which makes policy-making difficult. Other constraints exist which also limit the scope of feasible policy action. For example, considerations of equity may prohibit adoption of a fiscal structure which is more conducive to long-term growth. Again, concern with the efficient allocation of resources such as the avoidance of undue monopoly power, or excessive social costs, may limit policies which meet macro-economic criteria. Probably by far the most pressing form of constraint lies in the existence of international commitments previously entered into in good faith – possibly by governments other than the one currently enjoying power. Especially in the field of international trade, for example, agreements on quotas and tariffs, and the commitment to maintain a fixed rate of exchange, seriously curtail the freedom of manoeuvre.

Of fundamental importance to the formation of concrete policy proposals is the extent to which the government may intervene and interfere with the normal functioning of the private market sector. At one extreme, the nationalisation of a substantial part of the private sector will certainly aid the attainment of macro-economic ends since it removes the need to juggle with policy mixes to induce the appropriate response. At the other, a strong sense of individualism and belief in the virtue of private enterprise will impose a constraint upon permissible policy action. Constraints such as the ones we have listed here may, of course, be formulated in terms of competing objectives and analysed in terms of conflict. This indeed is the logical approach inherent in the concept of a social welfare function encompassing all members of society. From the more pragmatic viewpoint of decision-making, however, a fairly definite division of labour will apply. The macro-economic policy-maker will therefore look upon alternative objectives more in the nature of constraints.

The Instruments

Having outlined the policy objectives and indicated the nature of the constraints, we may now list the instruments which the policy-maker will normally have at his disposal. Since we will discuss the operation of the policy tools in much greater detail later in this volume a somewhat cursory review will suffice. However, it is essential that we clarify at the outset one fundamental point, namely the criteria by which policy instruments are to be classified.

This is by no means an insignificant issue. Policy tools are capable of being classified in a number of ways (7). For example, policies may be classified according to the government agencies which undertake the appropriate action. Thus fiscal policy on this criterion may be considered activities undertaken by the Treasury, monetary policy being action undertaken by the authorities charged with supervising the banking system and so forth. The great weakness of such a classification, apart from the fact that certain functions overlap more than one government agency, is that it would lead to certain activities being considered fiscal policy in one country but not in another. Clearly, this is an unsatisfactory foundation especially if one wishes to assess the comparative performance of policy instruments between countries. Alternatively, policy measures may be defined in terms of their primary impact. In many ways such a classification is theoretically appealing. According to this criterion, a decision to curtail public expenditures would be regarded as constituting monetary policy if the principal impact was to reduce the money supply. This may in fact be the case, if the measure generates a positive budget surplus and induces a multiple contraction of credit throughout the banking system. Indeed, reductions in the level of government expenditure have frequently been advocated as a means of reducing the money stock by advocates who contend that the volume of money is the most significant variable controlling the economy. On this basis should not the proposed change be regarded as monetary policy? Although this position is one which can clearly be defended, it is not the one which we choose to adopt in the present work. The position taken here is that policy measures should be defined in an arbitrary but consistent manner according to the nature of the instruments themselves. Thus, for example, we may consider any tax or expenditure change as part of fiscal policy irrespective of the reason for its enactment or the agency initiating the change. Likewise, we may regard any change in the discount rate, or in the volume of existing debt, as an integral part of monetary policy. It follows that once we have classified the available policy instruments we have implicitly defined the appropriate authorities. Thus, the monetary authorities can be looked upon as those agencies controlling the monetary instruments, the fiscal authorities those with power over fiscal instruments and so forth. It follows that any given agency may simultaneously constitute more than one decision-taking authority; alternatively, a government department may find itself part of one authority on one occasion but not on another. Conceptually, this question of agency identification need not detain us here; our purpose is more fundamental. It is to stress that unless care is taken in classifying instruments at the outset, little is to be gained by enquiring into the endless discussion of the comparative effectiveness of alternative policy measures.

One final point may be noted. Any policy change must be defined in the *ex ante* sense. The influence exercised upon *ex post* variables may be one way of judging the efficacy of the policy measure but it does not delineate the policy. The policy exists independently of any effects. Thus, for example, the introduction of optional methods of accelerating depreciation allowances for firms below a certain size constitutes a policy measure even though no firm subsequently exercises its option.

1. Fiscal Policy

We define fiscal policy to include any change in the level, composition or timing of government expenditures, or equally any change in the rate of taxation or the timing and composition of fiscal receipts. A change in the size of fiscal revenues does not itself indicate fiscal policy; it may simply be a normal response of the economy to some other stimulus, as for example monetary policy. However, a decision to change the fiscal structure so as to make it more or less responsive to other stimuli is part and parcel of fiscal policy.

Fiscal policy has long been heralded as the most effective way of controlling the economy. The pre-eminence of fiscal measures in much of the literature on compensatory policy is partly to be explained by the theoretical contribution of Keynesian economics which both questioned the operation of the quantity theory whilst simultaneously providing a respectable foundation for fiscal intervention. It is also doubtless a consequence of the enormous increase in the taxing power of modern government, to a large extent the consequence of the war effort, which enables the advanced countries directly to control 30–40 per cent of GNP.

In contrast, the taxing ability of the developing countries is much more limited; often the government sector will have difficulty in controlling much more than 10 or 12 per cent of the country's current resources. This indeed is perhaps the biggest single contrast between the rich nations and the poor. In the former, the level of taxation is usually determined by reference to the desired expenditure programme; in the less advanced economy, the causal direction is usually reversed. It is the level of potential tax revenues which dictates the size of the expenditure programme.

2. Monetary Policy

In monetary policy we include any change in the official discount rate, or Bank Rate, at which the Central Bank fulfils its rôle as lender of last resort. We also define monetary policy to include any attempt to vary the money supply by altering the cash reserve ratio or the net volume of bonds and securities outstanding, and we shall also include the adoption of selective controls such as, for example, hire purchase restrictions which are aimed at influencing the volume of credit. It will be appreciated that the money supply and the rate of interest may change of its own accord; nonetheless, it is clear that for monetary policy to be effective the monetary authorities must have the means to influence the money supply. Any autonomous determination of the money stock – as for example by a commitment to the international gold standard – must weaken its ability to control the economy in the direction intended. This is a point of some importance for the developing economies, for whilst the traditional gold standard is no more, many developing economies lack the banking facilities required to control a capital inflow.

One question of interest arises from attempts to distinguish a "tight" from an "easy" monetary situation. Should expansionary monetary policy be interpreted in terms of the change in the volume of money outstanding, or should it be inferred from the general movement of interest rates? The two may not always move in opposite directions as conventional theory predicts. In particular, recent theoretical work on this subject has raised the possibility that expansion of the money stock will occasion increases in the rate of interest. We return tc consideration of this issue in the appendix to chapter VII.

3. Debt Management Policy

Under the heading of debt management policy, we restrict ourselves solely to the attempt to change the age profile of the existing debt; that is to say, we are concerned only with the composition of a given volume of debt. Moreover, for our purposes, we are concerned only with that part of the debt which takes the form of government stocks and securities. Although, logically, the debt includes the money stock issued by the government we shall ignore this component of debt when discussing debt management policy. The decision to alter the size of the existing debt, as for example by the purchase and sale of securities on the open market, we have already delineated as constituting a part of monetary policy since this is the traditional manner by which policy-makers have sought to change the money stock. Other writers, however, have preferred to consider it as one aspect of fiscal policy since a change in the size of the debt is usually a consequence of a budget surplus or deficit. As we have already indicated, the actual definitions adopted are essentially arbitrary; this does not matter providing we are clear at the outset as to the meaning attached to each policy and as long as the classification used is consistently adhered to.

It will be appreciated that the composition (and indeed the size) of the debt will change of its own accord as the shorter-dated securities mature and as the "longs" become "shorts" (undated stocks excepted). Accordingly, conscious debt management intervention will be needed to maintain the existing composition. This raises an interesting issue as to what precisely constitutes a "neutral" debt management policy. Is a policy which leaves the composition of the debt unchanged to be judged neutral or should neutrality be defined with respect to the term structure of interest rates on government securities? This is a question which cannot be answered without first specifying the peculiar nature of debt management policy. Is debt management policy an independent instrument to be used to secure certain objectives or should it more properly be regarded as an aid to render other policy instruments more effective? Alternatively, should debt management be looked upon merely as the means of administering other policy decisions in the cheapest manner possible? These are all issues which we will take up later in this study.

4. Prices and Incomes Policy

Economic policy invariably reflects – if only after a suitable time lag – significant advances in economic theory and the findings of major empirical studies. Thus it is hardly surprising that the pioneering work of A. W. Phillips (8), which introduced the notion of a relationship between the rate of change of money wages and the degree of unemployment, should be followed by renewed interest in the possibilities of an incomes policy that could be interpreted as an attempt to transform the underlying relationship expressed by the Phillips curve. Conceptually, the Phillips relation supplied a link between the change in aggregate demand conditions and the resulting change in money wages, which in turn carried implications for the rate of inflation and the current account of the balance of payments. Incomes policy thus became looked upon as an instrument to promote greater price stability and balance of payments equilibria. Whilst a successful incomes policy would itself constrain the rise in prices, it was recognized that direct price controls would be an essential ingredient of any incomes policy if the co-operation of the trade unions was to be forthcoming. In addition, however, it was recognized that certain sectors of the economy might be relatively immune to aggregate policy measures and may even respond in a perverse manner in the absence of price controls. For example, attempts at a deflationary policy by reducing the level of aggregate demand may, in certain sectors, raise unit costs and hence prices if the latter are administered. A specific guide to price increases is then required if the aims of the original policy are to be secured. Price controls would also be conducive to creating a climate of expectations that the present inflation rate would decline. Indeed, it may be argued that the influence upon expectations underlies the essence of a prices and incomes policy, for if expectations of inflation are themselves a contributory factor to inflation, as implied by the many studies suggesting that the Phillips curve has been shifted outward over time (9, 10), then conditioning expectations towards a lower rate of inflation would promote a desirable inward shift of the curve. But it should be noted that *any* policy change reducing the degree of expected inflation would bring about such a desired change, and it may be argued that incomes policy is not the appropriate policy since it may exert severe repercussions upon resource allocation (11). With regard to recent United Kingdom experience, it might also be alleged that incomes policy has operated in a decidedly perverse manner by conditioning the expectation that real incomes will be maintained. Particularly was this the case under the Heath administration when the "threshold agreement" linked wage increases to the change in the retail price index in such a manner as to maintain the real earnings of most workers and to increase the real earnings of the lower paid. In view of the subsequent quadrupling of the price of imported oil, implying an immediate once and for all fall in real living standards, such a policy was at best unfortunate and has probably delayed the painful adjustment that the British worker is now being compelled to undertake.

Whilst the emphasis upon an imposed incomes policy is still comparatively new, it has long been recognized that price stability required an equation between annual wage increases and annual increases in gross productivity. Indeed, this was the logic underlying the rationale of the precursor of incomes policy, namely wage guidelines, and was neatly summarized in an early contribution by Weintraub (12). Arguing from the identity that money national income is simply current output multiplied by the price index and equal to the wage bill multiplied by the ratio of prices to labour cost, we have

$$Y^m \equiv OP \equiv (wN)k$$

where w is the average wage rate, N the volume of employment and k the mark-up factor. Then

$$P = \frac{(wN)k}{O}$$

But O/N is merely the average output per worker, A. Thus,

$$P = k\left(\frac{w}{A}\right)$$

It follows that if the ratio w/A is unchanged, if wage increases are offset by increases in productivity, there will be no change in final prices. A raising of the w/A ratio, however, would be magnified in its impact upon the price level by the mark-up factor k, which empirically had revealed great consistency. The appeal of Weintraub's formulation of the price equation lay in spotlighting the dual nature of a prices and incomes policy; wage controls to constrain the w/A ratio, and price controls to constrain or bring down the mark-up factor, k.

An interesting situation which suggests the need for some form of prices and incomes policy to reinforce more conventional measures arises in the case of foreign-owned companies which are not only comparatively immune to domestic policy control, but also exert a significant impact upon national wage negotiations. In the United Kingdom this situation is especially relevant to the motor-car industry where the sizeable American investment, enjoying access to the cheaper credit provided by American capital markets can grant wage increases which initiate similar demands throughout the entire industry. In the case of a voluntary prices and incomes policy, where the attempt is to induce both sides of industry to limit the extent of wage and price increases within any given period, crucial importance attaches to the rôle of the public sector. Voluntary restraint on incomes and prices can hardly be expected to be forthcoming from the private sector unless similar policies are seen to be pursued within the public sector. At the same time, however, it may be argued that the more successful the government is in restraining prices in the nationalized sector, particularly in those areas where industry is a heavy consumer (as for example, transport, fuel, postal and telecommunication services), then the easier it will be for the private sector to grant inflationary wage increases to maintain industrial peace.

5. Financial Policy

For the sake of completeness we include under this heading various measures aimed principally at influencing the external account. Thus we consider exchange rate policy, by which we mean both the decision to adopt a fixed or floating exchange rate, and also in the case of the former the decision to devalue or revalue, tariff policy, quotas, import deposit schemes and the like. One might also wish to include under this category fundamental questions of fiscal harmonization – as for example the decision whether to impose taxes upon the origin or destination principle* – *tax changes* under either principle would, of course, continue to be regarded as constituting fiscal policy. For the most part, we will not be concerned with analysing such policies in the later stages of this volume although we will allude to them from time to time especially when considering policy mixes.

6. Announcement Effects

Almost any policy – whether or not it is fully understood – is likely to carry "announcement" effects which influence the pattern of aggregate behaviour. For example, a sudden increase in the discount rate following the publication of unfavourable trade figures may condition expectations of a tough budget. In consequence, a spate of buying may be induced on the part of the public anxious to avoid the budget impact. There is some indication that the public does respond in this manner to the expectation of tax increases. Likewise, it has often been argued that the primary impact of a rise in long-term interest rates has depended upon the psychological impact on business expectations. There are inevitably difficulties in gauging the size of announcement effects but there can be little doubt that they do exist. This raises the interesting question of whether announcement effects should be considered a policy instrument in themselves and whether

* Under the destination principle indirect taxes are rebated on exported products which are therefore exported net of tax. The indirect tax rates prevailing within the country of destination are then imposed by the recipient country. This is the system commonly followed; it avoids distortion in competition owing to different tax rates prevailing in different countries. However, the origin principle, whereby exported products bear the indirect tax of the country of export, is favoured for the European Common Market since it allows the abolition of fiscal frontiers.

policy-makers should deliberately mislead the public about the state of the economy, in an attempt to induce behaviour which may ultimately justify the initial policy statement. At one extreme, one can imagine a whole stream of bogus monthly trade figures being used with beneficial effect on both the balance of payments and the stock exchange. However, the great danger underlying such techniques lies in the question of confidence; as soon as credibility is lost in official statements, the announcement effect is negated.* It is for this reason that no government could put much faith in a policy instrument of this sort and expect it to succeed for more than a brief period of time. Nonetheless, it is clear that announcement effects should be taken into account when framing policy documents and in particular that regard should be paid to the timing of such statements.

Approaches to Macro-Economic Policy

Broadly, there are two general approaches to the formation of economic policy, and both spring from the theoretical and practical contribution of two Dutch economists to economic planning. In one category, we have what has become known as the optimizing approach to economic policy associated mainly with the name of Henri Theil (13). At the other extreme, and arising largely from the work of Jan Tinbergen (14), we have the so-called "fixed targets" approach. In the following exposition, which is admittedly *simpliste* and fails to do justice to either of the authors mentioned, we illustrate these approaches by reference to the familiar Phillips curve.

The Phillips curve postulates the existence of an empirical relationship between the rate of change of money wages and the level of unemployment. From this, it is a relatively simple step to the proposition that a similar relationship exists between the degree of

* Although, in all probability, an element of discretion may well exist in reporting official figures. Consider, for example, the tabulation of import figures for any one month. If a ship docks on 29 September and takes three days to unload should it be included in the trade figures for that month or for October? If an element of discretion does arise, one can hardly blame the authorities for making use of it.

unemployment and the level of inflation. Such a relationship is depicted in Fig.I.1. below where inflation is measured on the vertical axis and unemployment along the horizontal.* The significance of the point A is that this is the degree of unemployment needed to maintain perfect price stability. It should be emphasized that not all economists would be willing to accept the concept of the Phillips curve and the empirical evidence is still the subject of much debate. Moreover, there are many economists who are decidedly unhappy about an explanation of inflation which says very little about monetary conditions, for the only theoretical underpinning of the Phillips curve hypothesis is that the degree of unemployment may be taken as an index of the pressure of demand upon prices generally; the monetary mechanism is ignored.

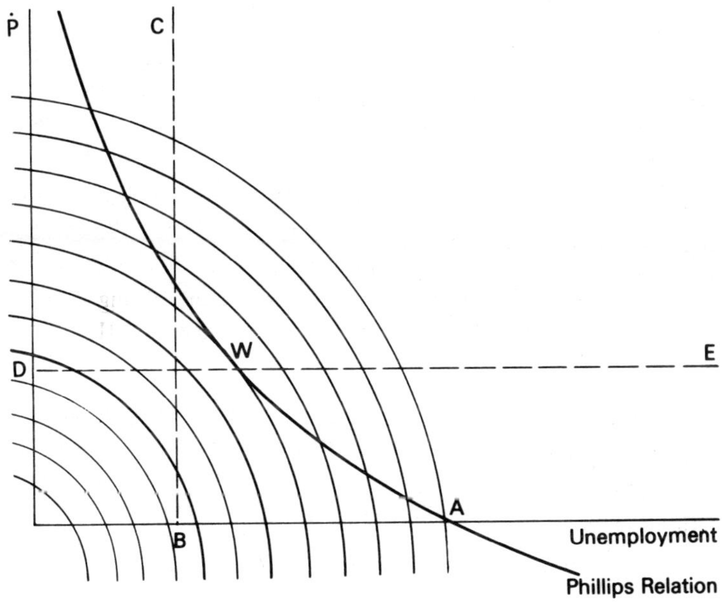

Figure I.1

* The placing of a dot above a symbol is a common mathematical convention to indicate the change in the variable with respect to time. Thus, if P is a general price index, then $\dot{P}$ is the rate of change in prices with respect to time, i.e. inflation in this instance.

Finally, even if the Phillips relation does exist, it does not necessarily imply that it will usefully lend itself to macro-economic decision making. This is because the Phillips curve is presumably the result of competitive behaviour in the labour market between trade unions on the one hand and employers on the other. Thus the introduction of policy tools to limit the degree of inflation by delineating the permissible range of the Phillips curve may give rise to behavioural responses changing the nature of the curve itself. These disclaimers are necessary if only to stress that for present purposes our use of the Phillips curve is purely illustrative; whether or not the Phillips curve exists does not negate its expositional convenience!

1. The Optimizing Approach

The optimizing approach to economic policy explicitly assumes that it is conceptually possible to specify the social welfare function. Once the social welfare function has been determined, that is, once the preference pattern of society with respect to all possible outcomes is known, the task of policy is simply to select whatever attainable combination will maximize welfare. Thus, for example, in Figure I.1, the objective function is summarised in the collective indifference curves superimposed upon the diagram. In this simple model, with only two policy objectives, the indifference curves indicate successively higher stages of collective well-being as they approach the origin. Clearly, the optimum position would be at the origin where perfect price stability is reconciled with full employment. However, the Phillips curve imposes a constraint by specifying all feasible combinations of employment and inflation. The policy decision-maker must select from this limited choice. If he is successful, he will juggle with alternative policy mixes to obtain a solution at point W, which maximizes the well-being of society given the predetermined indifference map. Implicit in this approach is the assumption that no one policy objective is sacrosanct: objectives, as well as instruments, are flexible. It is the task of the policy-maker to decide, in the light of all the available information, the extent to which any one objective must be compromised to maximize total well-being.

2. The Fixed Targets Approach

In many ways, the optimizing approach is theoretically appealing and being stated in terms of constrained maximization enjoys an affinity with traditional micro-economic techniques. For policy purposes, however, it may be contended that the fixed targets approach is more pragmatic. This latter version of policy-making neatly sidesteps the difficulties associated with approximating social welfare functions. Instead, policy goals are stated as constituting fixed targets from which no departure is permitted. In effect, this is tantamount to the decision-making authorities intervening in the rôle of dictator in specifying what the social welfare function should be. Once the objectives have been determined, policy-making then reduces to the search for an adequate armour of instruments to secure their attainment. Without delving into the mathematics involved, it may be demonstrated that to achieve any given number of policy objectives requires at least an equal number of policy instruments. If an inadequate number of policy tools exists, then new instruments must be devised to secure the objectives.

Let us assume, for example, that the decision-making authorities have decreed that the objective of price stability should be interpreted as no more than 5 per cent inflation per year, whilst the goal of full employment is consistent with 2 per cent unemployed. In this case, the fixed targets limit the acceptable region of Fig. I.1 to the area left of the vertical line BC and below the horizontal line DE. Moreover, given the Phillips curve, these twin objectives are incapable of being achieved simultaneously with the existing conventional tools of macro-economic policy. Let us assume, however, that incomes policy has yet to be devised. To what extent does the introduction of this new policy tool resolve the conflict between competing goals? Clearly, as indicated in Figure I.1, the existing policy measures are able to achieve either goal at the sacrifice of the other. The introduction of the new policy tool, therefore, may be looked upon as an additional policy measure to secure an additional policy objective, by affecting the appropriate inward shift of the Phillips curve. This is an issue to which we return in the Appendix to this chapter.

Assessing Policy Performance

Having outlined the essence of macro-economic policy-making, the question remains as to how its effectiveness should be assessed. Clearly, some measure of the impact of policy changes is desirable since it would provide an indispensable guide to policy-makers generally.

Unfortunately, there is no simple way of obtaining the relevant data to judge policy performance. This is because we seek to make a comparison with a non-existent situation; we wish to compare the performance of the economy given a policy measure with what would have occurred in the absence of policy changes. It follows that if the overall economic situation deteriorates following the adoption of a given policy, it does not necessarily follow that the policy was wrongly conceived. This cannot be determined without knowledge of what the course of the economy would have been if left to its own devices. The provision of economic forecasts is thus an essential element in the assessment of policy changes. Obviously, such estimates tend to be more accurate and possess higher degrees of confidence the shorter the period in question.

In order to illustrate what is involved, let us refer to Figure I.2. At time t we assume the level of income to be Y_t. If, at time t + 1, it is estimated that the economy would have attained the income level Y_h had the policy-makers not intervened, but in actual fact attained the level Y_a, then the ratio

$$\frac{Y_a - Y_h}{Y_t - Y_h}$$

provides an estimate of the success of the policy measures. It compares the amount of real output "saved" on account of policy action to the

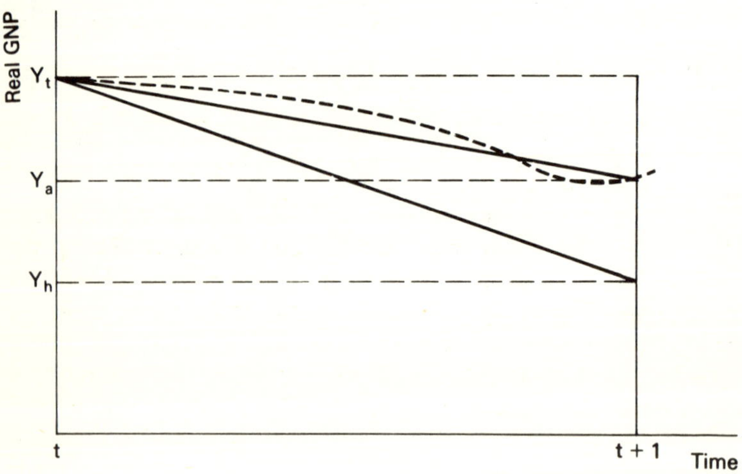

Figure I.2

amount which would have been lost in the absence of positive policy. If this ratio is equal to one, then we may consider the policy completely successful; if the ratio is zero, then the policy must be judged a complete failure. Moreover, it may be noted that if this ratio is negative, so that the point Y_a falls below Y_h, then the policy is operating in a perverse manner. We will return to consideration of such "negative" aspects of policy when considering the important question of time lags and macro-economic policy.

Measures such as the one we have discussed above are frequently used in the attempt to assess policy performance, especially in the effort to determine the stabilizing impact of alternative policy instruments (15). However, such measures must be considered defective for a variety of reasons. First of all, it is clear that the measure suggested above refers only to the effectiveness of a given policy on the level of real output. It ignores other policy objectives as, for example, employment. Thus, a policy measure which is judged effective in stabilizing real output and hence national income may not be considered effective in terms of stabilizing employment levels. Logically, we should have a different measure to judge the efficacy of any given policy on each and every policy objective which is influenced by the change. It may well be that no unambiguous index of policy performance will emerge but rather that certain policy instruments will become identified as efficient in securing specific policy objectives. Thus, for example, interest rate changes may be efficient in attaining short-term balance of payments objectives but relatively ineffective in influencing the domestic economy. This is clearly relevant to the fixed targets approach to macro-policy, for not only is it necessary to equate the number of instruments and objectives but it is also desirable to allocate the instruments to their most efficient rôle.

A more serious objection to the measure suggested in Fig. I.2 is that it ignores completely the long-term expansion path of the economy. Thus, two policies may have identical success in stabilizing the economy but one may add more to future growth potential. Again, and this is a weakness of the comparative static methodology, it ignores entirely the movement to equilibrium. Thus, for example, the policy indicated by the dotted line gives the same final measure of effectiveness as the one we have considered. However, it may be held preferable on at least two counts: first because the total loss of output is less, and secondly because in this case the economy has already regained its upward momentum (16).

When all these considerations are taken into account, it is clear that the assessment of policy action may confront as many difficulties as actual policy formation. Inevitably, the two are interlinked, and there can be little doubt that just as value judgements enter into the formation of specific policies, so too they will emerge in the assessment of comparative effectiveness.

Appendix Incomes Policy, Regional Policy and the Phillips Curve

When discussing the Tinbergen approach to economic policy, we used the example provided by the Phillips curve and considered how the adoption of an additional policy instrument could theoretically achieve the unsatisfied policy target by bringing about a favourable shift of the curve. In the present Appendix we examine two of the policy proposals which have been advocated in recent years as a means of achieving this result.

Incomes policy has always been looked upon as an instrument to assist in the attainment of price stability and by achieving the latter, to promote a favourable balance of payments. It was generally assumed that by restraining wage demands such a policy would be reflected in an inward shift of the Phillips curve at all levels of employment. More recently, however, this latter proposition has been questioned (17). Incomes policy justifies wage increases as being non-inflationary if they do not exceed the national increase in real output. Consequently, if it is predicted that the economy will continue to grow by some 3–3½ per cent per year, then labour as a whole may look forward to annual increases in real earnings of the same amount. Thus the introduction of an incomes policy may generate expectations of wage increases and influence wage negotiations in the direction of higher rates even if such increases are not indicated by the pressure of demand in the labour market. Hence, if the policy is successful in restraining wage increases in periods of exceptionally low unemployment it may be unsuccessful in preventing increases when unemployment is high. If this is the case, and it should be emphasized that the argument has been hotly denied on econometric grounds (18, 19), incomes policy serves not to shift the Phillips curve but rather to pivot it around a point. We illustrate such a situation in Figure AI.1, where the dotted curve portrays the trade-off between inflation and unemployment when incomes policy is in effect. It follows that incomes policy may work in a decidedly perverse manner, especially if it is accompanied by monetary and fiscal measures to deflate the economy in periods of balance of payments crisis. In this case, increasing unemployment is accompanied by a higher rate of inflation than that which would normally have occurred in the absence of incomes policy.

Whilst this phenomenon may explain the apparently paradoxical observation of inflation occurring together with substantial unemployment, it does not contradict either the logic of the policy or that of the Tinbergen approach. In Figure AI.1, for example, if the fixed targets are indicated by the hatched lines, then the introduction of an incomes policy makes possible their simultaneous fulfilment.

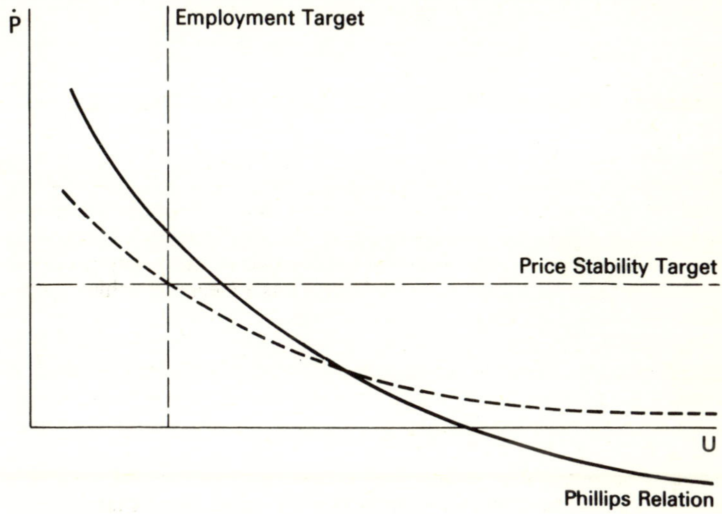

Figure AI.1

Unlike incomes policy, regional policy is not so intimately linked with the objective of price stability. Indeed, as we have already indicated, regional policy is more properly regarded as an objective in itself. Nonetheless, it is recognised that the promotion of regional policy may have favourable repercussions upon other goals so that the vexed question of trade-off need not arise; accordingly, it is permissible to regard regional policy as simultaneously both instrument and objective.

The relevance of regional policy to the Phillips curve lies in the fact that the presumed relationship between unemployment and inflation is generally considered to be non-linear. The pressure on wages (and hence prices) is normally considered to be greater the closer one approaches full employment. Thus the slope of the Phillips curve increases as the vertical axis is approached. If this is the case, then it follows that the aggregate level of inflation may be reduced if industry can be persuaded to re-locate in areas with greater unemployment. The resulting decrease in the numbers employed in the high employment areas will reduce the pressure on prices to a greater extent than the increase in employment in the low employment areas will increase it. We illustrate this situation with reference to the composite diagram of Figure AI.2. Part (a) of the figure describes the situation in the regions of high employment, Part (b) depicts the employment situation in the "regions", while Part (c) indicates the aggregate relationship. A transfer of employment of the amount $q-q_1$ from region a to b will imply a corresponding inward shift of the aggregate function for any given level of employment. Thus, a movement along disaggregated Phillips curves is consistent with shifting the position of the aggregate relationship.*

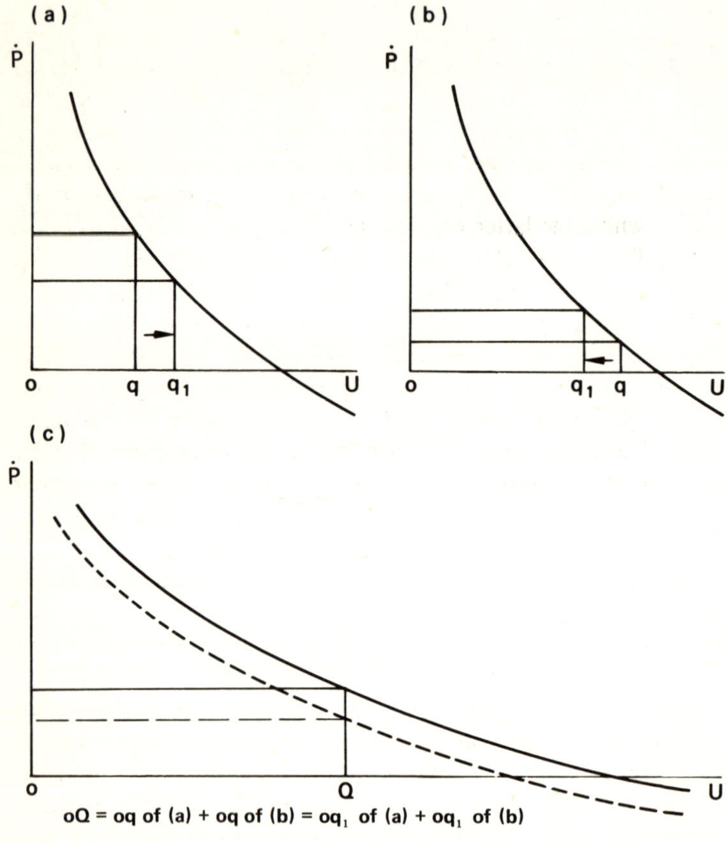

Figure AI.2

* It will be appreciated that the same result will be attained if the disaggregated Phillips relation is linear providing that the slope of the function for the high employment regions exceeds that of the low employment areas. Intuitively, this possibility seems eminently plausible.

Chapter II The Micro-Theoretic Foundations of Macro-Economic Policy

Before Keynes, or rather before the appearance of the *General Theory* in 1936, the accepted division in economics lay between the theory of Value and Distribution on the one hand and the theory of Money on the other. The former was analysed in terms of supply and demand, with the emphasis primarily upon the subjective marginalistic utility approach, whilst the latter was couched almost entirely in terms of the Quantity Theory (which we shall examine in detail in the following chapter). Moreover, this division, usually referred to as the classical dichotomy, was distinctly rigid. The volume of money, whilst determining nominal values, was held not to impinge upon comparative exchange ratios, or indeed upon any real variables including, in the long term, the rate of interest. The Keynesian revolution was in many respects an attack upon the classical dichotomy; an assertion that the volume of money was important as a determinant of investment spending, real output and employment *via* its impact upon the rate of interest. In place of the classical dichotomy Keynes suggested that the appropriate division lay between the economics of resource allocation (micro-economics) on the one hand and the theory of income determination (macro-economics) on the other. This distinction, it may be noted, was one perfectly in keeping with Keynes' social philosophy, and indeed that of many advocates of a mixed economy, for it led directly to the notion that government intervention was justified in order to achieve full employment income but thereafter the market system could be allowed to determine its allocation – a function which, with the exception of a few specific instances, it performed in a tolerably efficient manner. That today, this should be the accepted division in economics is a tribute to Keynes' achievement and influence.

So complete was the Keynesian victory, that macro-economics has become looked upon almost as a distinct subject independently of its micro-economics counterpart, and it has become commonplace in both theoretical and practical contributions to indicate macro-policy implications without any reference to the probable micro-economic response pattern of the individual units subject to the policy variables. An illustrative example of this tendency was foreshadowed in the concept of the consumption function. Whereas the standard micro-economics visualised consumer behaviour in terms of a rationalistic utility maximizing approach, which produced hypotheses incapable of being tested,* the Keynesian consumption function offered a guide to aggregate consumer behaviour, which, eschewing all mention of utility, led to hypotheses which lent themselves directly to empirical verification or rejection. Macro-economic policy formation thus became the province of simple regression analysis, divorced from rigorous analytical concern with the response pattern of individual units.

In recent years, a feeling of unease has crept into the economic literature with regard to policy recommendations formulated in this way. More and more, the conviction has grown that the poor performance of many Keynesian oriented policy measures has sprung from inadequate attention being accorded to the micro-economic response pattern of those subjected to policy change. This has been especially noteworthy with regard to the theory of money and of risk-taking where increasingly more and more attention has been given to subjective utility approaches and the conclusions incorporated into macro-economic policy formation. It has also been stimulated by the attempts to analyse inflation in terms of the Phillips curve which has generated interest in the supply and demand conditions underlying the labour market and their behaviour in periods of expected inflation (1).

It is with reference to this background that we must appraise the revolutionary work of Clower and Leijonhufvud (2,3), for what the latter have suggested is that Keynes was basing his entire thesis of unemployment on an implicit micro-economic analysis, or more correctly on the general equilibrium analysis of price determination as contained in Walrasian economics. In order to assess this viewpoint we will review briefly the essence of Walrasian price theory, which differs radically from the partial equilibrium analysis of Marshall – Keynes'

* For example, if increased income generates increased consumption of good X the good is held to be normal and the consumer is assumed to be maximizing his satisfaction. If, conversely, increased income generates a fall in consumption of good X it is held to be inferior and again it is assumed that utility is being maximized. In short, the underlying theory is consistent with any observed response pattern and is thus incapable of refutation.

foremost teacher. Regardless of the interpretation to be accorded to Keynes, it seems clear that as a result of this contribution the former rigid distinction between micro- and macro-economics is rapidly disappearing and may soon be as archaic as the classical dichotomy which Keynes sought to displace.

The Walrasian Theory of Price Determination

The Walrasian theory of price determination specifically allows for the interdependence of markets and accepts that a change in supply and demand conditions in any one market will exert feedback effects on markets elsewhere which in turn will exert feedback effects on the market initiating the change. It is thus in sharp contrast to the more pragmatic Marshallian approach which studies the impact of changes in supply and demand in any one market on the price prevailing within that market, under the assumption of *ceteris paribus*. In short, the Walrasian view of the market economy is seen in terms of a series of simultaneous equations describing market equilibrium conditions for each and every good. The question which then intrigues mathematicians is whether or not a solution to such a complex series of simultaneous equations does exist. In order for a unique solution to exist it is a necessary, but by no means a sufficient condition, that there be at least the same number of equations as unknowns.* Further, in order to be

* An equal number of equations as unknowns is far from being a sufficient condition to provide a solution to a series of simultaneous equations. For example, consider the following:

$$2y + 3x = 12$$
$$4y + 6x = 20$$

We have two equations and two unknowns but no solution exists as the equations are inconsistent with each other. Likewise, consider:

$$2y + 3x = 12$$
$$4y + 6x = 24$$

Again we have two equations and two unknowns and the equations are consistent but we cannot derive a unique solution since we have only one *independent* equation; the second being derivable from the first. The requirement therefore for a unique solution to exist is that there be the same number of independent consistent equations as unknowns.

A wellknown feature of the Walrasian system is that if we have n markets in the economy then there are only $n - 1$ independent supply and demand economically meaningful, it is necessary that the market clearing prices generated by the solution be non-negative.

The mere existence of a solution, even one involving non-negative prices, does not guarantee that behaviour in individual markets will be such as to secure it. This is the issue which intrigues economists; how can one be sure that the indicated solution will ever be attained? The Walrasian answer is provided by the process of *tâtonnement*, an artificial device whereby the market process gropes towards the equilibrium solution and moreover is prevented from engaging in exchange at non-equilibrium prices. This artificial device embodies the form of an auctioneer who calls out prices for each and every good. Prospective purchasers and vendors may then tender 'fictive tickets' indicating the quantities of each good they wish to buy or sell. Only when supply and demand are equated in all markets simultaneously is actual exchange permitted to take place. If this is not the case the auctioneer, in the light of the information he has received, revises his prices and the tendering recommences.

Clearly the process of *tâtonnement* is a mathematically convenient device; equally clearly, it is not a description of the way in which markets actually work. In the absence of the all powerful auctioneer prices would be established in various markets which in many cases would be non-equilibrium prices, yet nonetheless a certain amount of trading would take place at these prices – 'false trading'. Here we encounter a principal difference between the Marshallian and Walrasian theories of price determination which is crucial to the Clower-Leijonhufvud view of Keynes. In Marshallian analysis, if supply does not equal demand, an equilibrating adjustment occurs almost immediately upon the side of prices. False trading is not a notable feature of the model analysis. In contrast, in the Walrasian theory, in

equations. This follows from the fact that if n – 1 markets are in equilibrium then the nth market must also be in equilibrium. To see this let the nth market be the money market; if supply equates demand in all n – 1 goods markets there can be no excess demand for money (from sellers of goods) or excess supply of money (from buyers of goods). Supply thus equates demand in the money market which is accordingly in equilibrium. It is therefore always possible to eliminate any one supply and demand equation and still derive a general equilibrium solution. Moreover, this equilibrium is consistent with any price level prevailing in the nth market; the solution determines relative and not absolute prices. We have to step outside the Walrasian system to determine nominal values.

the absence of *tâtonnement*, false trading must occur as some vendors find bids acceptable to them. The adjustment, initially at least, is on the side of quantity changes with no change in the quoted price.

The Reinterpretation of Keynes

In the Clower-Leijonhuvfud interpretation of the *General Theory*, it is contended that Keynes took a Walrasian view of the economy, conceived in terms of interdependence between four all-inclusive markets; the markets for commodities, money, bonds and labour. Moreover, Keynes conceded that a set of prices could exist such as to simultaneously clear all markets, including the labour market, thus generating full employment income. However, in the absence of the benevolent auctioneer there is no guarantee that the market economy will establish the appropriate price vector. On the contrary, where disequilibrium prices prevailed quantity adjustments would occur under the impetus of false trading which in turn would exert disequilibrating feedback effects upon other markets.

By way of example consider the labour market. If the price of labour is too high to clear the market (let us say owing to an autonomous fall in export demand), there will not be an immediate fall in money wages but instead a decline in the quantity of labour employed. The decline in labour employment implies a decline in incomes which exerts a feedback effect upon commodity markets elsewhere – a fall in demand. But here again, the decline in demand is compensated not by an adjustment on the side of prices but rather by a reduction of the quantity purchased; a feedback effect is thus exerted upon investment expenditures as inventories increase and consequently the demand for labour falls even further. The above sequence demonstrates two concepts fundamental to Keynesian thought. First, that effective demand for goods depends upon actual income received (the consumption function) and may fall short of notional demand – defined as that level of demand forthcoming had labour been able to sell its desired quantity of labour time at existing wage levels, – and secondly, the notion that the importance of the multiplier lies in magnifying deviations from the equilibrating market quantities.

The Clower-Leijonhufvud re-interpretation of the *General Theory* attempts to re-establish Keynes' reputation as a major theorist. Hitherto, the conventional wisdom has been to portray Keynes' achievement primarily as one in macro-economic policy formation by indicating how governments could intervene to raise employment levels, whilst simultaneously denying him a rôle as a major theorist on the grounds that the Pigou effect negates his attempt to demonstrate that the classical system has no inherent tendency to achieve full employment. In the new view of Keynes, the Pigou effect is largely an irrelevancy. If unemployment is the consequence of comparative exchange ratios being out of line, and in particular by the price of capital being too high relative to the price of wage labour, then all round deflation, as implied by the Pigou effect, is of no avail. What is required is a decrease in the rate of interest relative to wages – hence the reason for Keynes' repeated advocacy of expanding the money supply and his general agnosticism concerning the efficacy of cutting money wages as a means of generating employment.

In stark contrast to accepted doctrine, which views the *General Theory* largely as an exercise in comparative statics, this reappraisal of Keynesian economics focusses attention on disequilibrium situations and analyses the resulting adjustments in dynamic terms. Ultimately, even in the absence of the auctioneer, adjustments will occur upon the side of prices as both workers and entrepreneurs experience the painful learning process that their reservation prices are too high. A classical full employment solution is not inconsistent with the underlying model yet nonetheless, in this interpretation, Keynes' achievement is very real. It lies in pointing out that the automatic adjustment of the classical analysis rests upon the highly artificial assumption of perfect price flexibility guaranteed by the auctioneer; in emphasizing that price rigidity is the consequence not of monopoly but of imperfect information and that in the absence of such *tâtonnement* the disequilibrium adjustment process could be extremely long; and further, in stressing that initial reactions to disequilibrium situations are more likely to widen the discrepancy between actual and equilibrium prices/quantity relationships. Keynes thus emerges as a major theorist of macro-economic disequilibrium. It is not easy for the conventionally trained economist to accept such a revolutionary re-interpretation of Keynesian economics and if this interpretation is correct, the question must be raised: why has it taken so long for Keynes' real contribution to be appreciated? To this question, Leijonhufvud's answer is clear and unmistakeable; it is that Keynes has been grossly misinterpreted by his own disciples who have viewed the *General Theory* as a radical departure from Keynes' previous work, rather than as a continuation of the economics of the *Treatise*, and who have chosen to present Keynes in the mechanical and restrictive simultaneous equation model of the IS–LM framework. In this view, the major defect of the popular IS–LM construct is that it assumes independence between the IS and LM functions whereas Keynes specifically allowed for a change in the money stock to influence consumption expenditures by generating wealth effects (via the increased capitalization of bonds as interest rates fall). It thus minimizes the role of monetary policy and exaggerates the gulf between the policy recommendations of the *Treatise* and those of the *General Theory*.*

The Keynesian debate has led directly to a reassessment of the usefulness of the macro/micro economic distinction. More and more, the real distinction is perceived to lie in the extent of aggregation and not in any fundamental difference in method or approach. From the viewpoint of macro-economic policy formation, one would not wish to disaggregate to the extent of the complete Walrasian system with a supply and demand equation for each and every good. Recognition of mutual interdependence does not negate the fact that some markets are more important than others. Yet, even if we limit ourselves to just four principal markets (the composite goods market, the money market, the bond market and the labour market) the fact remains that implicitly we must have a micro-economic framework applicable to each. Since each of these markets are characterised by supply and demand functions and prices they are amenable to micro-economic analysis. At the same time, since interdependence is fully allowed, the nature of the analysis is more in keeping with general rather than partial equilibrium. Thus, macro-economic analysis is essentially quasi-general equilibrium analysis, in which micro-economic tools are employed, and interdependence fully recognised.†

To emphasize this point consider the composite figure II.1. In part b, we portray the labour market where the supply of labour services is drawn from households and is a positive function of the wage rate,

* It may be noted that the IS–LM framework is predominantly a policy oriented tool emphasizing *comparative static* equilibria. Adoption of this framework may thus have led Keynesian oriented economists away from the theoretical dynamics propounded in the Clower-Leijonhufvud thesis.

† This terminology, and indeed the subsequent argument, derives from R. L. Crouch (4).

whilst the demand for labour includes the demand of firms and government and is negatively related to the wage rate. Part c of the figure conveys a conventional micro-economic analysis of the supply and demand for commodities where the former is a positive function of price and is provided by firms (and in some cases by government) and where demand is a negative function of price and includes the demands of households, firms and government. Part d depicts the bond market which we assume consists of bonds supplied by both government and business firms and demanded by households and again where the normal positive and negative relationships apply with regard to the price of bonds – indicated by the reciprocal of the interest rate. In part e we show the supply and demand for money, with the supply being autonomously determined by the government and the demand by firms and households being negatively related to the price of money – i.e. the rate of interest. To complete the overall macro-economic model we depict the volume of output as a simple function of the volume of employment (part a) which is a permissible assumption in short-term analysis when we may assume the capital stock fixed. We thus portray the macro-economy in terms of four markets, three transactors and the aggregate production function and we may analyse the economy in terms of changes in market conditions, transactors behaviour, or in technology – the latter reflected in shifts in the aggregate production function. A change in the supply and demand conditions in any one market will exert feedback effects upon other markets which in turn will impinge upon the market initiating the change. The nature of the induced responses will depend upon the nature of the micro-economic assumptions underlying the model analysis in each market, as for example the assumption of profit maximization, and the policy implications will reflect, if only implicitly, these basic assumptions. The applicability of the assumptions will differ between differing economies and indeed may differ between different points in time within the same economy.

By way of example, consider the labour market. Conventionally, macro-economic analysis builds upon the micro-economic foundation depicted by Figure II.1b where both the supply and demand for labour are a function of the real wage and where it is assumed that an increase in the wage rate will call forth an increased supply of work effort. However, this assumption has been questioned with reference to the agricultural sectors of less advanced economies where it has been argued that a backward bending supply curve may be applicable above a

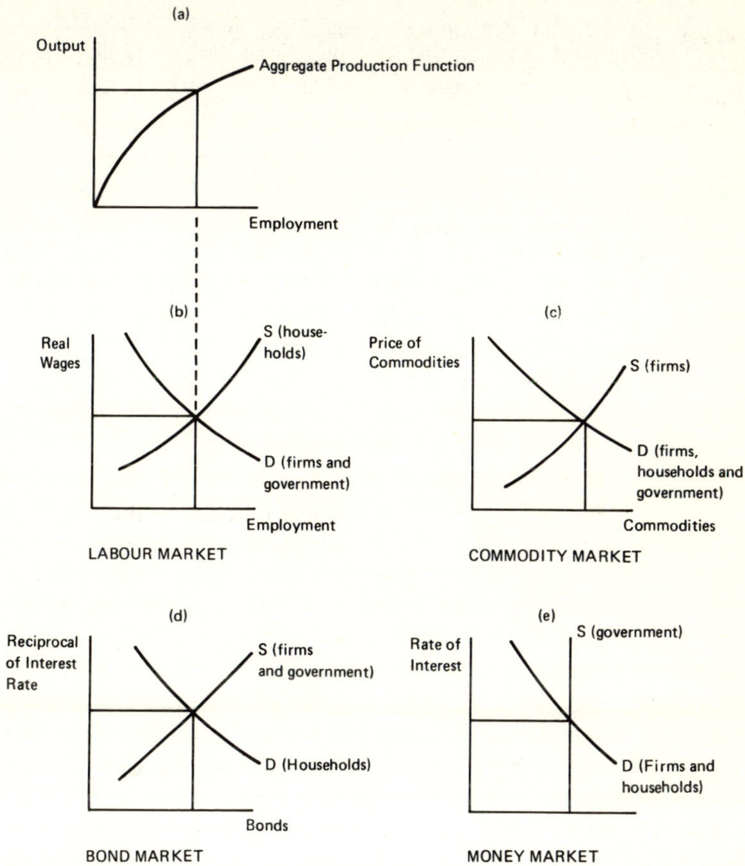

Figure II.1

certain wage. Clearly, this is an important consideration for policy-makers; taxation of agricultural income may generate increased output as well as revenue if this assumption is correct. In particular, it provides some justification for export taxes on primary commodities selling at fixed prices on world markets although such taxes are usually assailed as being detrimental to the attainment of balance of payments equilibrium.

These remarks concerning the labour market are purely illustrative. Similar considerations may apply to the market for commodities, the bond market and in particular to the demand for money. In each case, it is necessary to formulate a micro-economic framework to which the macro-economic policy proposal may be related. Failure to do so may not only lead to the propagation of policies which perform poorly, but may also limit the potential scope of macro-economic policies. For example, theoretical developments in the theory of economic growth have led to the popularisation of neo-classical models which imply a decidedly limited rôle for fiscal policy. However, in part this limitation is self-imposed by the nature of the micro-economic assumptions underlying the growth model. Particularly in the construction of the more esoteric growth models, there is an understandable tendency to incorporate extremely *simpliste* assumptions concerning the behaviour of consumer and investment expenditures. Such assumptions, typified by constant saving ratios, *ex ante* equality of savings and investment etc., are not derived from the standard micro-economic analysis of firms or households and implicitly they limit the relevance of the model analysis to policy action. A more sophisticated micro-economic analysis may supply the understanding necessary to the construction of new macro-economic hypotheses. The fact that the data available, particularly on inflation, employment and the balance of payments, requires the adoption of a macro-economic approach should not blind one to the need for a micro-economic foundation and a certain degree of disaggregation in order to understand the nature of dynamic interdependence. "The object of disaggregation is not to pursue partial equilibrium analysis but to examine the detailed working of the general equilibrium system." (5)

Having indicated, if only briefly, the nature of the micro-economic underpinning to macro-economic policy, we are now in a position to examine some of the policy instruments more closely. In what follows, we will pay particular attention to monetary and fiscal measures, traditionally the major measures of control. At the present time a heated debate ensues concerning the comparative efficacy of these respective policies. The former pre-eminence of monetary control was rudely shattered in the wake of the Keynesian revolution which not only questioned the effectiveness of monetary measures but also sanctioned and made respectable the competing claims of fiscal policy. In more recent years, the pendulum has begun to swing in the opposite direction and repeatedly stress is being laid upon the importance of the monetary variable. In order to understand the nature of this debate it is necessary to examine in some detail one of the oldest and most respected doctrines in economics, namely the Quantity Theory of

Money. As a prelude to our discussion of macro-economic policy generally, therefore, we will survey the evolution of this doctrine in the following chapter, paying particular attention to its modern interpretation and its relation to the Keynesian theory, and drawing out the respective policy implications.

Appendix The Micro-Economics of Stagflation

The unfortunate combination of higher rates of inflation with growing unemployment witnessed in recent years, especially in the United Kingdom and the United States, has presented a problem to orthodox macro-economic theory since it runs counter to formal model analysis. In most cases the problem is neatly sidestepped by invoking the conventional IS–LM apparatus and analysing the economy in real terms with prices conveniently ignored. Explanations of increasing inflation and growing unemployment are then usually presented in terms of a dynamically unstable Phillips relation with the instability explained primarily in terms of changing price expectations. We will consider this aspect of inflation in Chapter IV when discussing the implications of the quantity theory. For the moment, it is of interest to consider an alternative explanation for the phenomenon of 'stagflation' recently presented by Truu (6) which neatly illustrates the relevance of a micro-economic analysis to a macro-economic problem. Consider the Diagram A.II.1, which portrays the average revenue product and marginal revenue product curves of a firm or industry with respect to its employment of labour. With a wage level OV the amount ON of labour will be employed by the profit maximizing firm or industry. Assuming output to be a simple function of the volume of employment and given a negatively sloped demand curve for the product, there will be a determinate price/output relationship in the market. The rectangle, VWST may be considered as the surplus return on labour in the sense that it is the average revenue product minus the average wage paid multiplied by the total number of workers employed. Now let us assume that organized labour perceives this surplus return and under the threat of strike action forces an increase in the wage to OW. The profit maximizing firm will, according to static micro-theory, react by reducing its employment level to OM. Given our assumptions, output declines and with no change in demand conditions prices will rise. Hence the association of increasing unemployment with higher prices. Moreover, the adjustment process undertaken by the firm in response to the payment of higher wages creates precisely the identical

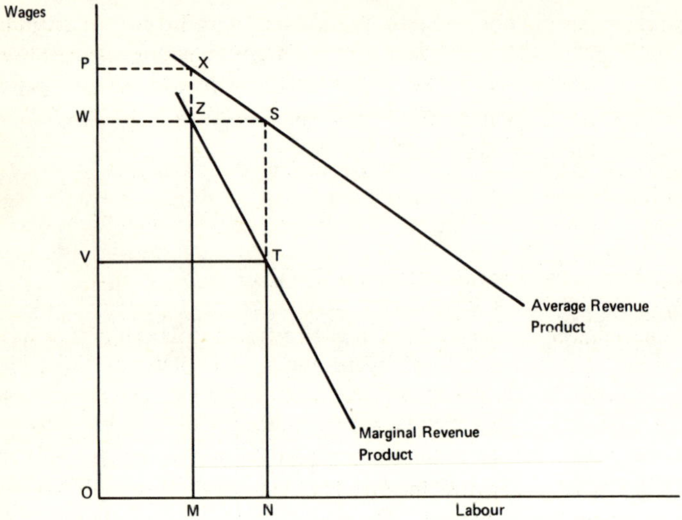

Figure A.II.1

conditions which precipitated the initial wage demand; it restores a surplus return indicated by the rectangle WPXZ.

This analysis is admittedly too simple, the more so for being stated in comparative static terms. It assumes that demand conditions are unaltered by trade union action and this procedure may be dangerous when generalizing the argument to the macro-economy. It further assumes that trade unions are willing to accept the consequences of their action in generating increased unemployment amongst their members. However, much of the force of these points is lost if the argument is conceived of in dynamic terms. In a growing economy both average and marginal product curves are continually shifting outwards over time as the normal process of income growth raises the level of demand. The trade unions are thus able to bargain for higher wages without necessarily having to accept unemployment amongst their members. Increasing unemployment within the economy is thus confined to non-members and in particular to the new entrants to the labour force. Under these conditions, output does not fall and may even increase but remains considerably below the full employment potential. In such an economy the most militant trade unions will be those in industries confronting income elastic demand conditions since these industries will be the ones experiencing the most rapid shift of revenue product curves. Such industries (in Britain the motor-car industry in particular), may exercise a decisive influence on national wage negotiations generally and may add to the pace of inflation by influencing wage claims and settlements in declining sectors or sectors experiencing little change in productivity.* This analysis, of course, assumes that the adjustment response by the firm or industry occurs on the side of prices, as opposed to output, and this is generally the case with prices being raised at discreet intervals usually following a wage agreement. It may be questioned whether trade unions are in fact as cynical as here portrayed, in being responsible for increasing the total volume of unemployment in pursuit of their own self interests. Two points seem worthy of mention. First, the extension of social security schemes, unemployment benefits, welfare payments and so forth have made it easier for trade unions to concentrate more on wage bargaining and less upon the employment consequences (8). The unions are thus able to pursue sectional interests without regard to national employment figures and presumably this tendency would be strengthened by the adoption of a negative income tax. Secondly, in an inflationary setting, frequent wage bargaining is essentially defensive in nature being an attempt to maintain real living standards. Annual wage demands are the only means whereby real living standards can be maintained by those sections of the population not subject to any prior agreement on increments. Further, it is not always realized that in an inflationary setting wage increases in excess of the rate of inflation are normally required in order to leave real income unchanged. This arises from the fact that marginal tax rates exceed average rates and this is especially true in the case of means tested benefits, where a wage increase may involve loss of a benefit and thus imply a very high marginal tax rate. Moreover, the rate of increase needed to maintain living standards intact in real terms is greater for the lower paid.† It is for this reason highly probable that any voluntary compliance by the trade union movement with an incomes policy, say by limiting wage demands to

* This latter point resembles closely the differential productivity thesis of inflation advanced by Edgren, Flaxen & Odhner (7). According to this doctrine, wage agreements which are justified by productivity increases, influence wage levels elsewhere, particularly in the public sector where possibilities of raising productivity per man are more limited. Such a theory of inflation would, in the British case, attach considerable importance to wage increases granted by the export sector following the devaluation of 1967, since this had the net effect of raising revenue productivity.

† Consider for example, a worker earning £1000 per year and after all allowances (of say £700) paying tax at a marginal rate of 1/3 on the last £300. His take home pay is £900. To compensate for inflation of 10% he will require take home pay of £990 implying a gross income of £1135 or a wage increase of 13.5%. Using the same example but with initial salary of £2000 the required increase is only 11.5%.

some previously agreed figure, would first require some improvements and safeguards for the lower paid workers. It was no doubt with this consideration in mind that the recent British version of incomes policy, initiated by the Labour Government in July 1975 with the support of both the TUC and the CBI, provided for a maximum *absolute* wage increase of £6 per week (reduced to £4 in 1976), implying a much large percentage increase for lower paid as opposed to higher paid workers. Clearly, if such policies are maintained for any length of time they will inevitably promote a narrowing of real income differentials with possibly adverse consequences upon the efficient allocation of resources. Ultimately also, they impinge upon accepted notions of equity and fairness, upon which much fiscal compliance depends, by inducing the highly skilled to seek out various fringe benefits and payments in kind, less controllable by incomes policy and less easily assimilated into the overall fiscal burden.

Chapter III The Quantity Theory of Money

Much of the recent discussion and controversy surrounding the issue of monetary versus fiscal policy for economic stabilization hinges upon the importance of the monetary variable. In general, the advocate of the monetarist viewpoint would argue not only that money matters but that it exercises a dominant influence upon the economy, so much so that other variables acting *independently* of the money stock have but a minor effect. The importance of the monetary variable is, of course, intimately linked with the quantity theory of money. The monetarist would normally adhere to the theory whereas the non-monetarist would tend to deny its conclusions or dismiss them as tautological. Unfortunately, an unbiased assessment of the pros and cons of the opposing positions is no simple matter because it is not always clear exactly what any particular quantity theorist is asserting. As is the case with most doctrines which have withstood the test of time, the quantity theory has undergone subtle but significant change. The quantity theory propounded today is no longer the theory put forward by economists in the tradition of Hume; moreover, it is not only the underlying assertion of the theory which has changed, or at least been subject to reinterpretation, but also the nature of the independent variable – namely money! At the root of much of the present debate is the vexed question of how money should be defined. Should it include bank deposits as is conventionally the case, and if so, should the latter be taken to include savings accounts (time deposits)? Before these questions can be answered it is necessary to determine what constitutes the essential distinguishing characteristic of money. Is it in providing a "temporary abode of purchasing power", in which case its scope becomes more embracing, or does it lie in its degree of liquidity – the ability to be quickly transferred into other assets with virtually no nominal loss – in which case its boundaries are more limited? Also, it is necessary to determine the time period which is relevant to the theory.

Is the quantity theory concerned with the short-run process of dynamic adjustment or is it primarily an exercise in comparative statics? Finally, do the policy implications differ with respect to differing time horizons?

To bring out the importance of this latter question consider the following quotation from one of the leading exponents of the modern quantity theory (1):

> What I and those who share my views have emphasized is that the quantity of money is extremely important for nominal magnitudes, for nominal incomes, for the level of income in dollars – important for what happens to prices. It is not important at all, or, if that's perhaps an exaggeration, not very important, for what happens to real output over the long period.

And

> I believe that the rate of change of the money supply by itself – . . . has a very important effect on nominal income and prices in the long run. It has a very important effect on nominal and real income in the short run. That's my basic conclusion about changes in the stock of money.

The Traditional Quantity Theory

The traditional quantity theory was first and foremost a theory of the value of money and its underlying assertion was the proposition that the value of money varied inversely with its quantity – with the latter being the causal agent. In the strictest interpretations it was held that a given percentage change in the volume of money would generate an equal percentage change in the price level although this rigid formulation of the theory was not essential to the doctrine but merely illustrative of it. It was not always clear as to what precisely constituted the mechanism by which an increase in the circulating medium achieved its effects but generally underlying the theory was the notion of a "wealth" effect. An increase in monetary wealth would naturally generate increased expenditures. If the volume of goods remained unchanged, this increase in demand would not be matched by any increase in supply and accordingly prices would rise. Implicit in this approach, and in many ways fundamental to the theoretical foundation of the theory, was a concern with the determinants of the demand for money. The latter concern, however, was never the purpose of the exercise but merely a useful tool to aid the analysis.

The antecedents of the theory go back a long way, well before the famous report of the Bullion Committee in 1810 (2) which presented a clear and compelling statement of the theory and paved the way for the dominance of its adherents in English political economy of the nineteenth century. Certainly, by the time that Irving Fisher presented his famous formulation in 1911 (3) he was no longer propounding a new doctrine but rather systematising a body of received opinion and developing an expositional framework hitherto without equal in the history of monetary economics.

The Transactions Approach

Fisher's famous equation of exchange, MV = PT, where M is the total money stock, V its velocity of circulation or the average number of times that each monetary unit is utilized in a given accounting period, T the total number of all transactions and P the general price level, is justifiably one of the best-known tautologies in economics. It is a tautology in that it asserts merely that total monetary expenditure is equal to the monetary value of all goods traded. By invoking certain assumptions it is, however, possible to transform the identity into a theory. If velocity is determined by habit, institutional arrangements, banking practices and so forth, then it may be assumed constant in the short term, and if T is also rendered a constant, which is not so unreasonable if we posit full employment output, then we obtain the well-known result:

$$M\bar{V} = P\bar{T} \quad \text{or} \quad P = \frac{M\bar{V}}{\bar{T}}$$

$$\therefore \quad \Delta M \Rightarrow \Delta P$$

Moreover, in this case, the relationship exists equiproportionately and a diagrammatic representation would trace out a rectangular hyperbola as indicated in Figure III.1. Thus far, the analysis is stated solely in terms of currency money, that is coins and notes in circulation. It is a comparatively simple matter to extend the theory to allow for bank deposits. Thus,

$$MV + M'V' = PT$$

where M′ is the amount of money held in the form of bank deposits and V′ its velocity. If V′ is assumed constant, $V' = \overline{V'}$, then again the strict quantity theory holds providing we make the additional behaviouristic assumption that the ratio of M to M′ is also constant. The latter assumption appeared to Fisher to be a plausible one to make: people would normally choose to keep a certain proportion of their monetary wealth in the form of cash and the remainder in the form of bank deposits and in the normal way of things such a ratio would be subject to only slow change over time.

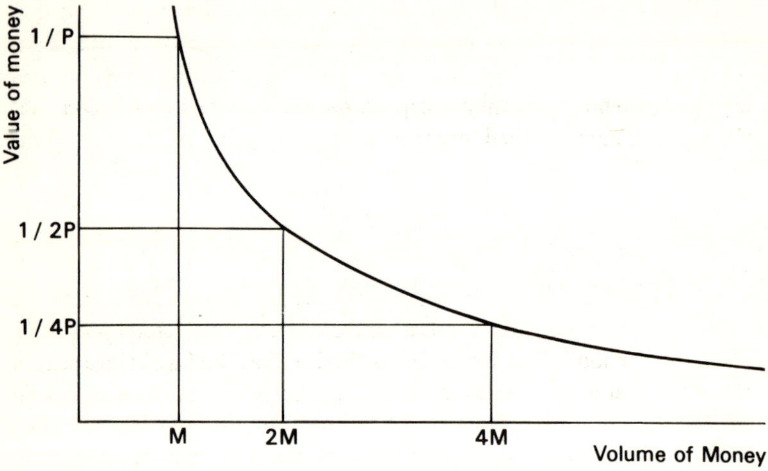

Figure III.1

Fisher's formulation possesses the great virtue of highlighting the assumptions necessary for the strict quantity theory to take effect. By the same token, it emphasizes the conditions under which the quantity theory would be disproved, a quality sometimes lacking in more recent treatments. Moreover, it is also of interest in being a decidedly macro-economic viewpoint of the pricing process; the relationship expressed is one between the aggregate money stock, total transactions and the aggregate price level. Two further points are of interest. The price level referred to is a general price index for all transactions occurring throughout the economy. As such it includes transactions in existing capital assets, second-hand commodities and so forth. Secondly, no explicit rôle is accorded to the rate of interest. Although it has been contended that Fisher did not ignore the influence of interest-rate changes entirely, they do not appear to exert a decisive impact upon the price level. This point is of some importance since much of the attack upon the validity of both traditional and modern quantity theories has been *via* interest rate effects.

The Cambridge Cash Balance Approach

An alternative formulation of the traditional quantity theory of money was propounded by the Cambridge school of economists, led by Marshall, Pigou, Robertson and Keynes. It should be emphasized that they did not consider themselves to be in any fundamental disagreement with Fisher; their prime concern was with the price level and for the most part they accepted the fundamental conclusion that the value of money varied inversely with its quantity. At the same time, however, they considered their own approach superior to that of the transactions version. The latter they held to be too mechanistic and on account of its broad aggregate nature to cloak the underlying motivations governing behaviour in money markets.

In this respect, it may be noted that the transactions version of the quantity theory implied a methodological departure from prevailing economic orthodoxy. It was to the orthodox that the Cambridge school returned. Just as the theory of value had yielded to utility analysis, so too would the theory of money. The value of money, just like the value of any other commodity, was to be understood in terms of supply and demand. In this respect at least, no dichotomy was to be maintained between the real and the monetary sectors. Since the supply of money was exogenously determined, either by the banking sector or by adherence to the international gold standard, it followed that major attention was given to the rôle of demand. It was this emphasis upon the subjective nature of the demand for money which provided the psychological insight lacking in the transactions version and which rendered the cash balance approach, in Pigou's words, "a more effective engine of analysis". Moreover, by specifying more precisely the constituents of the demand function, the Cambridge approach also indicated the conditions which would give rise to unstable fluctuations in demand. Thus, whilst the Cambridge approach may be shown to be formally identical to Fisher, in one sense it went further in indicating possible psychological and institutional factors which could deny the quantity theory.

Keynes *A Tract on Monetary Reform*

An illustrative example of the Cambridge version is provided by Keynes in his classic *Tract on Monetary Reform* (4). It is assumed that people have a certain demand for money in order to finance their day-to-day transactions. This demand for money will differ between individuals according to their tastes, habits, wealth and so forth, but nonetheless it can be aggregated and expressed as the power to command a certain number of consumption units. For analytical purposes, a unit may be taken as a basket of commodities representative of the consumer cost of living. If the actual volume of money which people are holding exceeds that which they demand to hold, then induced spending will occur upon commodities causing prices to increase.

If k is the number of consumption units which people wish to retain command over in the form of money balances, and n represents the total of currency in circulation, then the price level of consumption goods p is indicated by the Cambridge equation,

$$n = pk$$

Providing k remains constant, then we have the strict interpretation of the quantity theory whereby a proportionate increase in the volume of money generates a proportionate increase in the price level. As with Fisher, the simple equation may be expanded to allow for the existence of bank money. The expanded form of the equation is

$$n = p(k + rk')$$

where k′ is the number of consumption units which are held in the form of bank deposits and r is the reserve ratio maintained by the banking sector. Once again, providing k, k′ and r are maintained constant, the strict proportionality rule of the quantity theory holds.* However, Keynes is at pains to show that strict constancy of these

* A numerical example may help to clarify the argument. Assume the money stock in circulation totals £300, and that in the aggregate people desire to maintain command over 50 consumption units, half of which is to be kept in

variables is unlikely to be maintained. Moreover, he seeks to emphasize that they may change in response to a change in the quantity of money especially when the latter influence the prevailing state of expectations. The influence of the German inflation is clearly evident in this stress upon the interdependence of money and the demand for money. Thus, if an increase in the stock of money generates expectations of inflation it will lead to a decrease in the value of k and k′ and intensify the inflationary trend. It may also be noted that in the *Tract* a distinct rôle emerges for the rate of interest as a determinant of the price level since it governs in part the manner in which the rational individual will divide his monetary command over consumption units between k and k′. An increase in the rate of interest payable upon bank deposits will increase k′ at the expense of k and will normally lead to an increase in the price level. By linking a change in the money stock causally with a change in k, and by specifically introducing the rate of interest as a determinant of the price level, Keynes made a significant advance upon Fisher. Nonetheless, there is no fundamental point of disagreement. This is most easily demonstrated if we write the Cambridge equation in its more usual form and express the demand for money as a percentage of the real income of the community as opposed to a given number of consumption units. Thus,

$$n = pkR$$

where R stands for aggregate real income and k now represents the *percentage* of that income which it is desired to maintain in the form of money balances. Thus we may write,

$$p = \frac{n}{kR}$$

the form of cash and the remainder in the form of bank deposits. Assume further that the cash reserve ratio maintained by the banks is 20%. Then,

$$300 = p(25 + \frac{1}{5}.25)$$

$$\therefore\ p = 10$$

A 10% change in the money stock would imply, *ceteris paribus,*

$$330 = p(25 + \frac{1}{5}.25)$$

$$\therefore\ p = 11$$

and a 10% change in the money stock has occasioned a 10% change in the price level. Note also that the general price level itself depends upon the division between k and k′.

which we can compare to Fisher's equation

$$P = \frac{MV}{T}$$

Assuming that p = P,* and given that n = M, we obtain

$$\frac{MV}{T} = \frac{n}{kR}$$

$$\therefore \quad \frac{kR}{T} = \frac{n}{MV}$$

or

$$k\left[\frac{R}{T}\right] = \frac{1}{V}$$

Providing that the ratio of real income to total transactions remains constant the Cambridge k is proportional to the reciprocal of V. An increase in k implies a decrease in V and *vice versa* and demonstration of the strict quantity theory result of proportional changes in both money and prices demands constancy in each. This is hardly surprising. The Cambridge demand for money was purely a transactions demand and as such was implicit in Fisher's formulation. The beauty of the Cambridge approach lay in spotlighting and explaining the changes in k; in contrast, the mechanical nature of the transactions approach provided no insight into why the value of V should ever change. In essence, this was all that divided Fisher and the Cambridge school.

Patinkin and the Real Balance Effect

In 1956 there appeared a monumental work by Don Patinkin (5) which, *inter alia*, demonstrated the rigid conditions required for the strict proportionality rule of the quantity theory whilst simultaneously launching a severe attack upon the Cambridge analysis. Patinkin's main point of contention was that the advocates of the cash balance approach had failed to understand the nature of the quantity theory and this failure was revealed in the dichotomy which they maintained between the goods market and the money market. Far from integrating

* Which admittedly is a simplifying assumption since the P in Fisher's equation is a price index of all transactions including those of existing assets, whereas the p in the Cambridge equation is a price index of national income – i.e. current output.

the two, as had been claimed by the adoption of the same techniques of analysis of supply and demand, Patinkin held that the neo-classical economists had kept the two rigidly part. An increase in the stock of money was assumed to generate an increase in the absolute price level but to exercise no real influence upon the market for commodities. One purpose of Patinkin's elegant analysis was to show that only by exerting an influence upon the market for commodities, *via* the real balance effect, could the strict quantity theory be maintained. Part of Patinkin's attack revolved around the nature of the demand curve for money. Patinkin held that the Cambridge school had generally assumed the demand curve to be a rectangular hyperbola with constant unit elasticity. Indeed, a demand curve of this nature was generally implicit in the argument that a doubling of the money stock would induce a doubling of the price level and such a demand curve had been explicitly diagrammed in Robertson's book, *Money* (6). Patinkin used the real balance effect to demonstrate that the demand curve for money could not be a rectangular hyperbola, and moreover that such a demand curve would contradict the strict quantity theory assertion which the Cambridge quantity theorists were trying to establish! A brief outline of Patinkin's micro-analysis is presented below. In the context of the evolution of the traditional quantity theory its main achievement would appear to lie in making explicit the mechanism by which the "wealth" effect of a change in the money stock takes effect.

Conventional demand theory holds that the demand for any good is a function of real income and the price of all other goods and this treatment allows the construction of a demand curve and permits analysis in terms of income and substitution effects. Patinkin's point of departure is that it fails to consider the real value of one's cash holdings. Thus, a decrease in the price of any good increases the real value of cash balances and will thus generate a real balance effect in favour of increased consumption, in addition to income and substitution effects (providing the good is non-inferior). Failure to take account of the change in the real value of cash holdings due to price changes is tantamount to money illusion. Having indicated the nature of the real balance effect, the analysis is most easily approached *via* conventional indifference curves. In Figure III.2, assume an individual α has inherited monetary wealth to the real value of OY and receives a weekly income in terms of commodities of OX. Since he may transfer money into goods and *vice versa*, his initial location A is but one point on his budget line MM'. Let us assume that he would trade money for goods to arrive at his optimal position B, retaining OZ of cash and OT of goods. Suppose, however, that before he is able to trade, all prices, including the payment to factors, double. What are the consequences?

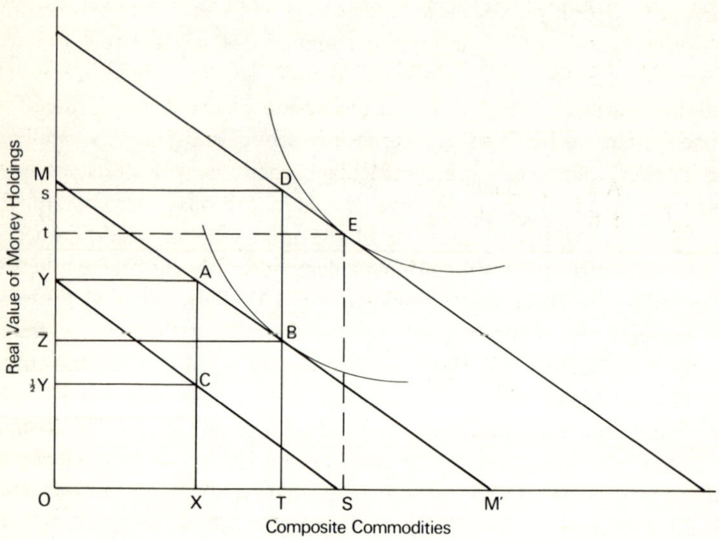

Figure III.2

The real value of α's money holdings are halved so that with his real income unchanged at OX his budget line is shifted parametrically inward to pass through the point C. However he may trade, this reduction in his total real worth will compel him to consume less of all non-inferior goods – including real money balances. Whereas his previous optimal consumption of real balances was indicated as OZ, his new equilibrium will imply consumption of something less than OZ. Since real money balances are equal to nominal money holdings divided by the price level, it follows that the enforced reduction in real balances must be accompanied by a less than proportionate increase in nominal holdings as prices double. Consequently, whilst his *nominal* holding of money will increase owing to the doubling of prices, it will certainly not double. α's demand for money is less than unit elastic; alternatively, α's demand for real money balances is not invariant with respect to the price level.

Having established the nature of α's demand curve for nominal money balances consider now the quantity theory. Let us assume that α had been successful in attaining his preferred position B on the initial budget line MM′. Suppose now that α's holding of money balances is suddenly doubled from OZ (= TB) to 2OZ (= TD). Consequently, whilst he finds himself at position D, his preferred position is now indicated by E where he can attain his maximal indifference curve. At his present position D he has an excess supply of real money balances equal to st and an excess demand for commodities equal to TS. If he is able, he will transfer money into goods to attain his chosen position. Suppose, however, that α's experience is generalised to the entire economy. All individuals awaken to find their real money holdings doubled. In this case, there will be a general excess of money and a general shortage of goods. In the attempt to adjust this situation, where all people are buyers and no one is a seller, commodity prices will be bid upwards by a process of *tâtonnement* without any exchange actually taking place. The process of inflation will be accompanied by the gradual inward shift of α's budget line (and indeed those of all other individuals) as the real value of his money holdings is progressively eroded. Inflation, therefore, progressively achieves the elimination of the excess supply of money and the excess demand for goods until equilibrium is again restored at the former position B. The real value of α's monetary holdings is now equal to its former level and since we had previously postulated that his real holdings had doubled it follows that the adjustment is only complete when the price level has also doubled. Hence, once again we reach the conclusion that a doubling of the money stock generates a doubling of the price level – given in this case that *all* money balances change equi-proportionately.

Since a doubling of money stock results in the ultimate doubling of all prices, it follows that the loci of points tracing out the relationship between prices and money will take the form of a rectangular hyperbola. This, however, does not represent the demand curve for money as the neo-classical school had supposed, but rather the market equilibrium curve which is the combined result of both a shift of the demand curve and an induced movement along it in response to an increase in the volume of money.

Patinkin's model may be considered an elegant refinement of the traditional quantity theory and its value lies in specifying precisely the necessary conditions for the strict proportionality of the quantity theory to hold and in analysing in detail the mechanism by which the change in the money stock takes effect – the real balance effect. Although Patinkin's analysis may be shown to be formally incomplete in failing to provide a full long-run equilibrium,* the integration of product and monetary markets through the real balance effect represented a significant advance upon earlier treatments. For the first time, the nature of the wealth effect is made explicit. What is not so analysed, however, is the manner in which the increase in monetary wealth comes about. A doubling of money balances is simply assumed and the analysis dwells entirely upon the resultant effects.

The failure to specify the manner in which the increase in monetary wealth is achieved must be considered a grave defect of the traditional statement. Clearly, if all money balances double overnight an immediate wealth effect is implied for all money holders throughout the economy. It can hardly be considered surprising if monetary expenditures increase in response. In practice, however, changes in the money stock do not take effect in this manner. Nor, in most cases, do people experience the happy visitations of helicopters carrying a surfeit of bank notes, which is the mode of transmission recently invoked by Friedman (8).

Conventionally, an increase in the monetary variable is not accompanied by an increase in net worth but rather by the exchange of one asset for another – i.e. by the public's sale of government securities on the open market. In this case, the "wealth" effect is absent. The same conclusion follows if the initial increase in the money stock is magnified by the existence of a fractional reserve banking system. Any resultant increase in bank deposits will be matched by an equal increase in liabilities. Consequently, it may be argued that there is no reason to assume that an increase in the money stock will exert any impact at all upon the economy unless it does so *via* the induced change in interest rates necessary to effect the increase.† This is precisely the Keynesian

* As was quickly pointed out by Archibald and Lipsey (7) and conceded by Patinkin in the second edition of his work, the equilibrium obtained is but a short-term equilibrium only since further changes will be induced for income recipients in future time periods. Moreover, if the analysis is extended to an infinite number of periods, general long-run equilibrium is found to be perfectly consistent with a unitary elastic demand curve for money – the real balance effect disappears. This raises again the thorny question of whether the quantity theory is a theory of short- or long-run equilibria or indeed whether it should be considered a theory of equlibria at all.

† A word of qualification is perhaps necessary. There will be a partial wealth effect arising from the increased capitalization of government bonds consequent upon the decline in interest rates. It has also been argued that a wealth effect may arise if the public look upon the existence of

position which leads to the conclusion that the net impact may be limited (especially if investment demands are interest-inelastic), or at least unpredictable. Hence the rationale for the Keynesian denial of the quantity theory. In contrast, the revised version of the quantity theory asserts that an increase in the money stock will generate fairly predictable increases in demands for commodities even in the absence of any change in net worth and acting independently of any interest-rate effect. This is the crux of the present dispute between the revised doctrine of the quantity theory and the Keynesian scepticism.

The Attack Upon the Quantity Theory

The traditional quantity theory had asserted that an increase in the quantity of money would be followed by a fairly predictable – if not always equiproportional – increase in the price level. At the same time, it was usually contended that other factors would exert little or no effect.

The attack upon the quantity theory developed along two distinct lines. On the one hand, it was argued that whilst changes in the money stock could indeed influence the general price level they would do so in an essentially erratic and unpredictable way. The extreme form of this argument concluded that changes in the money stock might exert no influence at all. Secondly, it was argued that other influences – notably the rate of interest – could exert a decisive and significant impact upon

interest-bearing government debt as constituting, in the aggregate, both a liability as well as an asset to the private sector. This they may do if they take cognizance of the increased taxation which is implied for the private sector in order to finance and service the debt. They will, however, possess no such sophisticated notions concerning the non-interest-bearing debt of the government, namely the money stock. Their possession of this will be looked upon solely as an asset. Consequently, the substitution of money for interest-bearing debt will have the net effect of cancelling a private liability and a wealth effect is implied. An even more ingenious argument has been invoked to show that any resulting expansion of bank deposits will also generate wealth effects by raising the market value of banking shares which presumably are held by the private sector. Whilst these theoretical niceties raise all sorts of interesting problems they presuppose a mode of behaviour upon the part of the public which hardly seems justified by casual observation. Regardless of the theoretical pros and cons the position taken here is that for policy purposes they may be ignored. For a most useful review of these and related arguments consult especially Smith (9).

the general price level. Both these theoretical developments were intimately associated with the economics of J.M. Keynes, who, as we have seen, had earlier advocated a variant of the cash balance approach of the quantity theory. Indeed, it may not perhaps be too great an exaggeration to conclude that the status of the traditional quantity theory was inversely related to the evolution of Keynes' thinking of monetary affairs – with there being no doubt that the latter was the causal agent.

Keynes and the *Treatise on Money*

In the *Treatise on Money* (10) the rate of interest emerges for the first time as a direct determinant of the price level. Hitherto, the rate of interest had been relegated to a comparatively minor and indirect rôle. For the most part, it was held that the significance of the rate of interest lay in its impact upon the quantity of money in circulation. A decrease in interest rates, for example, was expected to increase the demand for loanable funds and extend the quantity of bank credit. Thus, under the traditional quantity theory, the volume of money was the key variable and the significance of the rate of interest lay mainly in inducing marginal changes in the quantity of bank money outstanding.

In the *Treatise*, the comparative importance of money and interest rates is reversed. Now the rate of interest is able to exert a direct impact upon the price level through its impact upon saving and investment decisions, whilst the volume of money is now relegated to playing an indirect rôle, namely that of influencing the rate of interest. Moreover, the rate of interest may change on account of factors other than a change in the money stock and hence fluctuations in the price level become independent of changes in the money stock. The economics of the *Treatise*, therefore, constituted a major assault on the quantity theory of money as commonly understood. However, it is perhaps more accurate to argue that Keynes at this stage was not attempting to destroy the theory but rather to improve upon it by specifically taking account of influences previously ignored. Nonetheless, this change in the direction of approach was of major significance for the development of monetary theory. Until now, the impact of a change in the volume of money was assumed to take effect through some form of wealth effect leading to increased expenditures in commodity markets.

With the publication of the *Treatise* there emerges the Keynesian emphasis that the prime importance of changes in the money stock lies in the induced impact upon interest rates. The ensuing debate between these respective viewpoints continues to this day and is at the heart of the present controversy over the validity of the revised quantity theory.

The argument of the *Treatise* can be outlined fairly easily by invoking the system of equations that Keynes employed. National income (Y) is defined as the sum of factor payments (E) plus windfall gains (Q) where the latter represent actual sales proceeds minus the payments to the factors of production. Thus,

$$Y = E + Q \tag{1}$$

and Q disappears if only normal profits are being earned. Output (O) is simply equal to the combined output of consumption goods (R) and capital goods (C). Hence,

$$O = R + C \tag{2}$$

Saving (S) is defined as the difference between factor earnings and expenditure upon consumption goods. Thus,

$$S = E - PR \tag{3}$$

where P represents the price index of consumables. Investment (I) is simply the expenditure on capital goods. Accordingly, where P' indicates the price index of capital goods,

$$I = P'C \tag{4}$$

Finally the general price level (π) is merely the weighted sum of total expenditure divided by the level of output, so that

$$\pi = \frac{PR + P'C}{O} \tag{5}$$

Since PR = E – S (from 3) and P′C is simply I, we may rewrite equation 5 as

$$\pi = \frac{E}{O} + \frac{I - S}{O} \tag{6}$$

and we have derived an expression for the general price level which does not have money as an argument! Accordingly, prices vary either as the ratio of factor earnings to output varies – which may be interpreted in the current jargon as a variant of cost-push inflation – or alternatively as investment and savings diverge. Inflation due to the latter factor may be considered as constituting demand pull. Since the ratio $\frac{E}{O}$ may be assumed fairly constant if full employment output prevails, the major cause of fluctuations in the price level arises from savings diverging from investment. This is where the rate of interest enters to play a crucial rôle in the objective of price stability. That rate of interest which equates savings and investment we may term the natural rate. Changes in the value of money are thus associated with the market rate of interest departing from the natural rate. Why should such changes occur? On the one hand, a change in the volume of money may make credit conditions easier and lead to a general fall in interest rates; a departure of the market rate below the natural rate will generate inflationary tendencies as investment demands exceed the flow of savings forthcoming. Thus, the quantity theory re-emerges but this time in a new guise working through the indirect interest-rate effect. On the other hand, the market rate of interest may fluctuate as a result of changing expectations concerning security prices in the capital market. Thus changes in the price level may occur even without the prerequisite of an increase in the money supply. The influence of expectations in determining interest rates was a theoretical innovation in the *Treatise*. The importance of expectations was to become even more pronounced in the argument of the *General Theory* with even more profound implications for the quantity theory of money.

The General Theory

Whilst the argument propounded in the *Treatise* carried grave implications for the validity of the traditional quantity theory, it nonetheless maintained that an increase in the volume of money would normally generate an increase in the price level working through the change in interest rates. In contrast, the argument developed in the *General Theory* (11) was much more revolutionary in that it claimed that under certain circumstances even this effect would be absent. Two distinct lines of thought were involved in reaching this conclusion. First of all, the assumption of full employment output which had characterised the *Treatise* was dispensed with. The *General Theory* thus became a theory of the determination of the level of output and it followed that the adjustment to monetary disturbance could occur upon the side of output as opposed to prices. Today, this argument appears to have been fully accepted, at least in terms of short-run unemployment situations. Consequently, a popular form of Fisher's fundamental equation is often stated as

$$MV = PQ = Y$$

where Q is the current output level, P its price index and Y money national income. If velocity is assumed constant, then an increase in the money stock will generate merely an increase in the level of money national income; whether the adjustment occurs on the value of P, Q, or both remains *a priori* indeterminate.

Secondly, the *General Theory* indicated the circumstances in which an increase in the stock of money would exert no influence at all upon the rate of interest and consequently no impact upon the economy. This case, which has become known as the Keynesian liquidity trap, implied that at some minimal level of the interest rate the demand for money balances would become infinitely elastic and that additional increases in the money stock would merely be absorbed into idle speculative balances. The recipients of the increase in the money stock would not be induced to purchase bonds, thus lowering interest rates further, owing to the fear of realizing subsequent capital losses, and instead would be prepared to accumulate idle reserves. Now clearly, the velocity of an idle deposit is nil. Consequently, this process is accompanied by a general decrease in the average velocity of money. In terms of Fisher's equation, the increase in the money stock is exactly offset by a decrease in the velocity of money so that no change takes place in total expenditures and no impact is transmitted to the remainder of the economy. The quantity theory is denied. It should be emphasized that Keynes did not appear to attach much importance to this situation, except as an interesting theoretical possibility, and generally held that increasing the money stock would be accompanied by a decline in interest rates. Nonetheless, the analysis indicated that the decline in interest rates could be substantially limited and small variations in the rate of interest might not be expected to exert much impact upon investment spending. Any generalised statement about the effect of a change in the volume of money upon the aggregate economy could no longer be maintained. The traditional quantity theory had been eclipsed and swept aside in the upheaval of the Keynesian revolution.

The Revival of the Quantity Theory

The revival of the quantity theory of money is primarily due to the work of Milton Friedman and a group of adherents who, rightly or wrongly, have been dubbed as members of the "Chicago School". The association between the quantity theory and the University of Chicago is in part explained by Friedman's claim that the latter institution "was one of the few academic centers at which the quantity theory continued to be a central and vigorous part of the oral tradition throughout the 1930's and 1940's, where students continued to study monetary theory and write theses on monetary problems" (12). It should perhaps be mentioned that this claim has not gone unchallenged, notably by Patinkin (13). What cannot be denied, however, is that in 1956 there appeared under Friedman's editorship a most important volume entitled *Studies in the Quantity Theory of Money* (14), the product of the Workshop in Money and Banking at Chicago, and which more than any other event signalled the re-emergence of the quantity theory. It is this volume which has pivoted attention firmly upon the nature of the demand for money and the determinants of velocity and which has provided the stimulus for much of the empirical and statistical studies which have characterised later years.

The statement which emerges from this volume is strikingly different from the orthodox version of the quantity theory. Whereas the latter had been concerned primarily to explain fluctuations in the price level,

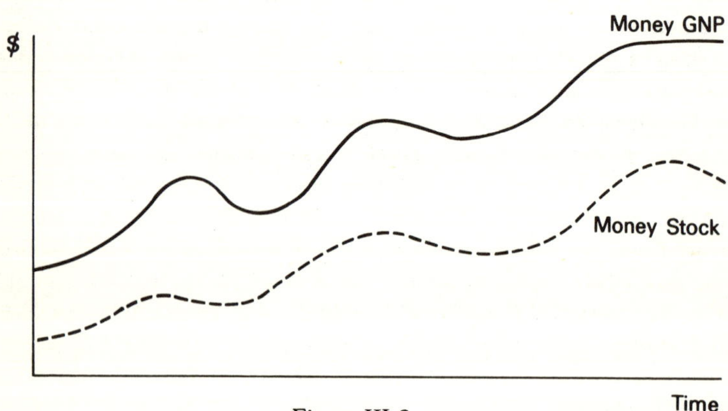

Figure III.3

the modern quantity theory is now a theory of the determination of money national income. The spirit of the revised doctrine can best be summed up in the suggested relationship of Figure III.3, where the money stock is the presumed causal agent. As a theory of money national income, it ranks as an alternative to the Keynesian theory which emphasizes income expenditure relationships and the multiplier process. The essence of the present debate between the so-called "Keynesian" school and the so-called "Chicago" school is simply which of these two statements is the more useful as a means of approaching national income determination (15). If the modern theory differs from the old, so too does the nature of the attack which has been launched upon it. Whereas the purpose of the attack upon the traditional statement was to deny the relationship between money and the price level, the modern theory is subject to a double-edged offensive. On the one hand, there are those economists who deny that any significant relationship exists between the volume of money and money GNP, relying for the most part upon variations in the money supply/GNP ratio; and on the other, there are those economists who concede the underlying relationship but dispute the direction of causation!

If the quantity theory is a theory of the determination of money national income, it follows that the impact of a change in the money stock can be either upon physical output or prices, or some combination of the two. In this respect, it is not unlike the modern Keynesian approach which argues that the impact of a change in the money stock will reveal itself either in output or in price changes, depending upon the extent of unemployed resources. However, in contrast to the Keynesian statement, the relationship between changes in the money stock and resulting changes in money national income is held to be much more predictable and the special case of the liquidity trap, whereby a change in the money stock exerts no effect, is explicitly denied. Further, the extent to which changes will occur upon the side of output or prices will depend in large measure upon the time period employed. It is Friedman's assertion that whilst changes in the volume of money may influence short-term movements in output employment and interest rates, in the long run these variables will approach their "natural" levels which exist independently of the volume of money. The significance of the revised quantity theory, then, is primarily on long-term nominal magnitudes, and in this respect it resembles closely the traditional statement, albeit in a far more sophisticated guise.

The Demand for Money

Of central importance to the revised quantity theory is the assertion that there exists a stable demand function for real money holdings. This, of course, is not to assert that the quantity of real money holdings remains unchanged but only that it varies in a reasonably predictable way in response to changes in a few key variables. For Friedman, the most important elements influencing the demand for money are the rates of return on money and other assets, both real and financial, the level of permanent income, and the ratio of non-human to total wealth. More specifically, we may write the demand for real money holdings as

$$\frac{M}{P} = f(r_m, r_b, r_e, \frac{\dot{P}}{P}, Y, w, u)$$

where r_m is the expected nominal rate of return on money and which will ordinarily be zero for money kept in the form of cash but may be either positive or negative with regard to money held in the form of bank deposits according to whether such deposits yield net interest or are subject to net service charges. r_b is the expected nominal rate of return on bonds, including expected changes in their prices, and likewise r_e is the expected rate of return on equities, allowance again being made for expected price changes. $\frac{\dot{P}}{P}$ is the expected rate of change of prices and hence the expected nominal rate of return on real assets if for simplicity, we ignore their expected yield. Y is permanent income and hence an index of total wealth and w that percentage of total wealth which is held in non-human form and thereby readily realizable – as for example property holdings. Finally, the variable u takes account of all other influences which may determine preference patterns generally. Thus, for example, an increase in the expectation of inflation would normally produce a decline in the demand for money holdings – i.e. a rise in velocity. Far from velocity being constant, as was tacitly implied in many of the more naïve versions of the traditional approach, it will respond to significant changes in the above variables in a predictable and rational manner. But – and this seems to be the essence of the modern approach – the above variables are normally subject to only slow change over time whereas the supply of money may experience abrupt change. If this is the case, and velocity is subject only to gradual change over time, whilst the money stock may rise and fall rapidly, the clear implication is that the demand for money is independent of its supply. The independence of supply and demand, i.e. between the money stock and its velocity, is an essential tenet of the revised doctrine.

If the demand for money does not show great variation in comparison to the supply, which may experience considerable and rapid fluctuation, then changes in the value of money – which as anything else are to be explained in terms of supply and demand – are almost always supply-determined.

To quote Friedman directly (16):

> It is clear from this discussion that changes in prices and nominal income can be produced either by changes in the real balances that people wish to hold or by changes in the nominal balances available for them to hold. Indeed, it is a tautology, summarized in the famous quantity equation . . . The quantity theory is not, however, this tautology. It is, rather, the empirical generalization that changes in desired real balances (in the demand) tend to proceed slowly and gradually or to be the result of events set in train by prior changes in supply, whereas, in contrast, substantial changes in the supply of nominal balances can and frequently do occur independently of any changes in demand. The conclusion is that substantial changes in prices or nominal income are almost invariably the result of changes in the nominal supply of money.

The preceding quotation also makes it clear why the interest-rate sensitivity of the demand for money is such a vital issue. Usually, a change in the supply of money is only possible *via* changes in interest rates. If the demand for money was highly interest-elastic, supply and demand would be interdependent and no precise causal influence could be discerned.

The increasing amount of evidence adduced from the empirical studies suggests that whereas velocity is by no means a constant it is sufficiently stable to allow the assertion that an increase in the money supply will exert a predictable impact upon expenditure decisions. It should not be assumed that the evidence is in any sense conclusive; findings differ, often significantly, and there is considerable controversy over the use of the time series data employed, lags in effect and the issue of causality.* Nonetheless, it would be fair to conclude that the

* For a discussion of the evidence and comments upon its validity, see especially Laidler (17), Kaldor (18), Goodhart (19), Walters (20), Bain (21) and Sims (22).

empirical findings have been accompanied by a formidable array of conversions, both in academic and non-academic circles, to the new orthodoxy of the revised quantity theory.

If the demand for money function is comparatively stable so that a change in money stock exerts a predictable impact upon money incomes, then the implications for the decision-making authorities are considerable. In particular, it implies that more concern should be paid to the volume of money and less to the question of interest rates, availability and so forth, which have generally been taken as an index of monetary ease or restraint. For the quantity theorist, high interest rates do not necessarily indicate a situation of tight money; on the contrary, they are more likely to indicate the consequences of substantial monetary increases in the past with inflation in the current period the consequence. The existence of high *nominal* rates of interest may merely reflect an increasing awareness of the effects of inflation by the lenders of capital.

Although the implications for the importance of the money stock are clear, it should be emphasized that Friedman and most of the adherents to the modern quantity theory do not claim that discretionary changes in the volume of money can be used as a viable instrument of short-term stabilization policy. Primarily, this is because of the uncertainty with respect to the time period required for the measure to take effect. Since they are concerned with the impact of a change in the *stock* of money upon the *flow* demands in commodity markets, it follows that the adjustment period may be long or short according to the change in the flow magnitude. The available empirical evidence would indicate some considerable variation in adjustment periods. Consequently, attempts at controlling the money stock to achieve short-term stabilization goals may be self-defeating and may heighten the degree of instability. Hence the reason for Friedman's advocacy of abandoning attempts at discretionary monetary policy in favour of permitting the money stock to grow at some pre-determined annual rate in line with the growth potential of the economy.

The Continuing Controversy

The fundamental point of issue between the traditional quantity theory and the Keynesian onslaught turns upon the crucial question of what constitutes an effective substitute for money balances. The Keynesian position is to contend that the only close substitute for money is alternative financial assets. It follows that if the monetary authorities increase the volume of money excessively a purchase of financial assets will occur and interest rates will fall. The reduction in interest rates renders money holding more attractive and other assets less attractive until eventually a new equilibrium is restored between the actual money stock and desired holdings. The implication is that the demand for money would be unstable or – what is the same thing – the velocity of money would be subject to considerable variation as a consequence of changes in its supply. Irrespective of the extent of the interest-rate effect, the conventional Keynesian position is to postulate that the induced consequences for investment and consumption spending would be limited. The limitation on investment spending derives from the assumption that investment demands are often interest-inelastic whilst the limitation on induced consumption effects implies that the wealth effect of a fall in interest rates (applicable to the holders of government debt, for example) is a minor factor in the consumption function.

In contrast, the traditional quantity theory had maintained that the only possible substitute for excessive money balances was goods and services; the rôle of financial assets was virtually ignored. Hence the common conclusion that an enlargement of the total money stock would increase the monetary expenditure on commodities thereby generating price increases. Implicit in this approach and essential to the validity of the doctrine was the assumption that the demand for money was comparatively stable – i.e. velocity comparatively constant – an assumption that was usually justified upon the grounds that the only demand for money was the normal transactions demand.

The modern revival and reformulation of the quantity theory straddles both these viewpoints. Money is looked upon as a substitute for all assets whether real or financial. An increase in the quantity of money will accordingly generate a general increase in demand for commodities in addition to exerting an impact upon interest rates. Although the immediate impact may indeed be felt in financial markets, complete adjustment will involve the commodity markets as well.

Of fundamental importance to the modern quantity theory is the belief that the demand for money is generally insensitive to changes in the interest rate. If the demand for money were to reveal a substantial degree of interest-elasticity, it would imply that a change in the money stock could be accommodated by a comparatively small change in interest rates inducing people to extend their demand for money to match the supply. Under these conditions little would follow from a change in the money stock; the impact upon commodity markets would be minimized and the enlarged money supply would simply be held at the lower interest rate implying a significant decline in the average velocity of money. If, on the other hand, the demand for money were decidedly interest-inelastic then the initial interest-rate change would not satisfy those people holding excessive money balances and direct spending on goods and services would occur, influencing the level of money incomes within the economy. Implicit in this contention of interest-rate insensitivity is the notion that the transactions motive dominates the asset motive in the total demand for money. Nonetheless, it is because money is regarded as an asset, able to serve as a temporary abode of purchasing power, that the relationship between changes in the monetary variable and increased expenditures is more indirect and more complex than traditional theory had supposed. And it is precisely because the relationship is thought to be so complex and involve longer time periods of adjustment, that the current advocacy of the importance of money does not necessarily imply that monetary policy is a viable countercyclical device.

Appendix Post-Keynesian Modifications to the Demand for Money

Whilst in keeping with Keynes' original statement, and whilst generally sceptical of the claims of the quantity theory, a number of contributions have taken issue with Keynes' specification of the demand for money and have proffered alternatives. The most important of these contributions are summarised briefly below. Apart from carrying important implications for the revised quantity theory of money, they also question the usefulness of maintaining the distinction between the transactions demand and the asset demand for cash as separate components in the total demand for money holdings.

1. Baumol and the Interest Rate Sensitivity of Transactions Demands

The logic of Baumol's model (23) leads to the assertion that the transactions demand for cash will respond, inversely, to changes in interest rates thus reinforcing, *ceteris paribus*, the interest elasticity of the total demand for cash holdings. It is assumed that the rational individual will prefer to transfer his income receipt into an interest yielding asset and then successively transfer portions of the asset back into cash to fulfil his transactions needs. The cost of holding idle transactions cash is the interest foregone; hence the incentive to minimize cash holding by increasing the frequency that one turns assets into cash. However, there are costs associated with liquidation of the asset – not least the cost of inconvenience. Hence the dilemma confronting the rational maximizing individual; how to allocate one's assets between cash and interest-yielding bonds, given that there are costs in holding cash and costs associated with turning bonds into cash. More formally, if Y is the income receipt, i the rate of interest, b the cost of turning bonds into cash and K the value of the bonds turned into cash to meet successive transactions needs, the question confronting the utility maximizer is how to determine the size of K – the cash holding per transactions period. Since the average cash holding will be K/2, the interest forgone by holding cash will be (K/2)i. The cost of turning assets (bonds) into cash will be determined by the number of occasions liquidation is resorted to; thus the liquidation cost is b(Y/K). Total costs are, accordingly,

$$TC = b(Y/K) + (K/2)i$$

which will be minimized when

$$\frac{d(TC)}{dK} = 0 \qquad \text{or} \qquad -bY/K^2 + i/2 = 0.$$

Solving for K yields

$$K = \sqrt{\frac{2bY}{i}}$$

and the transactions demand for cash, the average cash holding, is

$$K/2 = \tfrac{1}{2}\sqrt{\frac{2bY}{i}}$$

The rational individual thus acts to minimize the total costs associated with meeting his transactions needs, and a raising of the rate of interest will decrease his demand for transactions cash and vice versa. It may also be noted that if the act of liquidation where costless there would be no demand for transactions balances – a conclusion intuitively appealing.

2. Tobin and the Keynesian Asset Demand for Cash

The Keynesian asset demand for cash rests upon the assumption that individuals possess a concept of a normal or expected rate of interest. If the existing market rate of interest is in excess of the normal rate, then the expectation is that market rates will fall or alternatively that bond prices will rise. In such a situation, all asset cash would be turned into the purchase of bonds in the anticipation of making a capital gain and consequently the individual's asset demand for cash would be zero. Conversely, if existing market rates lie below that expected, the individual would possess a zero demand for bonds and his demand for asset cash would be infinite. The logic of the Keynesian position, therefore, is that the individual holds either asset cash or bonds but not both simultaneously; his speculative demand for money is summarized in Figure III.A.1. The conventional Keynesian aggregate demand curve for asset money holdings, depicted in Figure III.A.2., is accordingly derived from the assumption that different individuals possess different expectations about the normal rate between the points a and b.

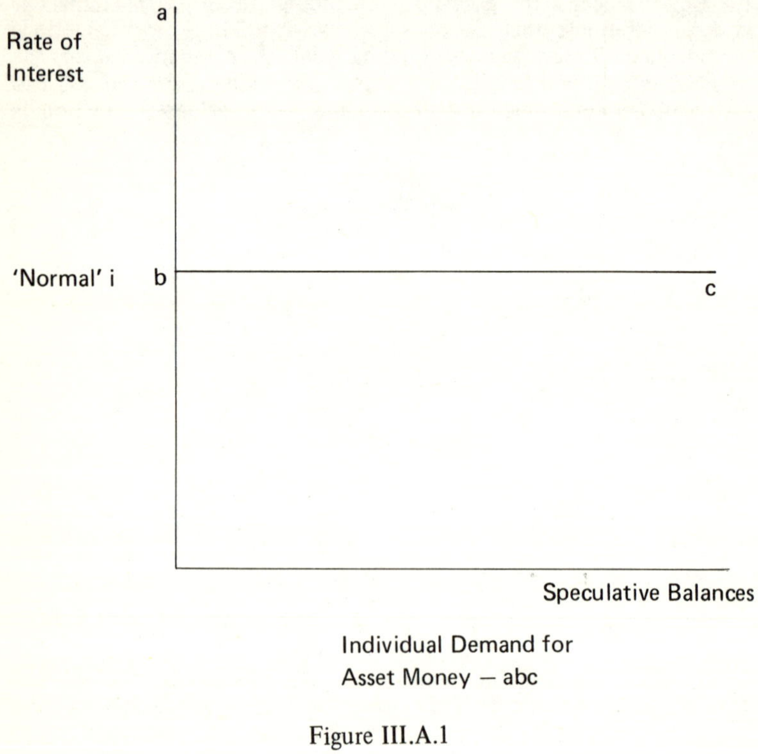

Figure III.A.1

The difficulty with such a statement lies in the fact that it does not accord with the observation that individuals are inclined to hold both speculative balances and bonds simultaneously. To meet such an objection Tobin (24) proposed a reformulation of the Keynesian demand for asset money which asserts that potential bondholders are *uncertain* about future interest rates. If uncertainty prevails, then investment in long dated bonds involves the risk of a capital gain or loss. The poten-

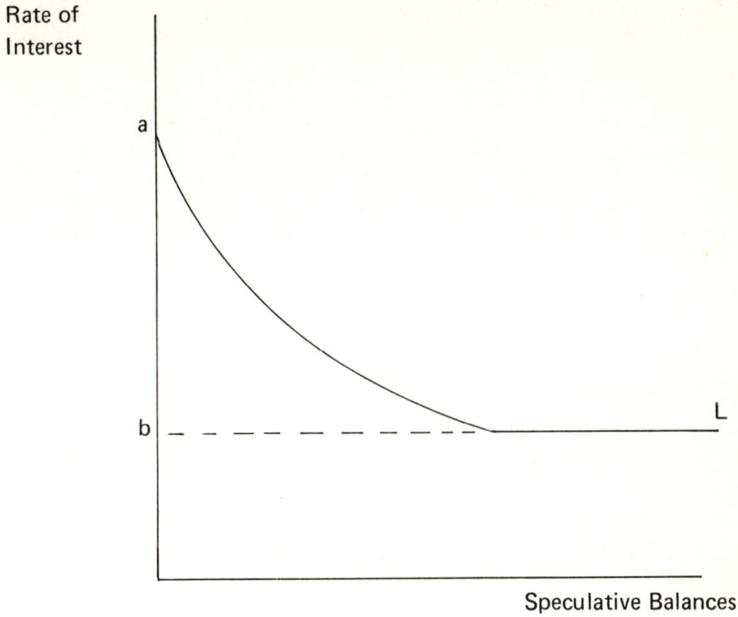

Aggregate Demand for
Asset Money – aL

Figure III.A.2

tial investor therefore must weigh the element of risk against the expected return his investment will yield. Optimal decision-making requires resort to conventional indifference analysis and suggests that normally the individual will hold both bonds and speculative balances.

The argument is summarized with the aid of Figure III.A.3. The lower portion of the figure depicts the allocation of total assets between idle cash holdings and bonds, whilst the upper portion illustrates the trade-off between risk, measured on the horizontal axis, and expected return,* measured upon the vertical. Let us assume the initial interest rate i^1. Then, as revealed by the indifference curves, the optimal combination will be OX of risk combined with an expected return OZ, implying an investment of OA in bonds and retention of YB in cash. Now consider the effect of an increase in the rate of interest. The interest line will be pivoted leftwards to i^2, raising the expected return associated with any degree of risk. How will the

* The expected return includes the expectation of a capital gain or loss possessing an expected mean value of zero.

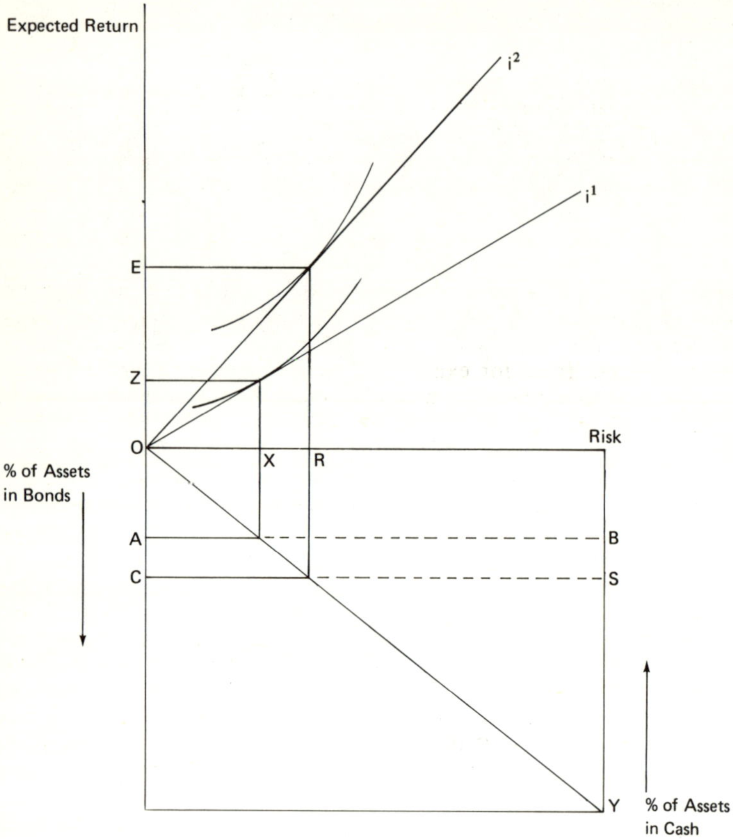

Figure III.A.3

individual investor respond? *A priori*, it is not possible to provide a definitive answer to this question. The rise in interest rates will incorporate an income effect, permitting the investor the luxury of undertaking less risk, whilst also promoting a substitution effect in favour of more risk as the cost of maintaining idle balances is now increased. If, however, as depicted in the diagram, the substitution effect is the stronger, the investor will increase his risk-taking and deplete his holding of asset cash. In the figure, the degree of risk rises to OR, the expected yield becomes OE, investment in bonds is indicated as OC and speculative money balances fall to YS. All that is needed to obtain the Keynesian result of an inverse relationship between the asset demand for money and the rate of interest is the assumption that the substitution effect outweighs the income effect in an analysis that reconciles the simultaneous holding of both cash and bonds.

3. Asset Choice Theories of the Demand for Money

Neo-Keynesian theories of the demand for money, strongly influenced by Tobin (25, 26) and associates at Yale, have also taken issue with Keynes' treatment of the demand for money upon the grounds that it is stated with reference to only one interest rate – that pertaining to long-term government bonds. In this view, money is but one asset in the entire spectrum of assets possessing varying rates of return, and the demand for money, or indeed for any asset, can be approached only in terms of its rate of return in relation to all other prevailing rates of return. It follows that the demand for an asset, including the demand for money, may alter solely due to a change in the composition of existing rates. Thus, for example, if the government intervenes in the open market to purchase long-term bonds whilst selling short, long-term rates of interest will fall whilst the short term rate will rise.* Since investment in real capital assets is more sensitive to long- as opposed to short-term interest rates, investment may be stimulated.

The asset choice (portfolio selection) approach focuses attention not upon the volume of money or the movement in the long-term interest rate as being the significant variable, in contrast to the Monetarist and Keynesian viewpoints respectively, but rather stresses changes in the structure of interest rates. Moreover, whilst both Monetarists and Keynesians would normally agree that an increase in the money stock will generate an expansion of nominal GNP (the former directly, the latter through the interest rate effect), the asset choice theory implies that an increase in the money stock could be contractionary, and vice versa. Such a situation is theoretically conceivable if the increase in the money stock is accompanied by a *comparative fall* in the rate of return upon real capital assets *vis à vis* alternative assets which would generate a switch out of real capital investment to restore portfolio balance.

* Such a policy, referred to as "the twist", has long been advocated as a means of reconciling balance of payments equilibria with higher growth rates.

Chapter IV Policy Implications of the Quantity Theory

If the quantity theory of money were merely a philosophical exercise in contemplating the probable outcome of improbable events, such as money descending like manna from the heavens, then one could enjoy the subtleties of the opposing arguments but one would be at a loss to understand the intensely heated nature of the exchange and the antagonism that the controversy has aroused. It is because the quantity theory of money carries important implications for policy involving fundamental normative positions (as for example the interventionist versus the non-interventionist stance) that the dispute has been so fiercely conducted and the enquiry pursued in a manner not always to be commended for its objectivity. In the present chapter we will examine some of the varied policy implications which derive from the basic doctrine and which have received considerable attention in recent years; these are the issue of monetary versus fiscal control, the possibility of cost-push inflation, and – a somewhat related question – the existence or otherwise of the Phillips curve. In addition, we will briefly examine the appropriate definition of the money stock when applying the analysis to an open economy and the balance of payments implications of a stable demand for money.

Fiscal versus Monetary Policy

The controversy surrounding the quantity theory is of vital importance to the issue of monetary versus fiscal control. The advocate of the new monetarism would insist upon the overriding importance of the monetary variable in determining nominal values and would also rely upon changes in the stock of money to explain short-run destabilizing movements in real output and employment and to be the prime cause of cyclical fluctuations generally. The influence of other factors – as for example fiscal variables – acting independently of the money stock would generally be denied. In contrast, the opponent of the quantity theory would tend to minimize the importance of monetary change *per se* and would emphasize other factors, in particular the public expenditure and taxation policies of the government. The emergence of fiscal policy into a position of respectability and later dominance as the principal means of macro-control went hand in hand with the eclipse of the quantity theory in the wake of the Keynesian analysis. Equally, the revival or restatement of the quantity theory has been accompanied by the reassertion of the claims of monetary policy and the questioning of the efficacy of fiscal variables.

It is for this reason paradoxical that the analysis of Keynes which was ultimately, even though unintentionally, responsible for the widely-held view that "money does not matter" carries important implications for active monetary policy whereas Friedman's own analysis and reassertion of the importance of money carries no such policy implications.

This is because, in Keynesian economics, the volume of money could, and in certain conditions would, change the level of *real* output and employment through its impact upon interest rates and investment spending. Such changes would be magnified in their impact upon the economy by virtue of the multiplier indicating that monetary policy may be a useful countercyclical tool. The downgrading of the monetary variable in Keynesian thought was largely the consequence of Keynes' disciples and post-Keynesian schools emphasizing, perhaps unduly, those particular conditions under which monetary measures would be ineffective (1). Thus in extreme cases, such as absolute liquidity preference for example, monetary policy would exert no impact. Further, in the pessimistic business climate of the nineteen-thirties investment demand functions were probably interest-inelastic and under these conditions the Keynesian logic would imply that "money would not matter much". Other measures, presumably fiscal, would be more relevant to policy.

In contrast, whilst Friedman insists that the money stock constitutes the ultimate determinant of the general price level and is thus of vital importance to the issue of inflation, and whilst changes in the volume of money are unrivalled in their ability to exert short-run destabilising impacts upon the economy, he does not advocate discretionary monetary policy. There can be no doubt that money matters and matters significantly, as the following quotation from one of Friedman's more recent publications testifies:

> I regard the description of our position as 'money is all that matters for changes in *nominal* income and for *short-run* changes in real income' as an exaggeration but one that gives the right flavour of our conclusions (2). [Italics in original.]

Nonetheless, this does not provide adequate justification for active monetary policy. This is because of both the length and uncertainty surrounding the time lag between the change in the monetary variable and the resulting income response which implies that discretionary monetary policy may operate in a decidedly perverse manner and generate destabilizing impacts. If, as Friedman claims (3), the lag may be anything up to two years, then expansionary monetary policy to stimulate a sluggish economy may take effect when the economy has already entered a powerful upswing and thus the net impact may be to add to the inflationary consequences. Equally, contractionary policies adopted during inflationary periods may exert their primary impact when the economy has entered a downturn and thus turn a minor recession into a major depression. It is indeed Friedman's assertion – which has not gone unchallenged (4) – that the great depression followed a period of monetary contraction and could have been avoided by more appropriate policies.

Friedman's statistical findings concerning the length of this time lag support both his theoretical and his policy conclusions. With regard to the former, it strongly suggests that the direction of causation is from money to income and not the other way around. Secondly, it supports his claim that discretionary policies (fiscal as well as monetary) should be abandoned in favour of greater reliance upon automatic stabilizers upon the one hand, and measures to reduce potentially destabilizing movements in the money stock upon the other. The advantage of automatic stabilizers over discretionary changes is that they take effect without delay. Time is required to collect and assess the data needed to establish whether or not discretionary changes are called for and still more time will lapse prior to their sanction and enactment. With regard to removing sources of disturbance, Friedman advocates that the commercial banking sector should be required to maintain 100 per cent cash reserves and thus be denied the opportunity to cause destabilizing movements in bank credit. Apart from the proposal that the money stock should be increased at a constant annual rate in line with the needs of an expanding economy no discretion remains for monetary action.

Friedman's findings upon the length of the time lag in effect of monetary action have raised considerable controversy, particularly with regard to the appropriate manner in which the lag should be estimated. We will touch briefly upon this subject in the following chapter. For the moment it is sufficient to note that other adherents to the revised quantity theory are notably less reluctant than Friedman in advocating active monetary policy and in particular in arguing the superiority of monetary versus fiscal policy action. Indeed, the controversy over whether the Keynesian or revised quantity theory offers greater explanatory power with regard to national income determination has been extended into a discussion of whether fiscal or monetary policy provides the superior form of control. Recent empirical work upon this subject, originating particularly in the Federal Reserve Bank of St. Louis (5), has come down emphatically upon the side of monetary control. In particular, the Andersen-Jordan findings concluded that monetary influence was stronger, worked more speedily and was more certain than fiscal policy actions. Indeed, in some cases it was held that conventional indices of fiscal policy action – as for example changes in the full employment budget surplus – exerted a statistically imperceptible influence upon the level of GNP. These interpretations, obtained largely from the results of multiple regression analysis using reduced form equations, have generated considerable controversy (6). Although we have looked upon discussion of empirical procedure as falling outside the scope of this work we will briefly indicate the nature of the underlying controversy since it is illustrative of much of the dispute surrounding the efficacy of respective policy instruments.

Generally, econometric studies of the effectiveness of policy instruments upon the level of economic activity rely upon either the structural model approach or the reduced form approach. The former, which in many ways is the more appealing intellectually, consists of constructing a model of the economy which describes the manner in which the key variables interact to determine the general level of economic activity. Such a model "explains" the behaviour of the economy in that a logical sequence of events is implicit in any autonomous change. A common example is provided by the Keynesian theory of income determination. Given the identity, $Y \equiv C + I$, consumption can be made a function of income, investment a function of the interest rate and the interest rate a function of the money stock.

In each case, a theoretical explanation underlies the functional relationship. An exogenous change in the money stock will change the interest rate, which in turn will affect the volume of investment and the multiplier – determined by the consumption function – will govern the resulting impact upon the equilibrium level of national income. For forecasting purposes such models can become very complex and involve the solution of a large number of simultaneous equations. Difficulties are inevitably encountered in estimating the coefficients which apply to the functional relationships of the model. Nonetheless, in principle it is possible for such models to be developed and solved for any endogenous variable. Thus, for example, from our simple Keynesian model the equilibrium level of income may be expressed in its reduced form as a function of the exogenous variable the money stock. The other endogenous variables enter only into the multiplier expressing the relationship between the change in the exogenous and the endogenous variable under consideration. It is this procedure which suggests resort to the reduced form approach. Why not simply take observed changes in GNP and express them as a function of the exogenous variables? Let us write $Y = f(X)$, where X represents the exogenous variables, and we avoid both the need for an intricate theoretical explanation and the difficulties associated with estimation of the various coefficients involved. Indeed, if our interest is in the respective claims of monetary and fiscal policy why not simply regress changes in GNP as $Y = f(M)$ and $Y = f(F)$, where M represents monetary and F represents fiscal policy, and compare the respective results? This is essentially the procedure adopted in the Andersen-Jordan approach. Two important points need to be emphasized. First, the validity of this approach – if it is to be accepted at all – depends crucially upon the exogenous nature of the policy variables. If the policy variable is not truly autonomous but is itself a function of GNP then a high correlation will be indicated but it will imply nothing about the power of the policy instrument. This is especially relevant to testing the importance of monetary policy because changes in the money stock may merely reflect changes in the level of economic activity and the expansion and contraction of credit which accompanies it. By the same token, it is obvious that fiscal policy cannot be gauged by changes in the level of the budget surplus because this will respond automatically to changes in the level of activity. Some other indicator – let us say changes in tax rates – will have to be adopted. But here we encounter a second difficulty, namely that the reduced form approach requires that exogenous policy variables be changed fairly frequently in order to derive statistically significant estimates of their impact. Tax rates often remain unchanged for a considerable period of time. If tax rates do remain unchanged during the period of observation then clearly no correlation will exist between tax rates and movements in GNP, and if the former is our chosen index of fiscal policy, then it is inevitably discredited. Since the money stock is subject to fairly frequent change, measures of this nature relying upon the reduced form approach may contain an inherent bias in favour of the effectiveness of the monetary variable.* Considerations of this nature raise serious difficulties for the investigator pursuing this method of approach. To a certain extent, the difficulties may be overcome by defining policy instruments more appropriately but even then the reduced form approach suffers from one grave – and for many observers fundamental – defect, namely the lack of any supporting theoretical framework. Correlation need not necessarily imply anything about causation and in the absence of a theoretical framework no causal impact can be inferred or its direction determined. Finally, it may be noted that Artis and Nobay (8) following similar procedures with United Kingdom data reached precisely the opposite conclusion – fiscal policy appeared to be more potent than monetary policy as a policy variable.

Cost-Push Inflation

The modern reformulation of the quantity theory places the blame for inflation squarely upon the shoulders of those responsible for controlling the money supply. If the authorities concerned allow the money supply to expand at a rate in excess of the increase in national output, rising prices will be the result. At least, this is the conclusion suggested by the revised doctrine. A corollary of the above is that if the authorities do not permit the money stock to outpace the increase in national output then inflation will not occur regardless of the attitudes

* This difficulty, it may be noted, does not arise in the case of the structural model since it may be assumed that changes in income caused by tax changes have generally similar effects as changes in income arising in other ways. Thus, the latter may be used as a proxy to test the comparative effectiveness of tax-rate changes on GNP. For this and related argument see especially Helliwell, Shapiro, Sparks and Walters (7).

adopted by trade unions towards wage negotiations. The logic of the argument would amount to a denial of the phenomenon of cost-push inflation – by which we mean here inflation initiated by the bargaining power of trade unions in raising per unit wage costs. This conclusion follows if we postulate a stable demand for money implying fairly constant velocity. In this case, and assuming for simplicity a fixed money stock, any significant increase in nominal wages can only come about if it is accompanied by a substantial increase in the level of unemployment. Since it is unlikely that the trade unions will behave in a manner guaranteed to put their members out of work, it may be argued that cost-push inflation is virtually impossible unless the monetary authorities passively react to meet the required increase in monetary circulation.

Indeed, it may be contended that one reason why cost-push inflation has come so much into prominence in the post-war years has been the commitment entered into by modern governments to maintain full, or near-full, employment. Such a commitment, it is alleged, not only permits trade union negotiators to ignore the employment consequences of inflationary demands but also amounts to the adoption of a passive stance upon the part of the monetary authorities to supply whatever money is deemed necessary.

The argument may be illustrated in terms of the simple macro-economic framework of Figure IV.1. In Part (a) of the figure we

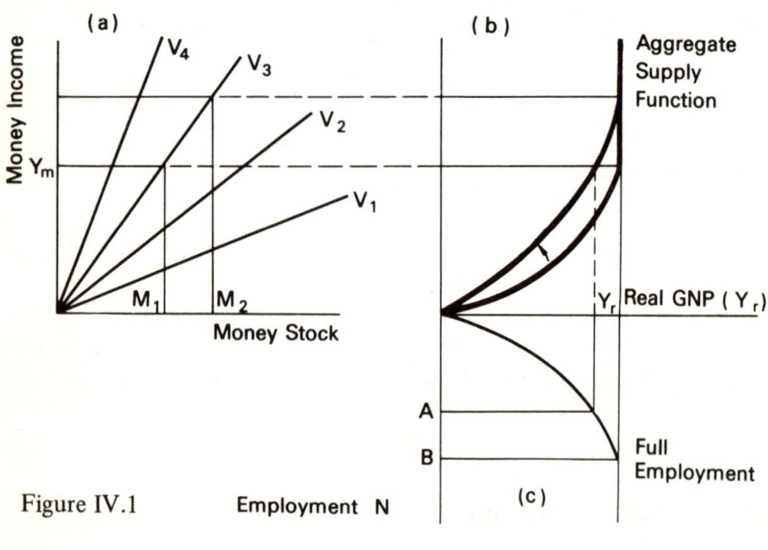

Figure IV.1

summarise the essence of the modern quantity theory where the level of money national income is positively correlated with the stock of money. The actual relationship will depend upon the velocity function, the radians labelled $V_1 - V_4$ indicating successively higher values of the income velocity of money. In keeping with the revised doctrine we assume relative constancy in the velocity relation; the radians are thus linear in character. Let us assume for purposes of illustration that we have a fixed money stock, M_1, and constant velocity indicated by the radian V_3. Then money national income is indicated as Y_m. In Part (b) of the figure money national income is translated into real income by invoking the concept of the aggregate supply function. The function is assumed to be non-linear owing to the assumption of diminishing returns and it attains a vertical range when full capacity output is reached. It will be noted that the aggregate supply function is drawn for a given price level. The price level is simply $\frac{MV}{Y_r}$; thus for an autonomous increase in prices the aggregate supply function would shift inwards indicating that a lower real output would be forthcoming from a constant level of monetary expenditures. Finally, Part (c) of the construct shows the technical relationship between employment and output and full employment of the labour force is assumed to coincide with, and indeed constrain, the capacity level of output. Now assume that the bargaining power of trade unions is sufficiently powerful to force an increase in wage costs, and hence prices, reflected in the inward shift of the aggregate supply function. If monetary expenditures remain as before, unemployment must be the consequence indicated by the distance AB. Full employment of the labour force can only be maintained if the money stock is increased to M_2 to maintain the former level of output. Hence the justification for the assertion that cost-push inflation depends for its existence upon the willingness of the authorities to expand the money supply.

Opponents of the quantity theory would generally assert that cost-push inflation can always be accommodated merely by an expansion of velocity. Moreover, those economists who stress the degree of "liquidity" in the economy – witness for example the celebrated Radcliffe Report (9) – would also argue that velocity can increase almost without limit. The comparative constancy of the velocity function in the past is held to be merely the consequence of the fact that the authorities have usually chosen to expand the money supply making velocity changes unnecessary.

The Phillips Curve

The reformulation of the quantity theory also carries implications for the alleged phenomenon of the Phillips curve. To paraphrase Friedman's argument, a function relating the volume of employment to the rate of change in money prices is fallacious since it implies a relationship between real and nominal magnitudes (10). Since the former is determined by real forces in the economy, and only temporarily influenced by the monetary variable, whilst the latter is entirely monetarily determined, it is clear that there is no reason to assume any relationship between the two. To draw out the implications of this argument more clearly, consider the composite diagram Fig. IV.2. Part (a) depicts the situation in the labour market where at the real wage W/P the equilibrium volume of employment is OQ and the extent of unemployment indicated by PQ – in the Keynesian sense of

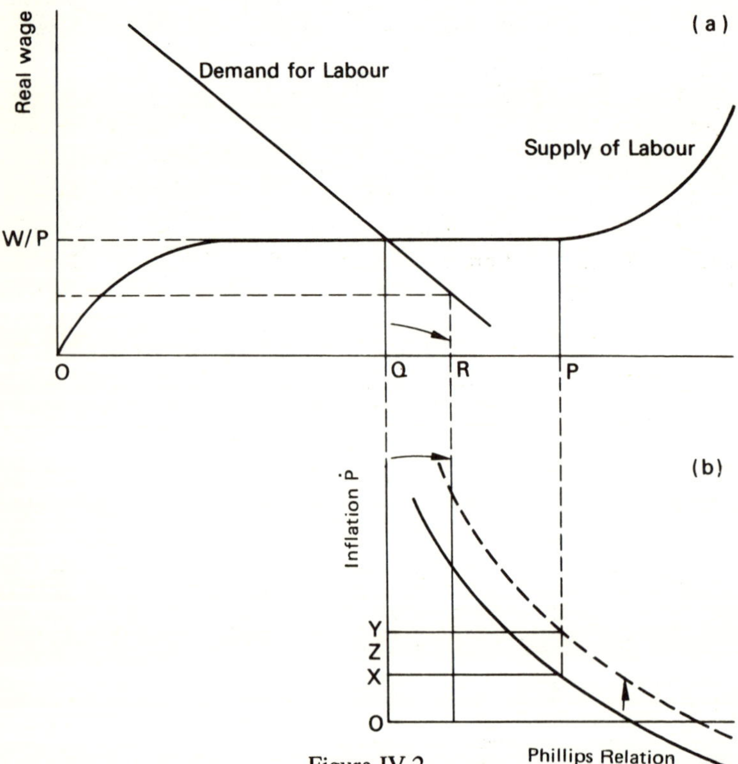

Figure IV.2

being willing but unable to find employment at the prevailing real wage. Let us now link this amount of unemployment to the Phillips curve portrayed in Part (b). We have a situation whereby the equilibrium amount of employment as determined in the labour market is accompanied by an inflationary trend of OX. What are the consequences?

Assuming that labour entered into a contractual agreement in nominal terms, the gradual effect of inflation will be to erode the real wage and create a disequilibrium situation in the labour market. The employment of labour will be initially extended as the employers respond to a decrease in the real wage whilst labour, traditionally, reacts with a lag. Accordingly, the increase in employment to OR will, given the validity of the Phillips curve, be accompanied by an increase in the rate of inflation to OY. This is most easily seen in terms of the diagram if we move the axis of the Phillips diagram inward by an amount QR equal to the expansion in employment in the labour market. Thus, we have the situation claimed by the Phillips curve, a trade-off between employment and inflation.

However, this situation will be short-lived. As soon as labour perceives that its real wage is falling or as soon as its nominal contracts expire, it will renegotiate for the former real wage and the employment level will return to its previous equilibrium. Moreover, in negotiating a further nominal contract, labour may fully allow for the inflationary trend of OX which had previously jeopardised its position. Whether we allow for this additonal sophistication, however, is not essential to the argument, for the increase in the nominal wage – whether it allows for expected inflation of OX or not – will increase the degree of inflation beyond the level OX for the equal employment of labour OQ. Consequently, the Phillips curve is shifted upwards and a new rate of inflation – say OZ – becomes associated with the employment level OQ. But the process does not stop at this point. Once more labour's real income is declining owing to the new level of inflation OZ – and this conclusion obtains even if labour had fully allowed for the expected inflation OX in forming the wage agreement. Thus, whilst a short-term trade-off between inflation and employment may exist as indicated, the long-run solution will be the constant amount of employment OQ and an ever accelerating inflationary spiral as the Phillips curve is continually shifted upwards. The existence of a temporary trade-off between employment and inflation arises from the fact that the degree of inflation is never correctly estimated: a dynamic money illusion persists in that expected inflation always falls short of the actual. It is Friedman's contention, however, that experience is the great teacher and ultimately the inflationary process will be correctly gauged in striking the wage bargain. When this solution is attained, the employment level remains constant and is linked to a constant rate of inflation; even the temporary trade-off disappears.

Like most of the other issues raised by the revival of the quantity theory, the assertion that the Phillips relation offers only a temporary trade-off between employment and inflation has aroused considerable controversy and has stimulated attempts to resolve the debate by econometric techniques (11). Like most of the recent empirical findings concerning the importance of money, the evidence is by no means unambiguous and is capable of lending support to both sides. An interesting point made by Laidler (12) in support of the Friedman position is that the existence of a trade-off between inflation and employment would imply that labour's real wage and share in national product would decline in periods of inflation – a conclusion which is not supported by the evidence. At the same time, however, denial of the permanent Phillips relation rests upon the belief that labour correctly gauges inflation in future time periods. One may readily accept this as being the case if inflation were to occur at, say, a steady 20 per cent per year – indeed in such a situation it is hard to believe that anything else could be possible – and one may expect the evidence culled from the experience of the Latin-American countries to give some support to the expectations hypothesis. But it is not so clear that where inflation averages substantially less, and where it is subject to considerable variation, labour or anyone else would behave in such a consistently rational manner. And even so, granted that the trade-off may be only temporary, the time period of adjustment may be so long as to allow the authorities use of the trade-off in formulating policy proposals.

If the expectations thesis is correct there will be a distinct Phillips curve for each level of expectation. In addition, if the rate of inflation is only imperfectly estimated, the long-run Phillips curve will not be vertical but will be much steeper than the short-run relationship. This is indicated in Figure IV.3 where we measure the rate of change in money wages on the vertical axis. Assuming productivity per head to be increasing at an annual rate of p% the employment level oa will be perfectly consistent with price stability. Wage increases in line with productivity changes should leave prices unaffected. If however, the

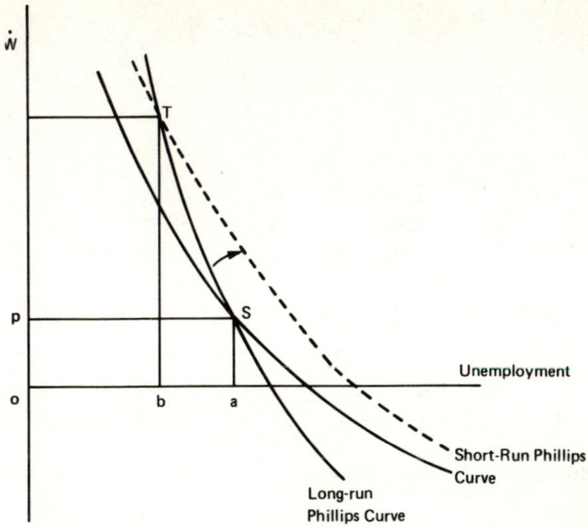

Figure IV.3

authorities attempt to reduce unemployment to the level ob, annual wage increase will now exceed the annual productivity change with inflation occurring in consequence. Subsequent wage bargaining conditioned by the inflationary experience will then result in an outward shift of the Phillips curve. The loci of points S and T trace out the long-term Phillips relation curve implying a more limited trade-off than that indicated by the short-term Phillips curve. One interesting implication of this analysis, noted by Laidler (13), is that in seeking to reduce inflation to a given target level the authorities are provided with a choice between accepting heavy unemployment for a limited time, or a lower volume of unemployment for a longer time. That is to say, the nature of the trade-off is time dimensional – a fact not without electorial significance. Consider for example, Figure IV.4. Let us assume an initial situation at point A on the short-run Phillips curve with unemployment of oa and inflation of ox. Let us also assume that this rate of inflation has been maintained for some time so that, with expectations being geared to recent past experience, it is equal to the expected rate of inflation. Suppose now that the authorities attempt to seek the inflation/unemployment combination indicated by point B on the long-run Phillips curve. Two choices are open to them. On the one hand, unemployment may be raised to oc by moving to position C on the short-run Phillips curve. This implies a fall in the actual rate of

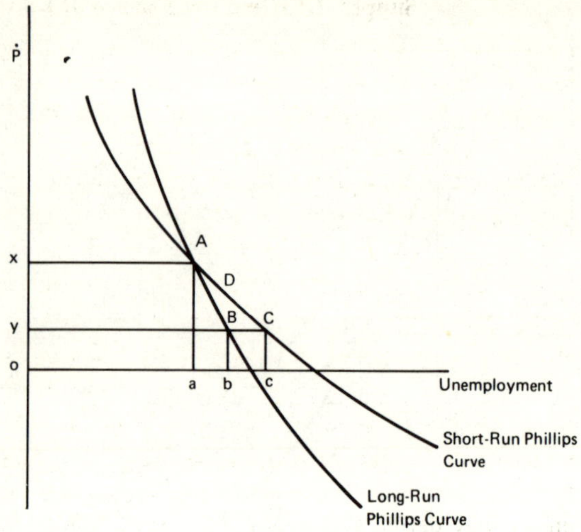

Figure IV.4

inflation to oy – less than the expected rate. The consequence, as expectations are revised in the light of experience, is an inward shift of the Phillips curve until eventually position B is gained. Alternatively, the authorities may curtail the increase in unemployment to ob and seek to attain position D. Here again, as actual inflation falls below that expected the Phillips curve is shifted inwards until the target combination is secured. However, the adjustment process will be quicker under the former policy since the greater the discrepancy between experience and expectations the faster will expectations be altered. Hence the nature of the trade-off between the intensity of unemployment and its duration.

Finally, it may be noted that the expectations hypothesis carries implications for the announcement effects associated with policy statements. Indeed, as the U.S. Council of Economic Advisers Economic Report to the President admits (14) the imposition of the wage freeze and price controls in August 1971, was undertaken with the expectations impact very much in mind and similar remarks undoubtedly apply to like measures enacted by successive British governments. However, inward shifts of the Phillips curve need not rely on a formal incomes policy; any measure, including, say, a commitment to IMF creditors to curb the public sector borrowing requirement, would promote the desired shift if it diminished expectations of inflation.

Definition of the Money Supply, DCE and the Balance of Payments

In sketching the evolution of the quantity theory we conveniently ignored the question of how the money supply should be defined. For our purpose this was an entirely permissible procedure because although the ultimate definition might be crucially important in assessing the empirical evidence, it is of minor consideration in the exposition of the theoretical content. However, in the context of the present chapter it is necessary to specify the quantum which the authorities may seek to control. In particular, with regard to a country having a substantial involvement in international trade, as for example the United Kingdom, it is important to enquire as to whether the conventional definitions are adequate as a guide to policy action.

If money is looked upon primarily as a medium of exchange, and if we are concerned principally with the means of purchasing domestic output, then we may define the money stock as including all notes and coins in circulation plus all current checking accounts held by private sector residents in their resident currency. Presumably, this definition would correspond most closely to the notion of money being used for transactions purposes. However, since time deposits or savings deposits are for the most part convertible upon demand into cash, despite the technical time delay normally associated with such deposits, a case could be made for their inclusion in the effective money supply. This second definition, however, leads us into difficulties, for may it not be argued that similar deposits held with post offices or other institutions such as building societies are equally withdrawable upon demand and should thus be included in the monetary base? The logical extension of this argument would lead to the proposition that almost any asset capable of being readily and easily transferred into cash would be classified as money and indeed this is broadly the position taken by those economists concerned with the overall degree of "liquidity" within the economy. The usefulness of the liquidity approach has been called into question in recent years, particularly by the adherents to the new monetarism,* and conventionally it is accepted that bank deposits differ – most probably in the motivation of the depositors – from other forms of savings with non-bank institutions. Whether we choose

* Implying as it does considerable scope for velocity changes. For a useful discussion of the appropriate definition of the money stock see Cox (15), which surveys the earlier controversy between Sayers (16) and Newlyn (17).

to include the time deposits of the banking sector or not, it should be noted that we specifically exclude those deposits held by non-residents. This is because such deposits are generally held for other purposes than the purchase of domestic output. With regard to the United Kingdom, for example, considerable non-resident sterling balances are often held within the country owing to the interest-rate differential which frequently prevails between London and other financial centres. In practice, the official definition adopted within the United Kingdom is even broader than either of the above and includes the foreign currency deposits of residents and the deposits of the public sector. The former are usually held for purchases or investment overseas whilst the latter change primarily owing to the lack of synchronization between payments and receipts and are not closely related to the volume of public sector expenditures. It is for this reason that secondary measures have been proposed and recently adopted in government publications of financial statistics (18).

Regardless of whether one chooses a narrow or broad definition of the money supply, its rate of change may be regarded as inadequate as an indicator of monetary ease or constraint within the context of an open economy. This is because the money supply will respond to changes in the external account showing a tendency to increase in periods of balance of payments surplus and contract during periods of deficit. The excess expenditure will be financed by a transfer of sterling into foreign currency and this will be reflected in a decline in bank deposits and a slower growth of the money supply generally. But this will in no way indicate a contractionary situation. Indeed the payments deficit may be the direct consequence of a relative lack of stringency in credit conditions generally; the slowdown in the money supply merely indicates that the credit is being provided from overseas. An external deficit may thus be looked upon as a source of credit to the domestic economy.

It is to deal with this problem that the concept of Domestic Credit Expansion (DCE) has been invoked. The concept has come into prominence recently particularly within the United Kingdom (19, 20), but it may be more properly associated with the theoretical and empirical work of IMF economists (21, 22). Put simply, DCE attempts to adjust the recorded internal money supply to allow for the changes induced by the presence of external surplus or deficit. As a first approximation, it may be equated with the increase in the money supply plus the deficit (minus the surplus) in the balance of payments.

We are now able to consider the implications of the modern quantity theory for the balance of payments. Stated briefly, under a regime of fixed exchange rates, the monetarist approach links an external deficit to an excess supply of money and a surplus to an excess demand. If the demand function for money balances is stable, then an increase in the monetary stock in excess of that which people wish to hold will induce additional spending. In the context of a closed economy the process ultimately generates rising prices, which eventually will eliminate the excess supply of money. Once we move to the more realistic open-economy model, however, rising prices are no longer the only available means to secure the optimal adjustment. Unwanted excess money balances can now be run down through the purchase of foreign currency reserves used to finance imports of goods and services and foreign securities. Given the extent of restrictions upon capital movements generally, it is likely that the bulk of the adjustment process will fall upon the current account. Hence the rationale for the assertion that a current trade deficit springs from an excess monetary supply. The excess monetary supply is, of course, eliminated in the process of adjustment that reveals itself in the growth of imports. Accordingly, as repeatedly emphasized by Johnson (23, 24) amongst others, the key determinant in the balance of payments is the extent of domestic credit expansion and not the actual money supply *per se*. Monetary policy is thus important because it determines the extent of domestic credit expansion. Precisely similar reasoning applies to the situation of a trade surplus.

The logical policy conclusion obtained from this analysis is that devaluation will be ineffective as a means of curing a payments deficit unless it is accompanied by measures to eliminate the initial source of that deficit – namely the excessive growth of DCE. Devaluation has the immediate effect of decreasing the real value of monetary balances held owing to the increased price of imports. It thus serves to eliminate, if only partially, the excess supply of money over the desired stock that people wish to hold. However, as long as the authorities continue to expand the money supply at a greater rate than people wish to add to their stock, the leakage into imports must continue and the payments deficit will be perpetuated indefinitely. This analysis must of course be modified under conditions of freely floating exchange rates. Now, monetary expansion will be reflected in a declining exchange rate and the consequent rise in prices rather than in payments deficits; none the less the power of monetary expansion is still considerable.

Import Prices and Inflation

It is commonly argued that one source of Britain's recent economic difficulties, and in particular recent inflation rates, stems from the rising price of commodity imports. Especially significant in this respect was the sudden rise in the cost of imported oil supplies given the limited substitutability between alternative energy sources.

However, the monetarist reformulation of the quantity theory logically leads to the denial that rising import prices can cause inflation, even assuming maintenance of fixed exchange rates.* Indeed, this may be regarded simply as a variant of the denial of the cost-push thesis. Provided the money stock is held constant and velocity changes limited – implying a stable demand function for money – the volume of total spending in the aggregate economy is fixed. If the price of imported oil rises – let us assume with the import volume constant – the consequence must be a fall in expenditure elsewhere. All that is involved is a change in comparative prices. The price of oil and oil-intensive products will rise but other prices will fall; the aggregate price index therefore will remain unaltered. Persuasive as this argument appears to be upon the surface, it would seem to rest upon the assumption that product prices are extremely flexible and more importantly flexible downwards. If this is not the case, if there is a tendency to hold prices constant when domestic outlays are now redirected to imports, then maintenance of the fixed money stock will imply quantity adjustments generating unemployment. Rising import prices, therefore, may be responsible for raising the level of inflation and the degree of unemployment simultaneously – suggesting an outward shift of the observed Phillips relation. At least, this is the analysis suggested by consideration of the short term. It may well be that the logic of the monetarist position is salvaged if the analysis is extended to one of long-run equilibria, for the ultimate consequence of the higher unemployment levels may well be a *lower* rate of price increase over time in the affected industries than would otherwise have occurred had import prices remained constant. In the monetarist view, the final analysis will incorporate the required change in comparative prices. Rising import prices can lead to inflation only if the monetary authorities are unwilling to accept the employment consequence of sluggishness in downward price flexibility and thus act to inflate the money supply. In short the policy implications of monetarism may be incompatible with the

* In principle, freely floating exchange rate regimes insulate the importing economy from the inflationary effects of higher import prices.

political realities, especially if, as in the case of the United Kingdom, the existence of strong trade unions and oligopolistic industrial structure imply that the adjustment process may be decidedly lengthy.

Appendix Trade Unions and Inflation – An Alternative Approach

We have seen that the logic of the monetarist reformulation of the quantity theory of money leads to a denial of the ability of trade unions to generate inflation. This is not to assert that trade unions do not have harmful (as well as beneficial) effects, as in the case of restrictive practices and feather-bedding agreements which lower overall productivity, but only that they are guiltless of the charge most commonly levied against them, namely that they are responsible for a raising of the *aggregate* price index. Provided the authorities strictly adhere to holding the money stock fixed, collective bargaining, which forces up wages and thus prices in one sector of the economy, must imply corresponding decreases in some other sector – or at least, in terms of a dynamic context, a lower rate of increase than that which would otherwise prevail. The result of collective bargaining therefore is to change *comparative* wage rates and hence *comparative* prices in favour of the unionized or more strongly unionized sectors.

Such a conclusion depends for its validity upon the assertion that velocity is constant or very nearly so, or is effectively constrained in its ability to rise. However, from the long-term viewpoint upon which monetarists tend to rely to reach full equilibrium, the scope for velocity changes may be considerable in the light of potential institutional changes, whilst in the short term, conventional analysis may suggest that successful trade union bargaining in one sector of the economy can generate price increases throughout all sectors. Consider for example the analysis depicted in Figure IV.A.1. We assume two sectors of the economy, the unionized and the non-unionized, both of which display maximizing behaviour as indicated in the equation of marginal revenue and marginal cost. For convenience we posit initially identical prices in both sectors, so that $P_u = P_n$. Total outlay on unionized output is simply P_uABC, let us say equal to U, whilst total expenditure upon the non-unionized sector amounts to P_nQRS, which we denote as equal to N. Total monetary expenditure is thus U + N equal to the fixed money stock multiplied by a constant velocity. We assume also that consumption outlay in one period is a function of income in the previous period; thus $C_t = f(Y_{t-1})$.

Now let us assume that trade union bargaining successfully raises wages in the unionized sector. Marginal costs rise in consequence and the new equilibrium is indicated with the higher price P_u^1. But since we had originally assumed maximizing behaviour, the unionized sector must have been operating upon the elastic portion of its demand curve.

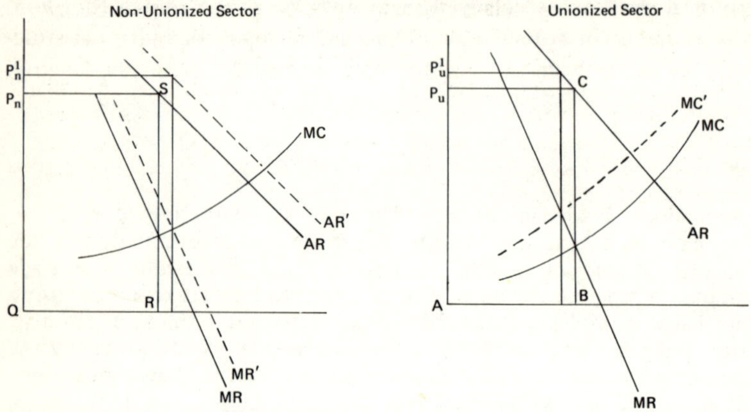

Figure IV.A.1

The increase in price, therefore, must imply a decrease in the total outlay upon unionized output. *Ceteris paribus*, with a constant level of monetary expenditure, total outlay must rise on the produce of the non-unionized sector. With marginal costs unchanged in the latter this will imply a raising of the demand curve and *normally* a higher price for the non-unionized output as indicated by P_n^1. The pressure of trade union bargaining in one sector of the economy, therefore, is able to generate price increases throughout all sectors – even without the assumption of imitative behaviour upon the part of non-unionized workers. Clearly, such a solution can only be a temporary one. With higher prices prevailing throughout the economy and the volume of monetary expenditure unchanged, real output and real incomes must fall in successive periods. With falling real incomes a decline in demand will be the indicated outcome in both markets. With complete price and wage flexibility in both sectors the ultimate solution would be consistent with no change in the aggregate price index but with prices no longer equal between the two sectors. The long-term inflation rate is thus unaffected by trade union bargaining; all that has been achieved is a temporary rise in unemployment consistent with the fall in real output. However, suppose perfect price flexibility does not prevail or is at least asymmetrical as between upward and downward movements. The attempt to maintain both prices and wages in both sectors must be accompanied by rising unemployment levels over and above that indicated in the monetarist solution. It is possible, in keeping with the Phillips curve, that rising unemployment will itself eliminate inflationary pressures. But, and herein lies the crux of the argument, will the unemployment levels arising from the attempt to maintain wages and prices be politically acceptable in a democracy? If not, the authorities will be compelled to inflate the money supply and reduce the unemployment level to some acceptable level, thus providing the finance to fuel the inflationary process. It is difficult to deny the logical outcome of the long-term monetarist case. Trade unions cannot cause inflation if the volume of monetary expenditure remains unchanged. But if the trade unions possess the power to alter the money stock, then the policy implication stemming from the monetarist view becomes an irrelevancy.

Chapter V **Monetary Policy**

By monetary policy we mean any *conscious* action undertaken by the monetary authorities to change the quantity, availability or cost (interest rate) of money. A broader definition might also take account of action designed to influence the composition and age profile of the national debt, as for example open market operations geared to the purchase of short-term dated securities and the sale of long-term bonds, but for our present purposes we shall consider this to be the separate issue of debt management.

It is important to emphasize the conscious element in our definition, because monetary conditions may change of their own accord, or owing to alternative policy decisions undertaken by the government. For example, suppose the government adopts a restrictive fiscal policy and raises taxation in order to cope with inflationary conditions or balance of payments deficits. The imposition of higher tax rates may be accompanied by the public drawing upon their bank balances to meet the new tax demands and, normally, assuming the banking sector does not carry substantial excess reserves, this will necessitate a reduction in the total money supply and most probably an increase in interest rates. Alternatively, let us suppose the government sharply reduces taxes to stimulate the economy and accepts the need for a budget deficit. The deficit will have to be financed either by the sale of government securities in the open market, or alternatively by the printing of new money. In both cases, acceptance of the deficit implies changes in the quantity, availability or cost of money. The decision-taker will (or should) be concerned with such monetary repercussions when formulating his policy; but he will hardly regard it as comprising monetary policy. By insisting upon the conscious element in our definition we are able to define monetary policy in terms which are free from ambiguity.

Irrespective of the definition we care to adopt, it is important to realize that our discussion of monetary policy implies nothing at all about the *importance* of money. The advocate of the view that "money matters" will generally assert that a change in the quantity of money will work itself out in a fairly predictable manner over time, an increase exerting an expansionary influence and a decrease exercising a contrary effect. The origin of the change in the money stock need not be of prime concern. As we have seen, the present-day quantity theorist would in all probability stress that the importance of a fiscal policy change lies in the induced repercussions upon the volume or availability of money outstanding. There need be nothing inconsistent in arguing that "money matters" whilst simultaneously maintaining that monetary policy as defined is ineffective either because it is countered by induced changes elsewhere (i.e. velocity changes), or because it takes effect with too long a delay. Indeed, one may endorse the importance of money whilst still insisting upon the primacy of fiscal policy if the latter exerts a more direct or predictable impact upon monetary conditions. This distinction between the importance of a variable and the importance of measures to influence it is one worth preserving in discussing almost any aspect of macro-economic stabilization policy.

The Eclipse of Traditional Monetary Policy

In traditional analysis, it was generally assumed that the effectiveness of policy action lay primarily upon the sensitivity of investment demand to changes in the rate of interest. It was further assumed that the rate of interest exercised a significant influence upon the flow of new savings. Since the banking sector could control the interest rate by expanding or contracting the money supply it could influence both the level of investment demand and the flow of new saving. Stability required the maintenance of that interest rate which would just equate the two – the so-called "natural" rate of interest.

The classical economist tended to believe that in the long term the rate of interest would coincide with the natural rate. In other words, the rate of interest would be determined by the "real" forces of productivity (investment demand) and thrift. In the long term the monetary influence was of little or no significance. In the short term, however, it was allowed that the monetary factor could play its part. And in much of classical analysis the monetary factor was largely exogenously determined by the operation of the international gold standard. An inflow of money due to a trade surplus and the consequent multiple expansion of credit by the banking sector could be accompanied by the market rate of interest diverging from its long-term natural rate. A market rate of interest below the natural rate would imply a significant expansion of investment demand in excess of the flow of new savings. So important was the cost of credit considered to be in determining investment expenditures that this divergence between market and natural rates of interest was often looked upon as the major explanation of the phenomenon of business cycles in much of classical thinking. A level of investment demand in excess of the inflow of new savings would imply a total level of monetary expenditures in excess of current output – with inflationary consequences. Conversely, a market rate of interest in excess of the natural rate would imply deflation.

As we have already seen, this was essentially the message which Keynes propounded in the *Treatise* and it is a comparatively short step to restate the analysis in terms of the divergence between *ex ante* investment and saving with changes in real output and employment occurring in consequence.* Because the classical economist dealt with a theoretical framework which focussed upon the price level this step was not to be taken until the appearance of the *General Theory* and changes in output had generally to be inferred from changes in the price level, the latter acting as a barometer of the state of trade. Whether we think primarily in terms of price or output changes, however, is really immaterial to the argument which seeks to demonstrate the overriding influence of the rate of interest upon investment demands and hence upon the level of activity generally. The policy conclusion to be drawn from all this is clear enough. Fluctuations in the level of economic activity could be avoided if the monetary authorities conducted their activities so that the market rate of interest was maintained as close as possible to its natural rate over time. Indeed, the opposition of Keynes to the maintenance of the gold standard was based largely upon the belief in the potential effectiveness of monetary policy and the imposed

* In these terms the natural rate of interest would be that which equated *ex ante* saving and investment implying no tendency for the income level to change; it is the rate of interest which maintains the *status quo*. As Keynes recognised in the *General Theory* (1), there would be such a rate of interest for each and every level of employment. In contrast, in the *Treatise* Keynes had assumed that the natural rate of interest would be unique. More than any other factor, this distinction highlights the intellectual gulf between the two works. For a contrary point of view see Shackle (2).

inability of the authorities to take appropriate compensatory action whilst being held to the "rules of the game".

If traditional theory had stressed the importance of the cost of credit in determining the investment decision then its demise was a consequence of the downgrading of the importance of interest rates as a controlling force in the economy. In this assault upon the importance of the interest rate – and in consequence upon the importance of monetary policy generally – three distinct factors combined: the intellectual revolution which accompanied Keynes' *General Theory*, direct empirical studies of business investment behaviour, and the experience and consequences of the Second World War.

In the former case, much play was made of Keynes' special case of interest-rate determination where the existence of a liquidity trap prevented the monetary authorities from being able to force the interest rate below a certain level.

Secondly, the *General Theory* was notable for its continual emphasis upon the unstable nature of long-term expectations and the importance of the latter in determining investment behaviour. False expectations, often based upon slender and deficient evidence and in which the facts of the current situation would exercise a disproportionate influence, were held to be the major determinant of the investment decision and to completely override marginal changes in the rate of interest. A decrease in the cost of capital would have virtually no effect in the face of a collapse of the marginal efficiency of investment schedule and conversely increases in the rate of interest would have little effect when expectations were buoyant.

To this theoretical base were added the empirical findings of the *Oxford Studies* (3) which concluded that investment demand was generally insensitive to changes in the rate of interest and that in many cases the rate of interest did not even enter into the investment decision. These findings, based upon sample questionnaire techniques, were reinforced by similar evidence from the United States where again the interest rate was held to be of minor significance to potential investors (4). Whilst in many respects deficient (5), these studies reinforced the prevailing belief in the interest-inelasticity of investment demand, a belief to be reaffirmed in the conclusions of the Radcliffe Report (6).

It was the practical experience and consequences issuing from the Second World War, however, which dealt the final blow to traditional monetary policy. The Second World War had necessitated a mobilization of resources upon an unprecedented scale, and in the time period available this had only been possible with the use of extensive direct physical controls. The success of such measures – and they had been undeniably successful in marshalling the war effort – led naturally to the belief that similar controls in an admittedly weaker version could be equally successful in the more relaxed conditions of peacetime in controlling the domestic economy. Moreover, the war effort had been financed relatively cheaply; individuals had lent money to the government at genuinely low rates of interest. Monetary policy which involved a decline in the capital value of government bonds would have amounted to a betrayal of trust; monetary policy thus abdicated in favour of the maintenance of stable bond prices, and the field of stabilization goals became the province of fiscal measures. The war had also achieved a sizeable increase in the potency of fiscal weapons. In the United Kingdom especially, the introduction of P.A.Y.E. and the extension of the personal income tax to literally millions of the lower-paid workers for the first time provided the authorities with a sizeable policy tool capable of swift implementation and yielding predictable results. Moreover, there was also a body of opinion which held that the advantage of fiscal *vis-à-vis* monetary policy lay in its ability to achieve more "equitable" results in that tax levies could be adapted to personal situations whereas monetary measures worked *via* the impersonal forces of the market. Indeed, in his influental *How to Pay for the War* (7) Keynes had argued the need for fiscal policy to safeguard the relative position of labour compared to capital owners during periods of inflation. Thus, by the end of the war, not only had traditional theory been intellectually discredited but it had already been effectively abandoned by the authorities and few advocates could be found in its defence.

The Re-emergence of Monetary Policy

Paradoxically, the re-emergence of monetary policy in the nineteen-fifties was also a consequence of the Second World War. The war had resulted in an enormous increase in the size of the public debt. The national debt was now a significant proportion of total outstanding securities; consequently any change in the yields payable upon government debt would have repercussions upon the yield obtainable elsewhere. Moreover, much of the public debt had been acquired by financial institutions which were decidedly conservative in their outlook. Their fear, so it was alleged, was to incur a capital loss as a consequence of a decrease in bond prices. In these circumstances, a rise in the rate of interest which would be accompanied by a decrease in bond prices would make them hesitant to sell their existing holdings in order to finance demands for loanable funds. They would prefer to hang on to existing assets until maturity in order to maintain their capital values intact.

If this analysis is accepted it follows that monetary policy to raise interest rates would effectively "lock in" such financial institutions in that they would be unwilling to finance investment demands. Thus, even if investment demands were interest-inelastic, monetary policy could still be effective by imposing limits to the supply of loanable funds. In contrast to traditional monetary policy which had emphasized the cost of credit to the investor, the "new" policy stressed the availability of funds for new investment. It will be noted that this sudden awakening to the potentialities of interest-rate changes occurred during a period of general business expansion and full employment. Many critics who had condemned monetary policy as being virtually useless in the years of depression now became advocates of the "new monetary policy" during an age of incipient inflation. Whilst still conceding the Keynesian position that the buoyancy of expectations was the major determinant in the will to invest, and whilst still insisting upon the general interest-inelasticity of the investment demand schedule, it was now recognised that investment could not be undertaken if investible funds simply could not be obtained. The new policy, therefore, was decidedly asymmetrical. In contrast to the traditional statement, which had assumed, tacitly at least, that changes in the cost of credit would have equal potency in periods of boom or depression, the new policy was only expected to be effective when it was desirable to curtail the volume of investment. A decrease in the rate of interest which would serve to "unlock" the financial institutions carrying large amounts of government debt could not be depended upon to induce investment spending in the wake of pessimistic business expectations. The nineteen-fifties, therefore, witnessed something of a partial resurgence in the belief in the efficacy of monetary policy.

It is obvious that the effectiveness of the new monetary policy will depend in no small way upon the maturity of the existing debt. The "locking-in" effect will be more potent the greater the maturity of outstanding issues and *vice-versa* since the potential capital loss is greater in the case of longer-maturing securities. The following example taken from Birnbaum (8) illustrates this point. The proportion of the capital value of a government bond which is "destroyed" by a one per cent increase in the rate of interest (in this case from 3 per cent to 4 per cent) is shown to be positively correlated with the period to maturity and to be virtually insignificant in the case of a bond with less than one year to run.

Years to Maturity	¼	½	1	5	10	15	25	∞
% of capital value lost	0.25	0.49	0.97	4.49	8.18	11.20	15.71	25.00

Thus for the locking-in effect to be effective requires that debt management policy be geared to lengthening the maturity of the existing debt during periods of expansion and shortening the debt maturity in times of contraction. However, there is little evidence to suggest that debt management policy was coordinated with monetary policy in this manner in either the United States or the United Kingdom, the two countries where the new monetary policy was widely endorsed. In the U.S.A. open market operations were deliberately restricted to the buying and selling of short-term bonds in order to avoid causing uncertainty and enhanced speculation. The so-called "bills only" policy thus effectively negated the strength of the locking-in effect. In the United Kingdom similar results obtained owing to the desire of the Treasury to finance its operations as cheaply as possible by re-issuing short-term securities and avoid the more onerous burden of interest rates on long-term bonds. Such considerations may suggest that the new monetary policy was never really given a chance.

Even with regard to longer-dated securities, the potency of the "locking-in" effect may be questioned on other grounds. It was soon pointed out that a relatively small interest-rate differential would be required to induce a financial institution to sell its government stock and provide investible funds even though a substantial capital loss was involved (9). Let us consider a simple example. We shall assume that a finance company invests £1000 in undated consols and obtains 6 per cent or £60 yearly on the investment. Let us also assume that a 7 per cent yield, or £70 per annum, would be required to induce the company to invest in a similar bond within the private sector – the differential reflecting an added premium for the greater risk associated with equity as opposed to gilt-edged investment. Now suppose the monetary authorities force an increase in the rate of interest to 8 per cent. The value of the consol immediately falls to £750. The finance company, it is argued, will be reluctant to sell in order to finance new investment spending because of the sizeable capital loss involved. It will prefer to hang on to its original investment, still retaining an income of £60 per year and hoping for an eventual decrease in interest rates to restore its original capital value. However, the required income of £70 per annum needed to induce a transfer of assets from the government to the private sector can still be obtained by investing the £750 at an interest rate of $9^1/_3$ per cent. And so the argument runs, in a tight money situation with investment demands interest-inelastic such an interest rate would be readily forthcoming. The force of this example lies in the fact that a sizeable increase in the discount rate to a "crisis" level has succeded in raising the required differential in yields between government and private sectors by only one third of one per cent. Moreover, the required increase in differential yield would be even less in the case of a bond with a finite life. If availability, and not the cost of credit, is the essence of the investment decision, then it may be concluded that the locking-in effect will not be a sufficient deterrent to investment.

The example is a highly simplified one and in many ways it may be regarded as overstating the case against the locking-in effect. It implicitly assumes that the government bond-holder is interested only in income yield and ignores its overall net worth. In the case of a government bond with a finite maturity date, however, where the ultimate capital sum is guaranteed the bond-holder may be unwilling to suffer a capital loss and thus deplete his net worth position unless additional compensation is forthcoming. A greater interest-rate differential may be demanded. Moreover, the example ignores the influence of taxation. If we refer back to our initial example but this time take account of a 50 per cent income tax, the post-tax yield upon the government consol is reduced to £30 per annum. If it is assumed that the same yield differential is required to induce private sector investment in the post-tax case as formerly, so that a net income of £40 is demanded, the private sector will have to offer an initial interest rate of 8 per cent. When the crisis rate of 8 per cent is adopted by the authorities the required differential rate is raised in excess of 10 per cent. Consideration of income taxation may strengthen the theoretical case for the locking-in effect.* Quite apart from these technical considerations, however, it may be questioned whether the availability doctrine could have succeeded in the extreme liquidity conditions which characterised the nineteen-fifties. The "new" monetary policy may have a greater chance of success in future periods as the national debt declines as a proportion of national income, especially if the attempt is made to lengthen the age profile of the existing debt.

This conclusion is broadly in line with the recommendations of the Radcliffe Report, which in many ways may be regarded as advocating a version of the locking-in effect in conjunction with the use of selective credit controls. The Report had dismissed the direct influence of the rate of interest upon investment expenditures – in the eyes of some observers too hurriedly† – but emphasized the ability of interest rates to control the behaviour of non-bank financial institutions and liquidity conditions generally. The Report took cognizance, however, of the need to avoid undue capital losses which would threaten the existence of many financial institutions. In doing so, the Report indicated a possible dilemma for the authorities – a dilemma which would be compounded by any commitment to protect the gilt-edged market generally. Moreover, it will be appreciated that the locking-in effect is crucially dependent upon the expectations of potential lenders. A raising of the interest rate will hardly be effective in locking in loanable funds if it induces expectations of further rises in the future. And in addition, interest-rate changes which lock in loanable funds also encourage the inflow of funds into those institutions which are able to raise their short-term deposit rates. Thus a financial institution may be able to increase its rate of lending even though it is unwilling to realise existing security holdings. Consideration of these issues weakens the theoretical appeal of the concept as a major policy device.

* Although, of course, the existence of capital gains taxation may be expected to diminish the force of the locking-in effect if capital losses are allowed against taxable income. In such a case, the bond-holder may have a direct incentive to sell government bonds when interest rates rise.

† In many ways the Report is notable for its comparative lack of empirical findings to buttress its conclusions and in some cases for reaching conclusions contrary to the weight of the evidence. For specific criticism along these lines see Gurley (10) and Walters (11).

The Importance of Velocity

Even if the "locking-in effect" is successful in curtailing the availability of funds for investment, attempts at restrictive monetary policy may fail if velocity increases in response. In the late nineteen-fifties especially, considerable emphasis was given to the importance of velocity movements being able to counter or completely offset reductions in the money supply. An increase in velocity is essentially an increase in the efficiency with which the existing money stock is being utilized. The question remains as to how this increase in efficiency is achieved.

First of all, restrictive monetary policy which raises the rate of interest also increases the opportunity cost of maintaining idle money balances. Both individuals and business companies will have an incentive to economise upon their transaction cash holdings. In addition, according to orthodox Keynesian theory, the speculative demand for money should decline as bond prices fall and as expectations of further falls are diminished. This general decrease in the demand for money permits a given money stock to finance a larger volume of expenditures and thus counteracts the attempt to curb the general level of economic activity.

In discussing the increase in velocity which characterises restrictive monetary conditions, the importance of the commercial banking sector should not be overlooked. As profit-making institutions they have a natural incentive to respond to money-market changes in a predictable profit-maximizing manner. As money becomes scarce potential investors are willing to offer high rates of interest to obtain investible funds. The commercial banks have thus the incentive to sell their holdings of government securities – especially their short-term bills where the extent of any capital loss is limited and yields are low – in order to make loans to customers willing to offer high rates of interest. It will be noted that this transaction implies no change in the total deposits of the banking sector. The sale of government securities to members of the public will destroy deposits in the same magnitude as they are created by the granting of new loans to customers. However, the importance of this activity with regard to monetary policy lies in the fact that the deposits which are destroyed by the purchase of securities will be for the most part idle deposits. Those that are created by advancing loans to would-be investors are on the contrary decidedly active. The net effect, then, is to turn idle into active deposits and thus cause a general increase in the velocity of circulation. Many proponents of the ineffectiveness of monetary policy have argued that the commercial banking sector has been the main culprit in permitting the expansion of velocity and have argued the need for tighter controls to permit policy measures to exert their full effect.

The changes we have been discussing postulate a relationship between the rate of interest and the velocity of money, which is normally measured by dividing final domestic expenditure by the money stock. If we depict this presumed relationship in Figure V.1, we obtain what we may choose to call the interest-velocity relation. We assume that within a given institutional framework there is some level of interest-rates at which velocity reaches a maximum

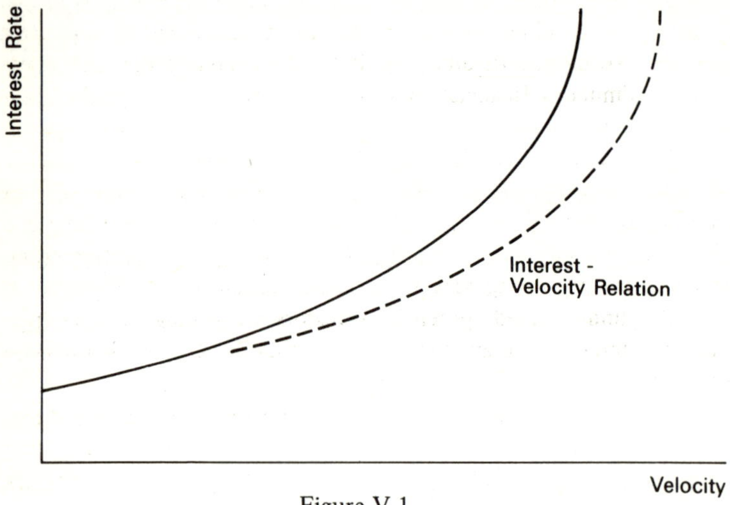

Figure V.1

at which point the interest-velocity curve becomes vertical. This situation will be obtained when it becomes physically impossible to economise upon transactions demands further, when all speculative holdings have been absorbed and when the banking sector has exhausted its holding of government securities and other similar assets which it is prepared to relinquish to finance investment demands. At this stage the velocity changes we have been describing can no longer offset monetary restraint. There is, however, another source of velocity change which we have yet to consider and which has been widely regarded as a major factor in rendering monetary policy impotent. We refer to institutional changes which have developed in the money market and in particular to the growth of non-bank financial institutions which are able to add to the amount of credit and thus increase the utilization of the means of payment. Although such non-bank financial institutions cannot create money – that is to say they cannot create legal tender – they are nonetheless able to expand the means by which investment may be financed.

There are two distinct issues involved. On the one hand the growth of non-bank institutions able to provide close substitutes for money implies that an increasingly larger share of expenditures is being financed by a sector no longer under the direct control of the monetary authorities. This argument relates to the important work of Gurley and Shaw (12) and has led to the demand that the normal powers which extend to the banking sector should also be extended to non-bank financial institutions. In addition, it has been argued that monetary restraint stimulates financial innovation in order to escape the main force of the restrictive measures and this reveals itself in an increase in the velocity limit (13). The two strands of thought are inevitably interlinked and they both imply a decreasing money/income ratio in response to contractionary monetary policies. Consider, for example, a restrictive monetary policy possibly reinforced by credit rationing by the commercial banking sector. In this situation with the supply of investible funds limited, potential investors are willing to offer high rates of interest to obtain the means of finance. Non-bank financial institutions (as for example a building society) are thus provided with the incentive to attract funds from depositors to finance these demands. By raising the interest-rate differential between their own deposit accounts and those of the commercial banking sector they are able to induce members of the public to transfer deposits from the banks. These deposits are then re-deposited within the banking sector by the non-bank financial institutions so that *in toto* the deposits of the commercial banks are unchanged. Consequently, there is no change in the volume of bank advances. However, the deposits of the non-bank financial sector have increased, permitting it to expand its loans and advances to potential investors. The extent of additional credit creation will depend upon the "reserve ratio" that the non-bank sector elects to adopt – which may be below those conventionally followed by the banking community and the net effect is to allow a given monetary base to finance an expanded volume of transactions.

The growth of non-bank financial intermediaries in response to tight money conditions may be looked upon as an institutional development increasing the permissible velocity of money. In Figure V.1 it is shown by an outward shift of the interest-velocity function as indicated by the dotted line. Such institutional changes develop in response to monetary constraint but generally do not disappear in times of comparative ease. Thus, over time the interest-velocity relationship will move continually to the right. It was perhaps this type of institutional development which led the Radcliffe Report to its conclusion that there is no limit to velocity changes and also to reject suggestions for controlling non-bank financial institutions (as, for example, interest-rate ceilings on non-bank deposits) upon the ground that other means of channelling liquid assets to investors would develop.

Whilst the expansion of non-bank financial intermediaries may have been an important factor in increasing the scope of velocity changes, both in raising the secular and short-run limits, many commentators have contended that the principal limitations upon the effectiveness of monetary policy lie elsewhere. On the one hand, it has been argued that the commercial banking sector, because of its substantial holding of short-term securities and its willingness to relinquish them to finance investment demands, has been the main culprit (14). On the other, and with particular reference to the United Kingdom, it has been argued that it is the unwillingness of the authorities to jeopardise the gilt-edged market in the interests of floating future government debt more easily which has rendered money policy ineffective (15). In this latter view, the unwillingness to sell sufficient gilts has meant that the money stock is, in reality, passively determined and alternative measures of control, as for example the introduction of special deposits*, cannot be expected to bear the full brunt of monetary control. Monetary policy can hardly be effective if the money stock is passively determined. For our purpose the interesting question is whether monetary policy could be effective if the authorities were to pursue a policy of monetary contraction. For whilst it may be true, as the Radcliffe Report appeared to imply, that in the long term there may be no limit to the institutional developments which increase the efficiency with which a

* Special deposits, a recent innovation in British monetary policy, are the additional cash deposits which the commercial banks can be forced to hold with the Bank of England. As such they may be compared with the American system of variable reserve requirements. For a useful discussion of this device see especially A.D. Bain (16).

given money stock may be utilized, in the short term it appears more reasonable to assume that such developments will be limited. If this is the case, monetary policy will exert an increasingly powerful effect as the inelastic portion of the interest-velocity relationship is reached. Increased velocity changes, therefore, will counter but not completely offset the force of monetary policy as interest rates are progressively raised. This immediately raises the issue of how high interest rates must be raised before monetary measures can exert their full effect – i.e. when the inelastic portion of the interest-velocity curve is attained. This is an important question because whilst in theory there may be no limit to the permissible level of interest rates, in practice there will be a feasible limit to what is politically acceptable in the short term. A practical interest-rate limit below the velocity ceiling will imply that monetary policy cannot be used with full effect and may have to be supplemented by fiscal and other measures. In contrast, a feasible limit in excess of the velocity ceiling will imply that monetary policy may be used with greater confidence. It behoves us, therefore, to enquire into the constraints upon the permissible level of interest rates.

The Institutional Limit to Interest Rates

Many factors combine to determine the permissible level of interest rates. One of the most important is undeniably the National Debt. A higher interest rate implies higher tax burdens to service the debt and in turn, since the debt is held in many cases by predominantly upper-income groups, such increased taxation may imply a transfer of income from the lower-paid to the better-off members of society. Secondly, for debtor countries such as the United Kingdom, a higher interest rate will also necessitate increased payments to those countries which hold sterling balances within the United Kingdom and thus constitute a charge upon the balance of payments. Moreover, with regard to the international sector, an increase in the rate of interest may induce capital movements from other countries with possibly embarrassing political consequences. Of even greater importance is the fact that an increase in interest rates will exert a disproportionate impact upon such activities as residential construction and home-owners buying their houses on mortgage. Such a group is not one to displease when considering electoral prospects. In addition, it has been contended that a restrictive monetary policy fosters the development of monopoly *vis-à-vis* other more competitive sectors of the economy in that the competitive sector is less able to pass on increased capital charges and also less likely to obtain alternative means of finance when conventional sources are depleted (17). Finally, the impact of increased interest charges is much more severe upon long-term as opposed to short-term investment projects (18). Thus it has been argued that restrictive monetary policy will tend to discriminate against growth investment where the pay-off period may be long-term. If this is the case, the implication is that restrictive monetary policy will conflict with the objective of enhanced growth, a conflict which might be avoided by the adoption of fiscal measures, or other more selective controls. All these considerations taken collectively would suggest that there is a limit to the feasible rate of interest within a democratic society.

There is some evidence to suggest that the interest-rate ceiling has shifted gradually upward over time; present discount rates would have seemed completely unrealistic in the decade following the war. In part, this gradual increase has reflected the world liquidity shortage which has led to one country after another taking measures to protect the capital account of its balance of payments. In addition, it is probably also the consequence of the fact that even the abnormal becomes regarded as the norm if it is maintained for a sufficiently long period of time. No doubt, it is also a reflection of a greater awareness of the existence of inflation that has characterised the post-war years which has led debtors to accept and creditors to insist upon higher nominal rates of interest. Thus the period of the "new" monetary policy has witnessed two contrary developments: the greater scope for velocity changes on the one hand paralleled by a greater ability to impose onerous interest charges upon the other.

Whether the interest-rate ceiling has risen sufficiently to permit monetary constraint to overcome velocity movements and exert its full impact must remain an empirical question. The ceiling may differ between countries as also may the scope for velocity changes. What does appear clear, however, is that as the permissible rate of interest has risen, so too has the importance of the cost of capital in the investment decision. When normal borrowing charges exceed 10 per cent and even 15 per cent an element of cost consciousness begins to emerge in consideration of capital outlays. Thus, ironically, the post-war movement in interest rates may have played its part in resurrecting pre-war monetary policy. The investment demand function may indeed be interest-sensitive at sufficiently high rates of interest.

Consideration of all these issues would suggest that there are strong theoretical reasons for believing that monetary measures to influence interest rates exert some impact upon the economy, whilst at the same time recognising that there may be serious constraints or limitations upon the effectiveness of such measures.

Money Multipliers and the Lag in Effect

Thus far, our discussion of monetary policy has concentrated almost entirely upon the interest-rate effect. We have looked at the influence of the rate of interest upon investment demands, upon the availability of credit and upon induced changes in velocity.* Traditionally, this is the manner in which monetary theorists have approached the question of monetary control. It is, however, a fundamental tenet of the "new monetarism" that what matters is changes in the volume of money *per se* and not any accompanying movements in the rate of interest. This is not to deny that such movements may exist nor that they may reinforce direct monetary change but only that such indirect effects are relatively less important and less useful as indicators of economic activity. Consider, for example, an increase in the public holding of monetary balances. Let us assume, for purposes of analysis, that this increase in monetary holdings is purely autonomous; what are the consequences? If the public possess a stable demand for money, an increase in money expenditures will occur with the excess amount of money being transferred either into commodities or alternatively into financial assets. In the former case, the increase in effective demand will

* For the sake of completeness, we should perhaps mention the influence of interest-rate changes upon the volume of consumption. Generally, economists have played down the importance of this factor but recent empirical evidence suggests that this may be an oversimplification (19, 20). An increase in the interest rate may reduce consumption on two counts: first because it implies a decrease in the net worth of those holding government debt – i.e. the locking-in effect extended to consumers – and second because it may induce additional saving. Although consumption has been assumed interest-inelastic, because of its importance in the composition of GNP, even a small elasticity could have a significant impact upon total expenditures – and theoretically a greater impact than that which would result from a much higher elasticity in the investment function. This latter point stems from Mayer (21).

exert a direct beneficial stimulus on output and thus raise money national income. In the latter, the public will increase their collective holding of financial securities. Normally, such action may be expected to induce a decline in net yields as security prices are bid upwards. However, this need not be the result. Suppose, for example, that the public voluntarily transfers its excess amounts of cash into deposits held with building societies. The latter may decide not to decrease the rate of interest paid upon such deposits but rather to increase the mortgages which they are willing to grant to home-buyers. The increased availability of credit thus granted to would-be house-purchasers may be reflected in increased buying of consumer durables. It is for this reason that the advocate of the new doctrine stresses the importance of the monetary variable and not any accompanying movement in interest rates. The money/interest-rate relationship may be weak or erratic; it is the amount of money and not its cost which is all-important to the determination of money national income.

The money multiplier is a concept which summarises the change in money national income consequent upon a change in the money supply. It may be likened to the Keynesian multiplier which relates the change in income to a change in autonomous expenditures. But the monetarist would argue that it provides a far more significant and predictable relationship. The money multiplier, however, is only a useful concept if the money supply changes autonomously or at least independently of income changes. Opponents of the monetarist position would usually deny the autonomous nature of monetary increase. Instead, they would generally hold that the money supply would respond to the increased needs of trade as the economy entered expansionary periods. Thus, an upward movement of the economy would naturally be accompanied by monetary increase as the banks expand the volume of credit. If this is the case, then the money supply and the level of national output would move together but no causal influence could be ascribed to the monetary factor.

It is for this reason that Friedman's analysis of the length of the lag takes on renewed significance. A lag of twelve to eighteen months would suggest *inter alia* the strong possibility that the direction of causation was from money to income. Although such an argument would be by no means conclusive* the longer the length of the lag the

* That is to say, even if the economy behaves in a Keynesian manner with a change in expenditures initiating income changes to which the money supply

greater is the temptation to make *a priori* judgements concerning cause and effect.

However, Friedman's findings have been subjected to intensive criticism (22). In particular, his analysis which relates the *change* in the money supply to the *level* of economic activity has been criticised as being methodologically unsound. A simple arithmetical example serves to demonstrate this point. Let us assume that changes in the money stock and changes in the level of economic activity occur more or less simultaneously regardless of the direction of causation. Let us also assume that the money stock remains a constant (say 10 per cent) proportion of money national income. Then if the economy is characterised by a continuously oscillating cycle as described in Table V.1, the money supply would behave accordingly and casual inspection of time series data would reveal the time paths indicated by the solid lines in Figure V.2. However, if we compare the *level* of money income with the *change* in money supply we find the relationship is one between the upper and the broken curve. Peaks and

TABLE V.1

	Time Period (years)									
	1	2	3	4	5	6	7	8	9	10(2) .
Money income	100	110	130	160	170	160	130	110	100	110. . .
Money stock	10	11	13	16	17	16	13	11	10	11. . .
Increase in money stock	−1	+1	+2	+3	+1	−1	−3	−2	−1	+1
Increase in money income	10	+10	+20	+30	+10	−10	−30	−20	−10	+10

reacts, time series data would normally show the money supply preceding income change. Consider for example the following. Suppose households increase their consumption by using hitherto idle savings. The initial impact would be for retailers to find their stocks being depleted and their bank balances being increased. Their reaction would be to increase their demands upon wholesalers who in turn would relay increased orders to manufacturers. At some stage – often only after some time has elapsed – productive activity will start up again. In the process the increase in income arising will most probably be financed by renewed credit made possible by the increased deposits now enjoyed by the banking sector. The expansion of credit follows and is caused by the initial expenditure decision, but it will generally precede the expansion of income which ultimately arises.

troughs in the change in the money supply now precede peaks and troughs in the level of economic activity by one whole time period and suggest a spurious causal relationship. That no reliance can be placed upon this sequence of events as an indicator of cause and effect can be demonstrated by comparing the *level* of the money stock with the *change* in the level of money income which would result in income fluctuations preceding those in the money stock. Comparison of changes in the level of money income with changes in the level of money stock would, of course, reveal what we have already assumed to be the case, namely simultaneous changes. Although Friedman offered

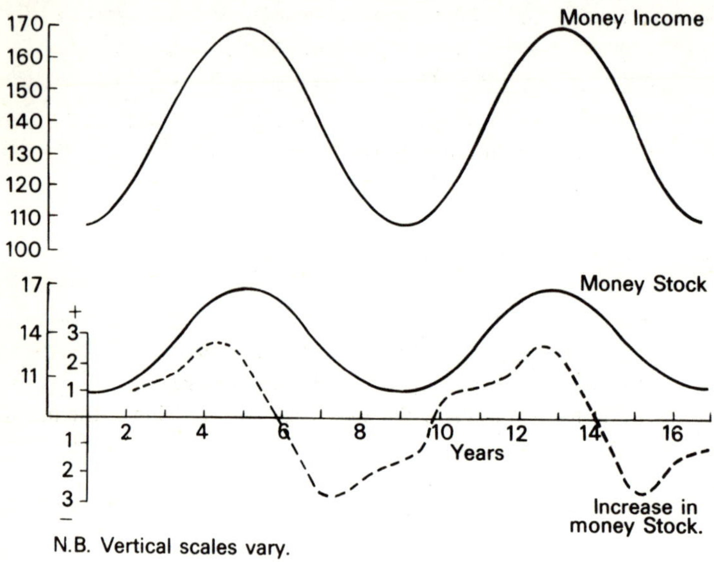

Figure V.2

considerable theoretical and statistical justification for adopting the procedure he does (23, 24), this example illustrates that the appropriate identification of the lag is no simple matter and should at least provide a warning against the casual use and abuse of time series data. In the present case, Friedman's analysis, quite apart from implying causation on behalf of monetary change, may suggest a time lag which from the policy point of view may be bogus. Intuitively, even if we postulate a stable demand for money function, one would expect some delay before the public adjust to a changed monetary situation; and equally, we would normally expect some interval to elapse before investors respond to a change in the rate of interest. Whether the lags preclude the effective use of monetary policy measures is still a debatable issue and one which has aroused considerable controversy (25, 26, 27, 28). One of the difficulties involved in identifying the lag is that a change in the money stock may not be followed by a changed response but rather by a quickening of the pace at which existing activities are being undertaken. Thus, for example, a decrease in the rate of interest may not generate new plans for investment but may speed up the completion of those already under way. Inevitably, issues of this nature intensify the difficulties associated with empirical research relying upon recorded data. And finally, even if fiscal policies can be shown to take effect with less delay, monetary policy possesses one great advantage in that policy changes can usually be initiated without the time required for legislative approval. Particularly with respect to the United States, this may be a consideration of no small importance.

Exogeneity of the Money Supply

Fundamental to the analysis of monetary policy is the issue of whether the money supply is truly exogenous in the sense that the monetary authorities can effectively control it. Monetarists generally argue not only that the money stock is the significant key variable in the macro-economy, but also that the authorities by acting upon the high powered money supply – the cash base – can exercise effective control over the total supply of money. In contrast, opponents of the monetarist view contend that the money supply is an endogenous variable responding through credit creation to the changing conditions of demand. In this view, the money supply is passively determined and it becomes futile to pursue monetary targets. Instead, the attempt should be to control interest rates as a means of influencing the overall level of demand.

To bring out some of the issues involved, consider the following specification of the total money supply*

$$M = C\left(\frac{1 + D}{R + D}\right)$$

* For a derivation of this equation see Bain (16) p. 67, or Chick (29) p. 21. For a discussion of the difficulties in determining the causal relationship between C and M consult Davis (30).

where M is the money supply, C the cash base, D the private sector's desired cash deposit ratio and R the reserve ratio maintained by the banks. The authorities can effectively control C, the amount of cash actually in circulation, and can obviously influence R in that minimum reserve ratios can be enforced. However, D, the optimal cash–deposit ratio, is effectively beyond control; and moreover the banks may, on occasion, elect to hold substantial excess cash reserves. Inability to control D would not be of great consequence if it displayed reasonable stability; it is argued, however, particularly by Tobin (31), that D responds to profit-maximizing behaviour on the part of the commercial banking sector confronted with a change in the cash base initiated by the monetary authorities.

Suppose for example that the authorities attempt to reduce the money supply by selling bonds in the open market. Presumably, they can induce additional sales by making the interest yield sufficiently attractive. The purchase of bonds depletes the banks' cash resources and – assuming the banks are fully loaned up – will force a multiple contraction of credit throughout the economy. Commercial banks, however, are profit-making institutions. They will have a natural tendency to resist being compelled to call in profit-making loans and advances and will thus be induced to seek additional deposits by raising deposit interest rates. Now if the cash–deposit ratio is sensitive to interest rate changes, the public may be induced to economize upon their cash holdings, thus offsetting in part the attempted curtailment of the money supply. To the extent that the cash–deposit ratio does vary, control of the cash base cannot imply complete control of the money supply. Monetarists, however, would contend that complete control is unnecessary provided the link between the high-powered money supply and the total money stock is sufficiently strong to permit changes in the cash base to exert a dominant influence. The link would, of course, be the stronger if, as Friedman has proposed, commercial banks were compelled to maintain 100 per cent reserve ratios.

Chapter VI **Fiscal Policy**

We define fiscal policy to encompass any decision to change the level, composition or timing of government expenditures or to vary the burden, structure or frequency of the tax payment. Fiscal policy may thus be considered as a double-barrelled instrument with both barrels being discharged simultaneously when required. Since fiscal policy normally influences the size of the budget surplus or deficit, the latter is commonly looked upon as an index of fiscal control. Such a view, however, must be regarded as fallacious since both expenditures and receipts will normally fluctuate in response to changing income levels whilst in no way indicating a policy measure. Any decision to change the responsiveness of either expenditures or fiscal receipts to changes in the level of economic activity, however, is very decidedly a part of fiscal policy.

In many elementary expositions, whilst it is conceded that a change in the budget surplus or deficit may merely indicate the responsiveness of the budget system to variations in aggregate income, it is nonetheless contended that a change in the level of surplus or deficit associated with *any given income level* does indicate positive fiscal action. In terms of Figure VI.1(b) below, it is held that a movement along the budget function illustrates the automatic response of the budget to varying income levels (often confused with the degree of automatic stabilization of the budget system) whereas a parametric shift of the function indicates discretionary fiscal change. This distinction, whilst conceptually appealing, is at best but a half truth. This is most easily seen if we consider the expenditure and tax functions in isolation before merging them to obtain the overall budget function.

Government expenditures will normally include some anti-cyclical component such as unemployment relief, price support payments and so on. Even though such features of public expenditures need not be (and in most cases have not been) incorporated with stabilization objectives in mind, they nonetheless provide a countercyclical element. Consequently, it is usual for some government expenditures to be negatively related to the level of economic activity. Likewise, since most tax structures exhibit proportional if not always progressive rate features, tax receipts are normally positively related with income. This situation is depicted in Part (a) of Figure VI.1. The overall budget

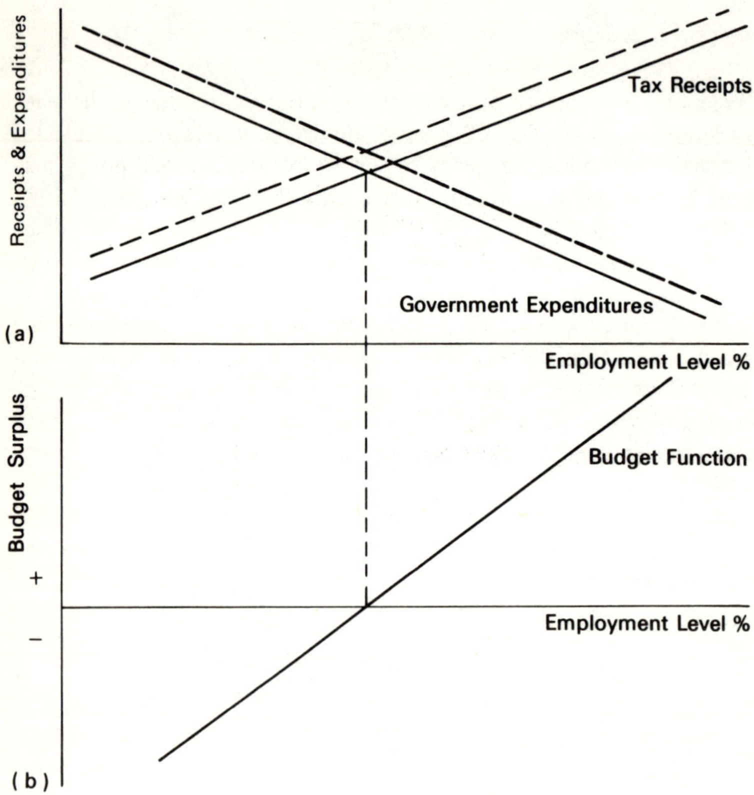

Figure VI.1

function shown in Part (b) is simply derived from the above and has its zero point directly below the intersection of expenditure and tax functions. Now consider a policy decision to raise expenditures and taxation by the same amount as indicated by the dotted lines in Part (a). No change is implied for the position of the overall budget function and in terms of the foregoing classification no policy change is indicated. However, two distinct policy changes have been enacted and moreover they will normally exert a positive influence upon the level of economic activity thus initiating a movement along the budget function.* Far from being but a passive reaction to a changing income level, such a movement summarises a policy decision not otherwise indicated in the lower portion of the diagram. Discretionary fiscal policy, therefore, need not imply a shift of the budget function. It is of course true that a shift of the function will usually imply a discretionary change, but it is equally true that no precise estimate of its restrictive or expansionary impact could be inferred from it. Consider, for example, a downward shift of the budget function by a given amount at the full employment income level. Such a movement would be consistent with either an increased government expenditure of this amount upon goods and services or an equal increase in transfer payments. Alternatively, it would be consistent with this amount being cut from the total tax bill. In all probability, however, the macro-economic impact of these measures would differ and may differ considerably when due allowance is made for the various import demands of the public and private sector. Considerations of this nature would suggest that whilst a given movement in the budget surplus may indicate the direction of change no great reliance should be placed upon it in forecasting the level of economic activity. This issue is clearly relevant to the question of monetary versus fiscal control for many of the empirical studies comparing the effectiveness of alternative policies have looked upon the full employment budget surplus as an index of fiscal policy.

Whilst the position of the budget function is often taken as indicating a stringent or relatively easy fiscal policy, its slope is often looked upon as summarising the degree of automatic stabilization incorporated into the fiscal system. The greater the slope of the function the greater the degree of automatic stability and *vice versa.* Such a view is also erroneous and for precisely similar reasoning to the above. The slope of the budget function summarises the degree of built-in flexibility of the overall budget to a change in income levels. The degree of automatic stabilization, however, refers to the stabilizing impact of a change in the budget surplus and cannot be assessed

* We refer here to the balanced budget theorem which we explore in more detail below.

without reference to a multiplier formula. Since the multiplier applicable to an expenditure change will normally differ from that associated with a given tax change equal changes in the size of the budget surplus will exert differing impacts according to how they are arrived at. Alternatively, a decrease in the slope of the expenditures function, compensated by an increase in the slope of the tax function so that no change occurs in the slope of the overall budget function, will be accompanied by a change in the degree of automatic stabilization incorporated into the fiscal structure as long as the expenditures multiplier and the tax multiplier differ. As an index and measure of fiscal policy, therefore, the concept of the overall budget surplus is one that must be used with considerable caution.*

An interesting question which arises when considering the budget surplus or deficit is how it will respond to a change in the rate of tax – particularly the rate of income tax. The issue is complicated because there are two opposing effects to consider. An increase in the rate of income tax will raise the revenue yield out of any given income level. At the same time, however, a tax increase will lower the value of the multiplier and lead to a decline in the income level. Which effect will predominate? This is a question which cannot be answered without resort to the more powerful tools of mathematics but the answer does, of course, depend upon the particular assumptions which are incorporated into the model analysis. Generally, in the more simple national income models and ignoring any disincentive effects of higher taxation, the result will be for the budget surplus to increase (2). The higher tax rate will more than offset the lower level of national income implying that there is no "optimal" rate of tax which will maximize the revenue yield. More complex and probably more realistic models incorporating accelerator-like changes in investment and allowing a greater rôle to the influence of expectations could well negate this conclusion and suggest that a tax cut might be the preferable way to remove a budget deficit. Such considerations are clearly relevant to the design of fiscal policy; certainly, there can be no doubt that definite answers to the above questions would greatly facilitate the task of the decision-taker.

* The distinction made above between built-in flexibility and automatic stabilization has been explicitly made by Smyth (1), who has demonstrated that under certain conditions it is possible for increased built-in flexibility to heighten the degree of instability within the system. This conclusion depends upon the adoption of a suitably lagged consumption function.

Fiscal Policy and the Multiplier

The concept of the multiplier is of vital importance to the analysis of fiscal policy. It is the valve which regulates the aggregate impact of any change in total expenditure; as such, it determines the impact of any change in government expenditures and an estimate of its size must be regarded as an essential prerequisite to the formation of fiscal policy. Secondly, the multiplier itself is, in part, determined by fiscal parameters and consequently it can be modified either to magnify or diminish the impact of autonomous expenditures arising elsewhere in the economy. Fiscal changes which serve to weaken the multiplier are generally referred to as built-in stabilizers; they reduce the extent of autonomous fluctuations. In Figure VI.2, for example, we portray the

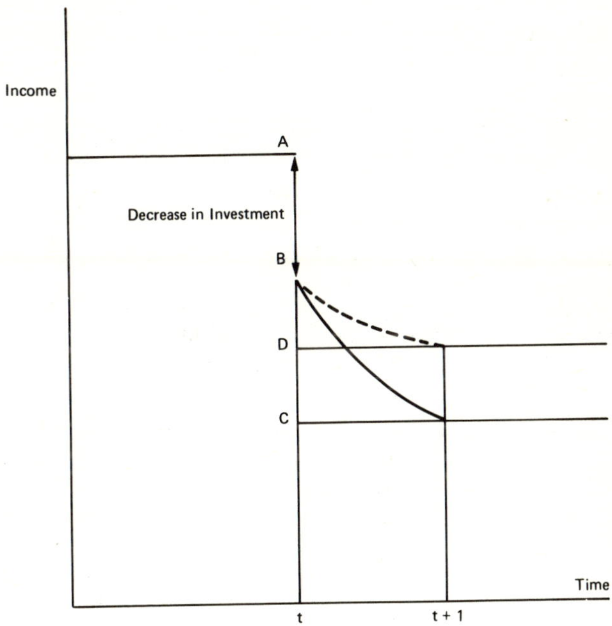

Figure VI.2

time path of the equilibrium level of income. For simplicity, we assume the income level is not itself a function of time: i.e. we abstract considerations of economic growth. Now assume at time t that an autonomous cutback in investment expenditure occurs indicated by the distance AB. According to conventional Keynesian theory the equilibrium level of income will decline by some multiple of AB owing to the operation of the multiplier. Pursuing the comparative static methodology we assume that equilibrium will be regained by time t + 1, with the total decline in income represented by the distance AC of which BC is accounted for by the multiplier. Now assume the same sequence of events but allow for the introduction of an automatic stabilizer. The stabilizer comes into operation in response to the initial income change – that is in response to the initial cut-back in expenditure. It reveals itself in a reduced value of the multiplier so that the equilibrium income level is now regained at a higher level of output. In the figure we show this by the path of the broken line. The total income loss is now AD of which BD is accounted for by the multiplier. In principle, therefore, the extent to which any fiscal provision constitutes a built-in or automatic stabilizer may be estimated by comparing the size of the multiplier before and after its introduction (3). In this way, it is possible to rank the various fiscal features in terms of their automatic stabilizing impact. In general, an efficient automatic stabilizer must possess one or more of the following characteristics (4). It must reveal a fairly immediate response to a change in the level of economic activity; such a feature, for example, would be possessed by a value-added tax *vis-à-vis* a flat rate excise levy. Secondly, it is desirable for an automatic stabilizer to exhibit flexibility in yield, so that in the case of a tax, for example, the percentage change in the yield would exceed that in the income level. Such a quality could result either from substantial flexibility in the tax base or from a highly progressive rate structure. Finally, it is desirable for an automatic stabilizer to be fairly large in relation to GNP so that any offset to income fluctuations is significant. For this reason, a proportional income tax would normally be a better stabilizer than, say, a highly progressive betting levy. For the modern economy, the most important of the automatic fiscal stabilizers are generally the corporation income or profits tax, the personal income tax and on the expenditure side the rôle of unemployment benefits. The corporation income tax is an effective stabilizer mainly because of the extent to which corporate profits fluctuate over the course of the business cycle, reflecting in part the importance of fixed costs. It is the change in the tax base in response to changing economic conditions which makes for considerable variation in taxable liability and contributes greatly to the built-in flexibility of the budget yield. The personal income tax is important as an automatic stabilizer mainly on account of its importance as a percentage of overall fiscal receipts and also because under a system of deduction at source or P.A.Y.E. it reveals an immediate response to changing income levels. The more progressive the actual rate structure the more the automatic stabilizing element is reinforced. The relevance of unemployment benefits to automatic stabilization is obvious enough, although their potency may be queried (5,6) but it is not always emphasized that the latter is also of major importance in reducing the size of the multiplier in the period of recovery, since their gradual withdrawal is concomitant with increasing employment.

It will be readily appreciated that this distinction between policy action which relies upon the multiplier as a fiscal lever, and that which aims at altering the multiplier itself, is closely related to one of the more controversial issues in macro-economic policy, namely that between dependence upon discretionary as opposed to automatic stabilizing devices. In general, discretionary fiscal policy will be more effective – or at least easier to implement – the greater the size of the multiplier whereas the advocate of automatic stabilization will seek ways to diminish the multiplier.

Arguments against discretionary policy measures depend for their validity upon the assumption of ignorance. Uncertainty with regard to the future course of the economy, delays in obtaining reliable and unambiguous economic indices and possibly misinterpretation of past policy successes may lead to the enactment of stabilization measures which exert perverse and destabilizing movements upon the economy. Even if present trends are fully known, there may be such a delay attached to any particular measure that it may exert its primary impact when the need for it has long since passed. Finally, a discretionary change by its very nature will carry announcement effects revealing the way the authorities view the economy and thus may provoke undesirable reactions. In contrast, automatic stabilizing devices place no premium upon factual knowledge. Their effect is to counter autonomous changes regardless of whether or not the authorities are aware of them. Since they are built into the economic system, they require no legislative approval before they can be put in motion, and indeed no new administrative machinery is needed which could delay their effects. Finally, automatic stabilizers may be more successful in striking a regional balance – in the sense of concentrating the offset where most needed – than a discretionary change which, due to administrative requirements, may concentrate initial effects where undesired by reference to any economic criterion. Announcement effects are absent although it must be remembered that the existence of automatic stabilizers may condition responses which would not otherwise prevail.

The arguments favouring reliance upon automatic stabilizers would probably go unchallenged if it could be shown that they were capable of consistently maintaining the economy at a high level, and preferably the full employment level over time. However, it has long been recognised that automatic fiscal stabilizers cannot fully offset an autonomous change but can merely dampen the resulting fluctuation (7). This stems from the fact that built-in stabilizers do not come into operation until some destabilizing change has occurred. Consequently, some income decline must occur, although theoretically the automatic stabilizers are able to attain a higher final income level than that indicated by position B in Figure VI.2 – that is to say, it is conceivable that they may be able to *more* than negate the operation of the multiplier.* Nonetheless, they would be powerless to prevent the initial decline. An economy relying solely upon automatic stabilizing devices, therefore, is not insured against cyclical downturn. Moreover, it must be remembered that automatic stabilizers cut both ways: they weaken the movement towards recession but at the same time delay the recovery. Technically, automatic stabilizers aim at stabilizing the economy, but they are completely neutral with regard to the level at which the economy should be so stabilized. There is consequently no guarantee that a system relying upon automatic devices would enjoy a higher *per capita* income level over time than an economy geared to

* Consider the case where the stabilizer takes the form of additional government expenditure proportional to lagged current income deviation from A such that the additional expenditure at time t is given by,

$$G_t = c(-Y_{t-1})$$

where Y denotes income deviation from A. Let the marginal propensity to consume be indicated by b, and assume that the initial decline in investment spending to be \$1. Then at time t the income deviation is given by,

$$Y_t = -1 + bY_{t-1} + c(-Y_{t-1})$$

so that equilibrium income deviation is given by

$$Y^e = -1/(1 - b + c)$$

and if $c > b$, $Y^e > -1$ (\$) and the income level is stabilized above B. For correction upon this point I am especially indebted to Professor Black of the University of Exeter.

discretionary changes. Indeed, there can be no guarantee that either system will generate a higher level of sustained *per capita* income than that which would occur in the absence of any policy whatsoever.

One of the most compelling arguments against too great a reliance upon automatic fiscal stabilizers arises from consideration of dynamic changes through time. In a growing economy which is characterised by an element of progression in its fiscal payments, it is usual for the growth in expenditures to lag behind the expansion of tax receipts. As a consequence, the budget surplus will gradually expand and, it is argued, will serve to slow down the normal expansion of the economy. Hence the need for discretionary fiscal changes aimed at reducing the fiscal burden and to counteract the element of "fiscal drag" reflected in the inherent tendency for the budget function to shift gradually upward through time.

Most advocates of fiscal policy would generally look upon the issue of discretionary versus automatic weapons not so much in terms of conflict but rather as one complementing the other. The value of automatic stabilizers in helping to maintain high employment levels and preventing autonomous disturbances from precipitating an irreversible downturn is freely admitted. At the same time, however, many economists would advocate the need for discretionary fiscal changes to accelerate recovery from unemployment – and in part to overcome the automatic stabilizers – and also would acknowledge the occasional need for tax reduction to give the economy the necessary stimulus to achieve higher growth paths. A compromise proposal which has been mooted in recent years is that of "formula flexibility" which may be regarded as an attempt to improve upon the element of built-in flexibility whilst avoiding the dangers associated with arbitrary discretionary changes. Such a proposal, for example, might be a previously legislated decision that all social security contributions be suspended or halved when unemployment reaches a certain figure and *vice versa*. The difficulty with this type of recommendation is essentially that of designing proposals which are sufficiently simple to avoid undue administrative burdens and inconvenience. In principle, however, such proposals possess the great virtue of seeking to vary the size of the multiplier inversely with the movement of national income so as to reinforce the effectiveness of discretionary measures in periods of recession and to weaken autonomous destabilizing movements in periods of prosperity.

The Balanced Budget Multiplier

The theory of the balanced budget multiplier is of special interest to the theory of fiscal policy for it is only in the case of a self-financing tax/expenditure change that other policy influences can be ignored. In all other cases, for example an expenditure increase financed by the sale of government bonds, changes in the outstanding money stock or in the term structure of interest rates are necessary to effect the initial fiscal measure. Accordingly, it becomes extremely difficult to determine what part of the policy impact springs solely from the fiscal action and what is really due to the use of other policy instruments. Much of the controversy concerning the potency of fiscal versus monetary measures springs directly from this difficulty. In the case of a balanced budget change, whilst repercussions will necessarily impinge upon the monetary sector with induced feedback effects elsewhere, the total impact is causally determined by the fiscal authorities. To this extent, it may be considered an example of a pure fiscal measure (8).

The essence of the balanced budget multiplier lies in the assertion that marginal propensities to consume will differ throughout the economy. If this is the case, a transfer of income to those with high marginal propensities to consume, financed by tax levies upon those with relatively low marginal consumption propensities will generate an expansion of income throughout the economy. The fact that the government sector is usually taken to be the sector with the high consumption propensity (MPC = 1) is really incidental to the theory, although it is in this context that the theory has been developed. The essence of the theory can be outlined diagrammatically in terms of the familiar national accounting framework. In Figure VI.3, the equilibrium level of income Y for a closed economy is indicated either in the upper portion of the diagram at the level where the aggregate expenditures function intersects the conventional 45° line, or alternatively in the lower portion of the figure at the point where the combined saving and tax receipts schedule equates the combined investment and government expenditure function. For simplicity we assume that investment expenditures are autonomously determined whilst consumption expenditures are a function of disposable income. Assume now that the government increases tax receipts to the extent of ΔT by imposing a lump sum tax and immediately spends the proceeds upon goods and services.* The net effect is to raise the aggregate expenditure function since the increase in government expenditures exceeds the induced fall in consumption. This occurs because whilst the entire tax proceeds are spent by the government, only a portion of the tax payment is financed by the cutback in consumption – the remainder is paid from savings. More specifically, the consumption function shifts downwards to the extent $\Delta T \times MPC$ whilst the government expenditures function is raised by ΔT. As long as the marginal propensity to consume is less than unity, the net effect must be to raise the equilibrium level of national income. Alternatively, in the lower portion of the figure the tax receipts function is raised by ΔT but the savings function falls by $\Delta T \times (1 - MPC)$ – again part of the savings being used to pay the tax. Consequently, the increase in the combined savings and tax function is less than the combined raising of the investment and government expenditures function since the latter is increased by the total amount of the tax proceeds. Accordingly, the equilibrium level of income is raised to Y' as indicated in the composite figure.

In this simple model, it may be noted that the expansion of income induced by the balanced budget fiscal change is exactly equal to the increase in government expenditures, which implies that the expansion of income is independent of the value taken by the marginal propensity to consume. This follows because the increase in expenditures, as already noted, is

$$\Delta T - (\Delta T \cdot MPC) = \Delta T(1 - MPC)$$

To obtain the ultimate increase in income, a normal multiplier must be applied to this expenditure change. But the multiplier in this simple closed economy model is simply $1/(1 - MPC)$. Thus the total increase in income is given by,

$$\Delta T(1 - MPC) \cdot \frac{1}{(1 - MPC)} = \Delta T.$$

Income expands, therefore, by the extent of the government expenditure irrespective of the value of the marginal propensity to consume.

* If the government were to use the proceeds to make transfer payments to members of the public at large, and if the recipients had identical marginal propensities to consume as the taxpayers, then clearly no effect is discerned; the balanced budget multiplier is zero. Normally then the balanced budget multiplier refers to the direct expenditure by the government upon goods and services. If the government were to give the goods and services away without charge, a similar qualification would apply as indicated in the following section.

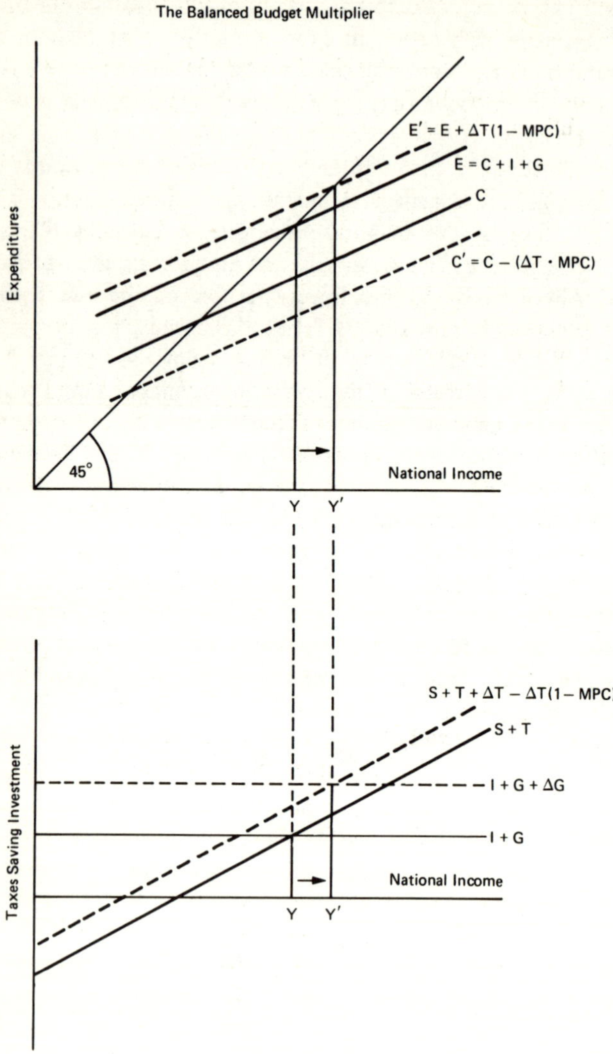

Figure VI.3

The implication is that a knowledge of the determinants of consumer behaviour is not required in order to assess the impact of a balanced budget fiscal change. Nor is this conclusion modified by the introduction of imports into the model, providing that government expenditures are used exclusively to purchase domestic output, for this case is then akin to a fall in the marginal propensity to consume on behalf of the private sector.

Given the assertion, a number of interesting propositions follow. First of all, it follows that a budget deficit is unnecessary as a means of realizing full employment income providing the principle of the balanced budget multiplier is pursued far enough. As long as marginal saving propensities are positive within the private sector the full utilization of tax proceeds by the government will continue to raise income and employment levels indefinitely. Paradoxically, it is the theory of the balanced budget multiplier which provides the Keynesian justification for non-deficit finance. Secondly, the argument illustrates that expenditure changes are normally more high-powered in their impact upon the economy than equal cost tax changes since part of the latter is siphoned off into saving outlets. Dollar for dollar, an expenditure change would appear to be the more efficient means of achieving stabilization goals but there are good political reasons why the government may prefer to choose the tax device when it feels the need to stimulate the economy.

It is perhaps of more interest to examine the qualifications which limit the wholesale applicability of the theory. First of all, any disincentive effects of higher taxation have been ignored in indicating the essence of the theory. The extent to which additional taxation deters productive effort remains an empirical question which has yet to be satisfactorily resolved but it is clear that consideration must be given to such an issue. Related to this question is the important objective of economic growth and the fact that the government using the balanced budget multiplier principle is able to substitute public for private goods. To a large extent then, this substitution may reflect investment for consumption goods and the question arises as to the extent to which this transfer can be effected without impairing the incentives of the existing work force. A more fundamental qualification involves the external sector in the case where the public sector imports goods and services. This aspect is of some considerable significance for the less advanced economies where the importing propensity of the private sector may be low – in the face of prohibitive tariffs and quotas on consumables – whilst that of the public sector may be comparatively high if the latter is importing essential capital items. In this situation, the balanced budget multiplier could easily be negative and tax-financed expansions of expenditures may depress the domestic economy whilst simultaneously worsening the external account.

It is also assumed that neither the government expenditure nor the higher level of taxation confronting consumers will adversely affect the present level of investment spending. With regard to the former, if the objective is to raise the level of income and employment then care must be taken to ensure that the government programme is not directly competitive with the private sector. Wasteful expenditures, the Keynesian example of pyramid-building being an illustration, may better serve the cause of securing full employment income than, say, socially useful investment in house-building.

One of the more interesting qualifications to the balanced budget theorem concerns expenditures by the government upon goods and services which are then given free of charge to needy recipients in the form of welfare payments (9, 10). If the recipients experience a real income gain, which we assume will normally be the case, they may attempt to raise their overall level of saving. Since they cannot save out of payments in kind, except in very trivial instances, they will attempt to modify their saving patterns out of alternative income. In the extreme case, if welfare recipients experience an income gain which they value equal to the cost of the service, and if they possess the same marginal saving propensities as those of the taxpayer then there will be no impact upon the level of national income. This extreme case will seldom if ever occur, partly because welfare recipients will in all probability possess lower marginal saving propensities, but also because they will be unlikely to value payments in kind as equal to the cost of the service provided unless they can be readily traded or transferred into alternative income (11). In most cases, therefore, the balanced budget multiplier will still be positive. Nonetheless, this qualification is of interest for one implication of the analysis is that in all probability the balanced budget multiplier would decline should welfare payments in kind be replaced by payments in cash – perhaps, for example, by the adoption of a negative income tax.

Finally, it should be noted that we have grossly simplified the analysis by implictly assuming income taxes zero. Once we allow income taxes to enter the analysis we are confronted with difficulties in defining a balanced budget fiscal change. If we assume an increase in lump-sum taxation equal to increased expenditures when income taxes are positive, we have an example of a 'pure fiscal measure' in the short-run, but with income taxes positive the expansion of income must imply an expansion of total tax receipts in excess of the additional expenditure. The budget surplus will expand by an amount equal to the increase in income multiplied by the average rate of income tax, with medium-term and long-term monetary consequences. The fiscal change has accordingly ceased to be pure. Alternatively, if we define a balanced budget fiscal change to mean increased expenditures financed by increased lump sum taxes *plus* the induced expansion of income taxes, then we have a situation of budget deficit in the short run with short-term monetary effects. This illustrates yet again, the great difficulty of drawing a meaningful distinction between monetary and fiscal action which would be both useful and unambiguous.

Fiscal Policy and the Consumption Function

The foregoing analysis has indicated the importance of the consumption function to fiscal intervention. Indeed, the emergence of fiscal policy as a respectable policy tool is intimately linked with Keynesian analysis which made the consumption function a pivotal point in national income determination. If the marginal propensity to consume out of disposable income is fairly significant and stable, it immediately follows that a fiscal change to influence post-tax income will have an important effect upon consumption expenditures. It is, therefore, of considerable importance to note that recent theoretical and empirical work on consumer behaviour has suggested that consumption may not be such a simple function of post-tax income (12). In particular, it has been argued that consumption is more properly related not to disposable income as conventionally measured, but rather to an estimate of "permanent income" or the discounted expected income over time. If this is the case, then a countercyclical fiscal change to influence the level of current disposable income will exert but a minor effect upon the level of consumption expenditures. This conclusion is reinforced if the fiscal measure is expected to be of short duration only. Thus the theoretical implications of the new theories of the consumption function tend to weaken the case for fiscal policy generally and, in particular, they question the wisdom of reliance on changes in the personal income tax as a countercyclical device.

Whilst the theoretical implications of the modern approach to consumer behaviour must be freely admitted, it should be noted that they do not weaken the effectiveness and potency of balanced budget fiscal changes. Indeed since the new theories of consumer behaviour assert that changes in measured disposable income exert their primary effect upon the level of measured savings and since the balanced budget multiplier theorem depends for its validity upon the assertion that the government is able to transform savings into expenditures, the lower the propensity to consume out of measured disposable income by the private sector the greater will be the initial impact of a balanced budget change. By the same token, the lower value of the marginal propensity to consume will reduce the multiplier impact exerted upon the initial change. In the simple model, as we have already seen, the net change is such that the opposing influences cancel out and the balanced budget multiplier is independent of the value taken by the marginal propensity to consume. Finally, it may be noted that should the model analysis be extended to allow for income taxation, then the potency of the balanced budget fiscal change is actually greater the *lower* the value taken on by the marginal propensity to consume (13, 14). If the modern theories of consumer behaviour are correct, this theoretical curio may be of interest in explaining why tax surcharges to match increased war expenditures are insufficient as a means of combating inflation (15).

The Composition of Fiscal Policy Measures

Thus far, we have considered fiscal policy largely in its Keynesian context of altering the level of aggregate demand. Indeed, this approach is implicit in the standard Keynesian analysis of fiscal policy which visualises the equilibrium level of income being determined where the combined expenditures function intersects the conventional 45° line. Personal taxation can be used to raise or lower the consumption function, business taxes and tax incentives may alter the investment schedule and, of course, the government may vary its expenditures function almost at will. Policy combinations such as the above may be used to keep the income level at its full employment point avoiding both extremes of unemployment and the inflationary gap.

The deficiency of this approach lies in its uni-dimensional view of the objective function which necessarily leads to excessive concern with the volume of aggregate expenditures. Fiscal policy, however, is also concerned with their composition which permits consideration of other policy objectives. Thus, for example, the fiscal burden may be directed more towards consumption than investment activity in the interest of stimulating the overall rate of growth. By using taxation in conjunction with debt retirement it is possible to affect a transfer of resources away from consumption towards investment expenditure – a policy proposal, which we shall examine in the following chapter, and one which has great appeal for those economists attaching overriding importance to capital formation in the growth process (16). Similarly, balance of payments objectives may be better served by shifting the tax burden more towards the service sectors and away from the manufacturing sectors if exports spring predominantly from the latter. In the United Kingdom, the introduction of the former Selective Employment Tax, which discriminated against the service sectors had precisely this idea in mind as one of its stated objectives. Such attempts to control the composition of aggregate expenditures may be reinforced by policies designed to change the composition of government expenditures.

In addition, when considering the implementation of fiscal policy it is necessary to consider the manner in which the tax burden is allocated between its direct and indirect components. The importance of this issue is underscored by the fact that indirect taxes may account for as much as 50% of total taxes raised in many advanced economies (more in certain developing economies), and yet for the most part indirect taxes are ignored in conventional portrayals of fiscal policy. The reasons for this are not hard to seek. Indirect taxes raise difficult questions of incidence, and of price illusion, and tax induced price changes are not easily analysed in terms of the conventional Keynesian model analysis. This would not matter unduly – indeed it would be a permissible simplification to treat indirect taxes as direct – if the indirect/direct tax ratio did not materially affect the nature of the macro-economic analysis and of the policy conclusions which spring from it. The fact is, however, that the macro-economic impact may differ and differ significantly according to whether tax changes involve direct or indirect taxes. Briefly, we will indicate two areas where the direct/indirect tax ratio may be of consequence.

a – The Real Deflationary Impact of Indirect versus Direct Taxes

It has long been argued that indirect sales taxes exert a greater *real* deflationary impact than equal yield direct taxes. Initially the statement was largely Keynesian in origin resting as it did upon the belief that sales taxes are more regressive than direct taxes and that the lower paid possess higher marginal propensities to consume. Important work by Cary Brown (17) demonstrated that this result still obtained, even if identical saving propensities applied to all taxpayers and regardless of whether indirect taxes generated money illusion or not. The explanation arises in the fact that part of an income tax is paid from savings whereas a consumption tax must fall entirely upon consumer outlays and thus exert a greater deflationary impact. It is important to note that this conclusion depends upon the assumption that income taxes have no impact upon prices whereas the sales tax is assumed to be passed forward 100% in a once-and-for-all price change.*

Thus a greater *real* deflationary impact is combined with a once-and-for-all inflationary increase in the price level. This apparent paradox has led many commentators to question the logic of the argument once the analysis is extended to the labour market under the assumption that wage bargaining is linked to changes in the cost of living (18). In addition, it may be noted that Brown's analysis compared the effects of an income tax – *with sales tax rates zero* – with the effects of an equal yield sales tax – *when income tax rates were zero.* In a modern economy the more appropriate assumption would be a comparison of direct and indirect taxes with both tax rates positive. Whilst this does not invalidate the basic analysis, when this is the case, it is not possible to maintain that a given increase in the *rate* of a sales tax will be more deflationary than a given increase in the *rate* of an income tax; indeed, it can be maintained that the opposite conclusion follows (19). If indirect taxes do exert a greater deflationary impact, then the adoption of a more indirect/direct tax ratio – perhaps necessitated by membership of a Common Market – will require offsetting compensatory measures elsewhere.

b – Balance of Payments Impact of Indirect versus Direct Taxes

Considerable controversy has arisen in recent years over whether or not the balance of payments is significantly affected by the composition of tax revenues. Both in the U.K., and the U.S.A. it has been argued that an increase in the indirect/direct tax ratio at the expense of

* This assumption is one commonly employed in the attempt to include price changes in macro-economic analysis. It may be noted that it implies a denial of the theory of incidence developed in most public finance treatises. It is also, perhaps, fair comment to note that the status of the economics profession is hardly enhanced by those texts which adopt one theory of incidence when dealing with micro-economic aspects of public finance and yet another when dealing with stabilization goals – especially when no justification for this sudden *volte-face* is forthcoming.

corporate income taxation would materially aid exports. The argument springs from the existing international conventions concerning the rebate of taxes on export products. Stated simply, the G.A.T.T. rules permit the rebate of indirect taxes. The rationale for this position is the following. Indirect taxes influence prices by altering marginal cost conditions whereas direct taxes affect neither marginal cost or marginal revenue and theoretically should leave profit maximizing output and prices unchanged. Thus, the rebate of indirect taxes is justified since otherwise exported products would be placed at a tax-induced disadvantage in export markets, but no such rebate is called for with regard to direct taxes. The existing convention, therefore, is to allow the *full* rebate of indirect taxes on exported goods which are then subject to the normal rates of sales tax prevailing within their country of eventual consumption. It follows that no tax-induced advantage or disadvantage is conferred owing to different economies having differing rates of sales taxation. At the same time no rebate is allowed for direct taxes.*

The logic of the G.A.T.T. conventions has been questioned on a number of points. First of all, it has been argued that permitting the rebate of indirect taxes in their entirety is to take an unusual view of incidence and assume that no portion of the tax is absorbed by the seller. If however, the seller does absorb part of the tax, then the granting of a full rebate will allow him to price his product more favourably in export markets than in his domestic market. Moreover, the advantage is greater the higher the rate of indirect tax which suggests that high indirect/direct tax countries may be placed at a competitive advantage in international trade. Secondly, it has been argued that to maintain that direct taxes do not affect prices is to take a rigid micro-static view of the corporation income tax. On the one hand, a high rate of corporate tax may reduce innovation, the supply of funds and the incentive to take risks, ultimately reducing international competitiveness. On the other hand, econometric studies have suggested that the corporation income tax is passed forward in the form of higher prices -- in some cases by more than 100 per cent (21). Considerations of this nature would suggest that high indirect/direct tax countries may be placed at a competitive advantage in international trade and they

* It may be noted that this permits the rebate of a value-added tax but not that of a payroll tax despite the fact that the two may be shown to be formally identical in their effects (20).

suggest that replacement of part of the direct corporate burden by a tax on value added would aid the external account.

The Timing and Assessment of Fiscal Policy Measures

In the enactment of fiscal policy measures it is important that due attention be given to their timing so that their impact may be concentrated at the most favourable moment from the viewpoint of stabilization purposes. Moreover, this comment applies equally to budgetary measures which have been adopted for reasons other than meeting macro-economic policy goals. There are two distinct but inter-related issues involved with regard to the timing of policy measures. First, it will be recognised that the central government will normally have a certain area of discretion with regard to grants to local authorities, for example, and may speed up the actual rate of payment in the pursuit of stabilization goals. Moreover, it should not be forgotten that the government is a considerable employer of labour. Not only will its attitude to public sector wage demands exert repercussions throughout the labour market, but it will also have some say as to when to meet a previously negotiated wage settlement. Back-dated increases to public sector employees may be so timed as to exert their maximum impact at peak periods of seasonal unemployment.

Secondly, it will be appreciated that the foregoing survey of fiscal policy has greatly over-simplified the task of the fiscal policy-maker in presenting the issues primarily within the framework of comparative statics. Tacitly we have ignored the question of time, a convenient expositional device which permits us to hold *desired* values constant whilst we make the required policy changes necessary to adjust actual values. In point of fact, however, the policy-maker is faced with the difficulty that both desired and actual values are themselves a function of time. Further, once we take account of the time dimension, we implicitly recognise that there are lags and delays associated with the implementation of any given measure; the general preference for tax and transfer changes as opposed to expenditure changes, for example, is partly due to the fact that they can more readily circumvent the various time lags involved (22). Once we admit of lags in effect we open up the possibility of fiscal policy operating in a perverse manner and exercising destabilizing impacts upon the economy (23).

By way of example consider a simple dynamic model for a closed economy such that national income is given by the sum of consumption, investment and government expenditures and let consumption be a lagged function of the income level in the preceding period. For simplicity assume that average and marginal propensities to consume be equal at 0.5. Let investment expenditures equal twice the change in consumption over the previous period implying an accelerator model of investment behaviour with the accelerator coefficient equal to 2. Finally, let government expenditure be autonomously determined at $1 billion. Then, as the reader may readily verify by recourse to numerical example, the time path of income will be that as indicated in Figure VI.4: that is to say, continuously oscillating fluctuations in income will be generated which will never die out and will be maintained at a constant magnitude over time.*

Assume now that the government ceases to be satisfied with this

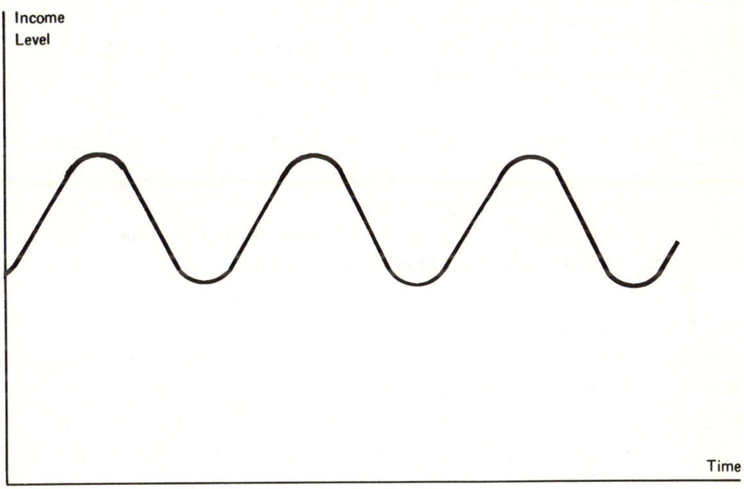

Figure VI.4

* In the initial period the income level is $1B – equal to the Government expenditure at time t. In the next period, t + 1, income rises to $2.5B being composed of $1B government expenditure, $0.5 Billion induced consumption expenditure stemming from the income level of the previous period, and $1B of investment expenditure arising from the change in consumption between time t to t + 1. In period t + 2, income rises to $3.75B and so forth. The example here is in fact taken directly from Samuelson's pioneering article in business cycle theory (24).

situation and instead aims at a target level of income by introducing additional expenditures (positive or negative) which it varies in a contracyclical manner, according to whether or not the income level of the previous period exceeds or falls short of the target level. The government thus acts with a one period lag in the manner that consumers do, and moreover, taking cognizance of a multiplier of two, always attempts to increase expenditure by half the shortfall when the income level falls below the target level. Alternatively, the government will always attempt to reduce expenditure by half the excess when actual income exceeds the target level. In this case the fiscal authorities are behaving in a manner which on the surface appears soundly conceived and may be expected to aid the attainment of stabilization goals, and yet it can be easily shown that the net result is to increase the degree of instability and intensify the magnitude of income fluctuation (25). The reason for this state of affairs is not hard to seek. It stems from the fact that the government is behaving in essentially an automatic fashion, responding to but *one* indicator of economic activity in a predetermined manner and ignoring altogether the response of the private sector. Thus the government's response to a given shortfall in income is the same irrespective of whether the private sector is increasing or reducing the level of aggregate demand. The analysis is clearly relevant to the question of formula flexibility. Simple mechanical rules which appear superficially attractive as a means of securing stabilization goals may heighten the degree of overall instability if they on occasion reinforce the response pattern of the private sector.

Admittedly, the example provided here is *simpliste* in the extreme, but nonetheless it illustrates one of the dilemmas confronting the fiscal policy-maker when dynamic considerations are allowed, and suggests the distinct possibility that discretionary policy may be destabilizing. This issue has grown in prominence in recent years mainly as a result of a number of independent studies which have argued that fiscal policy has been on balance destabilizing in the U.K. Since the United Kingdom is a country in which fiscal policy changes can be enacted fairly rapidly, in contrast to the United States where it may not be possible to obtain the required legislative sanction without considerable delay, the charge is a serious one and if sustained strengthens the case for reliance upon automatic fiscal stabilizers. However, at the present time the verdict must remain an open one; far from indicating incompetence upon the part of the fiscal authorities this issue has raised the difficult problem of how fiscal policy should be assessed.

It is clearly inadequate to argue that an inverse correlation between the percentage deviation from trend of public expenditure on goods and services and the percentage margin of unused resources is evidence of destabilizing fiscal policy (26), partly because it ignores entirely what is happening to taxes but also because the adoption of lagged relationships can alter the sign of the relevant correlation coefficient. Equally, findings to the effect that the lag of unemployment (signalling the need for policy measures) behind the growth rate of GDP (the variable to be controlled) led to restrictive measures taking hold only after the growth of aggregate demand had already slackened sidesteps the issue of which objective fiscal policy is pursuing (27). Criticism along these lines led Worswick to refute the charge that fiscal policy within the U.K. has been on balance destabilizing (28).

In assessing whether fiscal policy has been destabilizing or not the question may be phrased as to whether the actual income fluctuations would have been greater in the absence of a positive fiscal policy. This is the position adopted by Bristow, *with regard to taxation only*, who also rejects the destabilizing hypothesis (29). It is also the position adopted by Hansen, in probably the most ambitious attempt to date at assessing fiscal policy (30). His starting point is to estimate the total impact of the budget for seven O.E.C.D. countries over the eleven year period 1955–1965. Subtracting the estimated impact from actually observed GNP data provides an estimate of the 'pure cycle' – the hypothetical progress of the economy for each country in the absence of budget measures. Comparing the actual GNP data and the hypothetical or pure cycle GNP data with the trend growth rate of GNP – i.e., the average GNP growth rate – provides a measure of whether the budget is stabilizing or not. Provided the actual GNP data fall closer to the average growth rate than the pure cycle data the budgetary process can be considered stabilizing and vice versa. Perfect stabilization would be indicated by coincidence of actual GNP data with the average GNP growth rate.

Significantly, the United Kingdom was the only country surveyed where fiscal policy was found to be positively destabilizing. This situation, where actual GNP data deviates more from the trend than the pure cycle data is illustrated below in Figure VI.5. However, the question is immediately raised as to why we wish to measure the success of fiscal policy in minimizing deviations from average actual growth rates? When the Hansen findings were adjusted to measure the success of fiscal policy in relation to the potential or full employment growth rate the results are strikingly different and judged to be stabilizing, on the whole, in the United Kingdom (31). Furthermore, during the period in question, the fiscal authorities in Britain were more probably concerned with the balance of payments objective rather than that of income growth in the short-run. It is rather hard to be judged by reference to a policy objective one is not momentarily pursuing. Finally, one may legitimately raise the issue why should fiscal policy be judged in isolation from other countercyclical policies?* In the following chapter, for example, we shall argue that there need be nothing inherently inconsistent in combining a restrictive monetary policy with an expansionary fiscal policy. If such assessments are going to be made, and they will undoubtedly increase as more data becomes available (32, 33), would it not be preferable to list all policy objectives and tools together, determine which of the former have priority in the eyes of the policy-makers, and then attempt to assess the success of stabilization policy *in toto*?

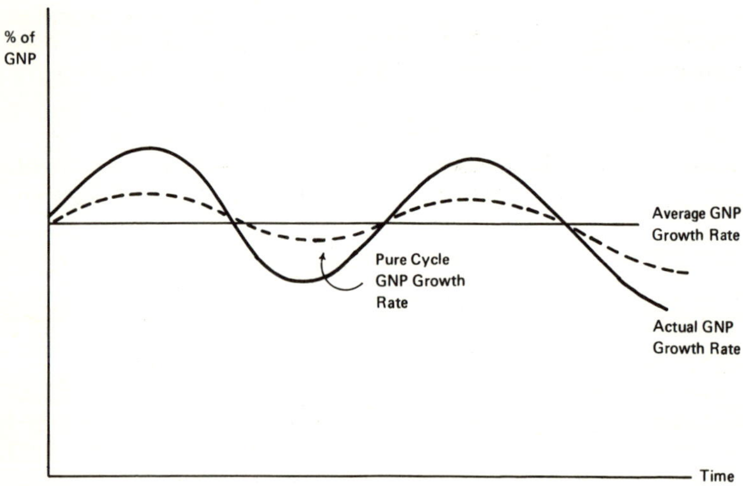

Figure VI.5

* In the Hansen study, it should be noted that the pure cycle is by no means completely pure since it includes other countercyclical policies – notably monetary policy and monetary policy conceived of in the expectation of budgetary management!

Appendix The "Failure" of Keynesian Fiscal Policies

The comparative success in maintaining near full employment in the post-war period is usually explained in terms of the Keynesian heritage and the ability of the fiscal authorities, adopting Keynesian-type policies, to so "fine tune" the economy as to maintain the appropriate level of aggregate demand. This view, however, has been challenged from two distinct points of view. First, Matthews (34) has argued that over the post-war period fiscal policy has been largely deflationary and that full employment has been more the result of the secular growth of labour scarcity relative to capital on the one hand together with extremely buoyant world demand for exports upon the other. Secondly, and more recently, the so-called "New Cambridge School" has challenged the applicability of Keynesian-oriented measures to an open economy such as the United Kingdom possessing a substantial involvement in international trade. The essence of this position, neatly summarized by Eltis (35), rests upon the proposition that if the volume of exports is insufficient to cover the full employment level of imports, then Keynesian-type measures to promote employment will be revealed in a payments deficit.

The New Cambridge view relies for its validity upon a simple national income accounting *identity* combined with an assertion concerning the *behavioural* response of the private sector with respect to saving and investment. The national income identity for an open economy, *ex post*, is simply

$$G + I + X = T + S + M$$

where the symbols represent government expenditure, investment, exports, tax yield, savings and imports respectively. Rearrangement gives

$$(G - T) = (S - I) + (M - X).$$

It follows at once that if we postulate the behavioural assumption that the private sector surplus $(S - I)$ is a constant or virtually so, then any increase in the government budget deficit is immediately transmitted into an increase in the external payments deficit on current account. The paradoxical result then obtains that the external deficit is determined solely by the public sector's borrowing requirement; for any given budget deficit "changes in exports, import prices, etc. make a lot of difference to real income but none at all to the balance of payments, however paradoxical this may at first sight appear." Deficit-financed expansion of domestic demand will ultimately thus lead to payments deficits, forcing curtailment of the expansionary process. Moreover, this conclusion stands whether or not the exchange rate is allowed to float – provided we accept the behavioural assumption incorporated into the accounting identity. The alternative cure for unemployment, therefore, must lie in export expansion plus import substitution; with a stable private sector financial surplus, this implies a fall in the payments deficit upon the right-hand side of the equation matched by fall in the budget deficit as the rise in domestic incomes induces rising tax yields.

The idea that increased budget deficits ultimately reveal themselves in a worsening external payments position is not particularly new in itself. Indeed, if the budget deficit is financed by increasing the money supply, it is precisely the conclusion reached by the monetarist school. Moreover, many economists would concur that the only long-run solution to Britain's current economic problems in the post-oil crisis period lies in a policy of export-led growth. What does appear to be the novel feature of the New Cambridge view is the assertion that the required increase in *net* exports is more readily obtained through the imposition of import controls (36). Devaluation, of an amount politically acceptable to competitors overseas, is ruled out as being ineffective to generate a sustained improvement in the external balance. Moreover, devaluation possesses the drawback of higher import prices, which may trigger wage demands, ultimately eliminating the competitive advantage so obtained.

The belief that import controls are the means to reconcile full employment output with the absence of a payments deficit is of particular appeal to the trade union movement, especially in those sectors where traditional industries are experiencing secular decline. In many cases, secular decline has been confused with the availability of cheap foreign substitutes. Also, however, there is a growing body of opinion in both academic and governmental circles that import controls may be the only way out if the depreciation of the pound continues to yield such seemingly minor results.

Any return to a fully fledged protectionist economy, however, would appear to be ruled out at least as long as the United Kingdom is dependent upon IMF support. Moreover, there are strong theoretical arguments against the case for import controls. Quite apart from the fact that import controls do provide shelter for inefficient industries, and thus ultimately influence adversely the long-term allocation of resources, they imply a diversion of expenditure to domestic output. Indeed, this is the means by which domestic output and employment are stimulated. The resulting rise in incomes will raise the level of demand, which will ultimately spill over on to three possible sources of supply: an increase in the volume of permitted imports, encroachment upon the volume of existing exports, or absorption of the enhanced domestic output. In the case of the first two possibilities there is no guarantee that the expected improvement in the payments deficit will be forthcoming. The case for protection, therefore, depends crucially upon the degree of excess capacity that already exists within the economy and which can be readily marshalled to enlarge domestic output.

Quite apart from the specific case for import controls, the underlying basis of the New Cambridge view has been seriously challenged.

On the one hand there are those economists who question the validity of a statement resting upon a national income equation identity without the requisite theoretical underpinnings (37). In particular, the attempt to correlate the public sector deficit with the external payments deficit, without even considering the manner in which the public deficit is to be financed, is held to be a grave omission. Will it not make a considerable difference if the public sector borrowing requirement is met by overseas loan as opposed to the sale of new bonds to the public at large? And equally, will it not make a considerable difference if the deficit is met by the sale of bonds as opposed to an expansion of the money supply? Finally, the stability of the private sector's financial surplus is subject to considerable dispute, although this is an empirical issue whose resolution depends largely upon the time period under consideration. The conventional Keynesian position is to assert that the private sector's surplus increases as incomes rise and falls as incomes decline – by an amount determined by the marginal propensity to save. Whilst considerable variation in the surplus is observed over the short run, the New Cambridge view would appear to be that ultimately private sector spending also responds – possibly through accelerator-type changes in investment outlays – so that the private sector's marginal propensity to spend is effectively unity.

Whatever the final outcome of the debate, it seems clear that the simple Keynesian closed-economy model of income determination is inapplicable to an open economy experiencing increasing liberalisation of trade and capital movements. Yet, ironically, it would seem the simple closed-economy model, examined in real terms with the money stock conveniently excluded, underpins a good deal of official thinking upon policy decisions.

Chapter VII The Monetary-Fiscal Policy Mix

Thus far, we have looked upon monetary and fiscal policy measures as being alternative means of achieving stated goals. Much of the present discussion is couched in these terms, a fact which sharpens the controversy over the comparative efficacy of respective policy measures. From the practical view of policy formation, however, the decision-taker will have resort to both measures simultaneously; he may combine fiscal and monetary policy to determine the most appropriate policy mix for any given situation.

Fortunately, a theoretical framework already exists for analysing the combined impact of monetary and fiscal changes. We refer to the well-known Hicks-Hansen IS/LM analysis which is usually presented as embodying the standard Keynesian theory of income determination.* In many ways, the IS/LM framework is defective as a means of analysing policy choice. It suffers from a decidedly mechanistic view of the macro-economy, and by focussing attention upon the simultaneous determination of interest rates and real GNP it is particularly unsuited to the study of price determination and inflation. Moreover, by assuming a closed economy the conventional treatment abstracts from perhaps the most important constraint upon policy decision-making generally, namely that imposed by the international balance of payments. In addition, the very simplicity and ease of manipulation of the IS/LM construct serves to cloak the fundamental assumptions of the model. A moment's thought will show that the IS curve implicitly

* We assume that the reader is sufficiently familiar with the derivation of the IS and LM curves as not to require its reproduction here. For a standard derivation see almost any macro-theory text, as for example Dernburg and McDougall (1), McKenna (2), Shapiro (3). A useful introduction emphasizing the qualifications inherent in the analysis is provided by Laidler (4).

summarises assumptions about both the investment interest relation and the consumption function. Equally, the LM curve summarises assumptions concerning the nature of the supply and demand for money. The policy conclusions implicit in the model are in reality pre-determined by the nature of these assumptions. It is hardly surprising that the conventional IS/LM portrayal, being derived from the attempt to popularise and extend the Keynesian theory, should carry an implicit bias against monetary policy generally and in particular against the new monetarism. Consider, for example, the standard diagram as depicted in Figure VII.1. The horizontal portion of the LM curve expressly assumes the Keynesian liquidity trap and reveals, as indicated by the dotted line, that monetary policy is completely ineffective in influencing either the income level or the rate of interest if the IS/LM intersection occurs in this region. Equally, Figure VII.2 displays a vertical IS function derived from the assumption of a completely interest-inelastic demand function and again the conclusion follows that monetary policy is of no avail. Yet it is part and parcel of the new doctrine that monetary changes will influence expenditure decisions irrespective of the investment response. In short, the new monetarism would imply that the IS curve and the LM curve are interdependent in that a change in the money supply would directly affect expenditure decisions.

A similar interdependence had been argued by Keynes who recognised that increasing the money supply would imply an increased

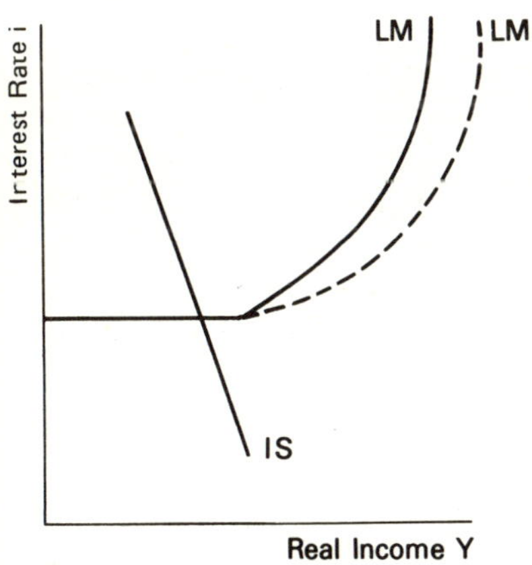

Figure VII.1

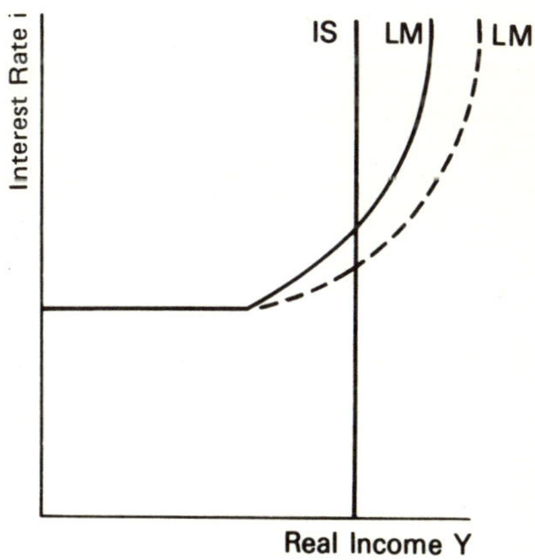

Figure VII.2

capitalization of bonds, *via* the interest rate effect, and would stimulate the consumption of bondholders. Thus the implicit independence of the IS and LM functions assumed in most elementary expositions not only conveys a bias against the new monetarism but also distorts the economics of Keynes. This is precisely the view adopted by Leijonhufvud in his reinterpretation of Keynes and it suggests that Keynes is closer to the monetarist position than claimed by conventional Keynesians – a view re-echoed by Friedman.* Indeed, it was precisely in order to bring out both the similarities and differences between his own statement and that of Keynes that Friedman has recently outlined his theory in terms of the IS/LM framework in two contributions (6, 7) which – as might have been anticipated – sparked off a lively controversy (8, 9, 10, 11). The interdependence discussed above suggests that a shift of the LM curve will exert feedback effects upon expenditure decisions and hence upon the IS curve. Equally, however, a policy induced change in the IS curve might influence the position of the LM function. This latter proposition has been suggested by Holmes and Smyth (12) in arguing that the demand for money is a function not of the level of income but rather of the level of disposable income. Consequently, an increase in the level of taxation, which induces a fall in the IS curve, will also reduce the demand for money – akin to an outward shift of the LM curve. Theoretically, the combined effect could imply a positive tax multiplier but even if this conclusion seems too extreme it nonetheless suggests that the impact of fiscal policy may be blunted. This effect, it should be noted, is additional to the element of automatic monetary stabilization already built into the IS/LM framework, which reveals itself in an extension of investment expenditure (due to the decline in interest rates) in the wake of fiscal contraction.

Despite all these necessary qualifications the IS/LM apparatus remains a useful expositional device for the classification of alternative policies and for drawing out the implications of combined monetary and fiscal action. Moreover, the analysis can easily be extended to allow for consideration of the external sector (13, 14). In the following figure, Figure VII.3, we simply superimpose a balance of payments function

* "Rereading *The General Theory* . . . has reminded me what a great economist Keynes was and how much more I sympathise with his approach and aims than with those of many of his followers" (5)

upon the standard IS/LM diagram:* the balance of payments function summarises all those combinations of interest rate and income which maintain equilibrium in the external account. It will have a positive slope because if exports are assumed exogenous, an expansion of income will be accompanied by a deterioration of the trading account owing to the induced inflow of imports. Maintenance of equilibrium,

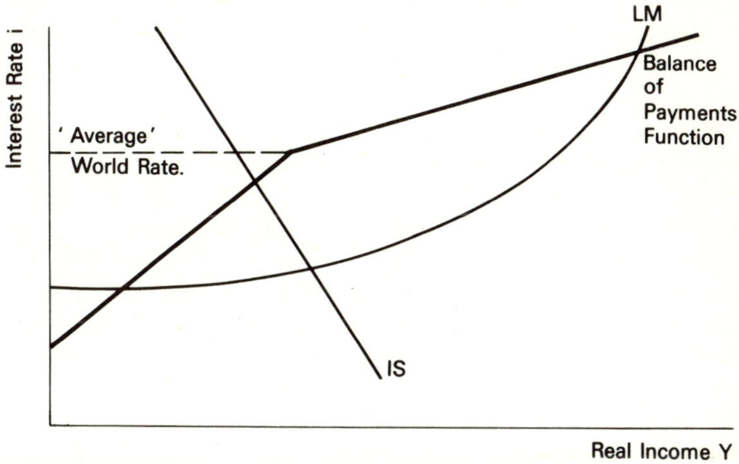

Figure VII.3

therefore, will require a compensating improvement upon the capital account – i.e. a raising of the interest rate. There is no reason, however, for the function to be linear. In the diagram we specifically assume that the responsiveness of capital inflows to a change in the rate of interest will depend crucially upon interest rates prevailing elsewhere. Below the average prevailing in alternate financial centres, a raising of the interest rate is hardly likely to induce substantial capital inflows whereas when it rises above the "world" average the response will be much more immediate and significant. At the same time, we may reasonably assume that the import effect of a given rise in income is likely to be

* Although perhaps the straightforward superimposing of such a function represents too great a simplification, for the slope of the IS function will normally differ for the open economy. For clarification of this point see Wrightsman (14).

approximately the same regardless of whether the increase occurs at a high or a low level. Hence the justification for the kinked nature of the balance of payments function. The diagram is purely illustrative, however, and equally plausible alternative constructs could be derived. And once more, it should be emphasized that the policy implications are inherent in the construct which one chooses to adopt.

Consider, for example, Figure VII.4. We assume an initial situation determined by the intersection of the IS and LM curves which implies both unemployment equal to AB and balance of payments deficit

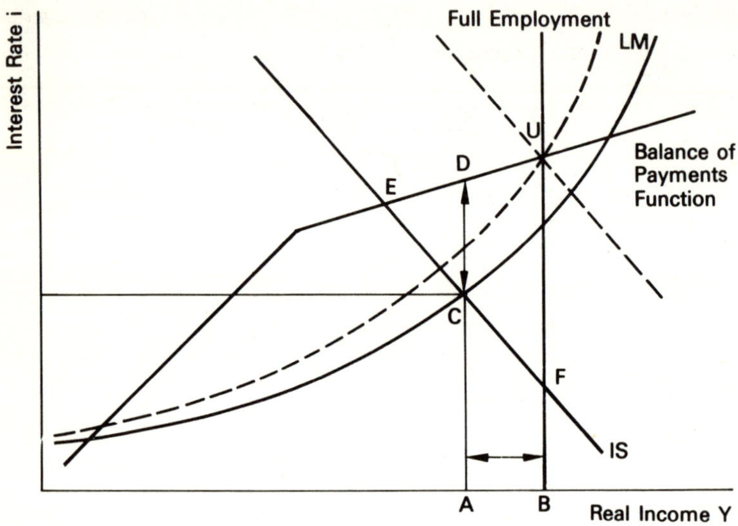

Figure VII.4

indicated by CD. Given this situation, either monetary policy or fiscal policy acting independently is able to secure *one* of the policy objectives. Thus, a contractionary monetary policy could gain the equilibrium E curing the trade deficit whilst an expansionary monetary policy could take the economy to point F and meet the employment objective. Similar reasoning applies to expansionary and contractionary fiscal policies. But complete equilibrium at U, indicated by the dotted lines, requires the combined interaction of both instruments simultaneously, namely an expansionary fiscal policy in conjunction with a restrictive monetary policy. Both instruments are required to attain the dual objective which provides a practical illustration of Tinbergen's principle of the necessary equality between the number of targets and policy instruments. It will be noted that both the required policy measures serve to raise the rate of interest, a factor decidedly relevant to our earlier discussion concerning the possibility of an institutional limit to interest rates. If the institutional interest-rate limit prevents the adoption of the combined policy measure, then no possible solution is indicated other than a successful devaluation which effectively lowers the balance of payments function for any given income and interest-rate combination. Indeed, the very existence of unemployment and persistent external deficit would suggest overvaluation of the domestic currency.

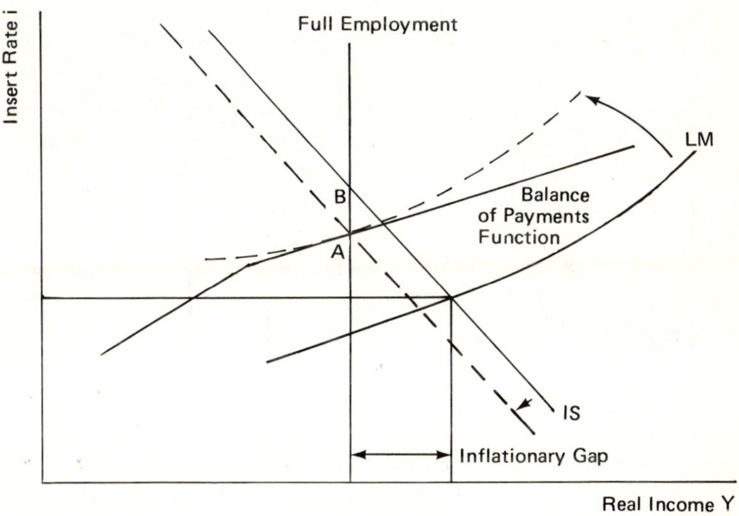

Figure VII.5

If balance of payments deficits are normally associated with inflationary conditions – and if for simplicity we assume the latter can be depicted by the IS/LM equilibria falling to the right of full employment – then Figure VII.5 may be considered as representing a more typical situation. Once again, complete adjustment requires the simultaneous use of both monetary and fiscal policy so that eventual equilibrium is obtained by the intersection of the dotted lines at point A. However, in this case, monetary policy operating alone is able to attain full employment and cancel the deficit – as depicted in the movement to position B. In contrast, whilst fiscal policy is able to secure the full employment objective it is unable, acting alone, simultaneously to abolish the deficit. This may be looked upon as an alternative way of demonstrating the comparative superiority of monetary *vis-à-vis* fiscal policy in achieving external equilibria – a policy conclusion to which we will return later. For the moment, however, perhaps it is sufficient to note that the equilibrium attained by the sole use of monetary policy in pushing the economy to point B will not usually provide a permanent solution. This is because position B implies a balance of payments surplus which in turn implies an inflow of capital funds. It will not always be possible for the monetary authorities effectively to neutralise a persistent capital inflow and if this is the case the resulting increase in liquidity will eventually shift the LM function outwards, once more generating inflationary tendencies. It was precisely this type of situation which characterised the German economy in recent years and led to demands for the revaluation of the German mark to produce an equilibrating raising of the payments function. One advantage of the extended Hicks/Hansen analysis lies in highlighting the equilibrating nature of alterations in the official rate of exchange. It is indeed unfortunate that the financial policies accompanying the formation of the European Economic Union have rendered this method of adjustment much more difficult to effect owing to the insistence upon fixed exchange rates – at least between those countries still committed to membership of the "currency snake". Although the Snake of linked currencies is allowed to float against outside currencies, no one member nation can alter its exchange rate unilaterally. Whilst the maintenance of fixed exchange rates is seen as a logical first step to the adoption of a common currency unit,* the existing diversity within the Common Market countries, particularly with regard to inflation rates, requires more flexible exchange rate adjustments – so much so that the principle deficit countries, Italy and the United Kingdom, have been forced to withdraw from the Snake.

Whilst the IS/LM framework is pedagogically useful in describing the combined impact of monetary-fiscal action, it is particularly unsuited to the analysis of policy proposals for economic growth. This arises directly from the fact that the IS function does not distinguish between consumption and investment expenditure decisions at any given income

* For a stimulating discussion of this and other issues see especially Forte (15).

level. In turn, this is the consequence of the IS function summarising positions of *ex ante* equality between saving and investment functions. It is thus conceptually possible for a given point of intersection between the IS and the LM function, implying a unique income level, to be derived from two sets of quite dissimilar saving and investment functions. Or, to make the point in a slightly different way, a parametric outward shift of the investment function, which implies a higher volume of investment spending for any given rate of interest, may be so compensated by an inward shift of the saving function, implying a voluntary cutback in consumption, as to leave the original IS curve unchanged. Presumably, however, the ratio between consumption and investment will exercise a determinate influence upon the growth rate of the economy and the policy-maker may justifiably be concerned with the precise manner in which any given equilibrium is attained. Whilst it is possible to disaggregate the IS/LM framework to allow for such considerations, the resulting insight is only gained at the expense of expositional clarity and for certain purposes alternative approaches may be preferred. The model we adopt in the following pages was not developed with the growth objective principally in mind, and although it may be usefully extended in that direction we will first of all consider its initial concern with specifying the appropriate uses of monetary and fiscal policy.

The Mundellian Model

Mundell's celebrated article (16) explicitly assumes that changes in the size of the budget surplus may be looked upon as an index of fiscal policy whilst changes in the rate of interest are indicative of expansionary or contractionary monetary policy. As we have previously indicated, one may entertain reservations about delineating policy changes in this manner but for present purposes we will adopt these assumptions as a simplifying step in the analysis. It is further assumed that a decrease in the size of the budget surplus will be expansionary and *vice versa*, whilst the level of investment is inversely related to the rate of interest. With regard to the external account, we posit that exports are exogenous, imports are a positive function of the level of income and foreign capital is sensitive to movements in the domestic rate of interest. Given these assumptions, we can reproduce Mundell's model and derive his important conclusion that, given the constraint of a fixed rate of exchange, appropriate stabilization policy requires that monetary policy be directed at external objectives and fiscal policy at internal goals. Moreover, failure to follow this policy prescription can cause discretionary stabilization policy to exert a perverse effect and render the resulting situation worse than the one it was designed to correct.

In Figure VII.6, below, we reproduce Mundell's original diagram. The XX function describes the loci of all those combinations of budget surplus and interest rate which ensure full employment without inflation. The function has a negative slope since it is assumed that a decrease in the budget surplus, presumed expansionary, will require an offsetting cutback in investment expenditure through higher interest-rate charges, if the aggregate income level is to remain unchanged. Likewise, the FF schedule summarises all those budget surplus-interest-rate combinations which are consistent with balance of

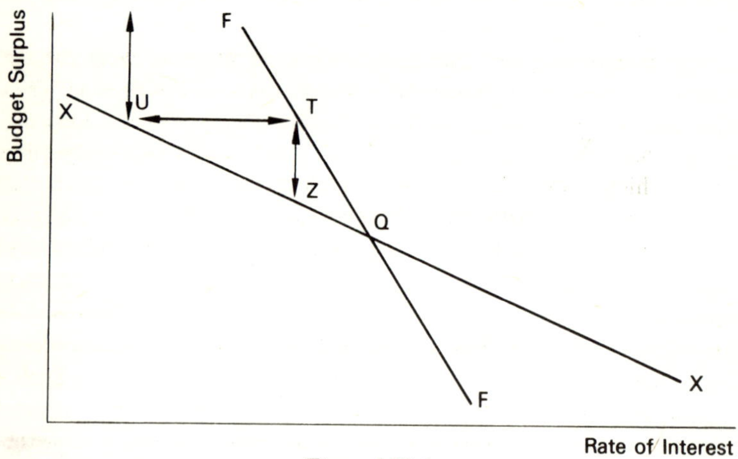

Figure VII.6

payments equilibria. The FF function is also negatively sloped since with exports assumed constant any increase in imports arising from the expansionary impact of a lowering of the budget surplus must be compensated by an improvement upon the capital account *via* an increase in the rate of interest. Since both functions are negatively sloped it is of interest to enquire into which function possesses the steeper slope. Given the model, the unequivocal answer to this question is that the external function will have the steeper slope. To see this, consider the balance of trade account implicit in the internal function. With exports exogenous and imports a simple function of the income level, it follows that the trade account (exports minus imports) must everywhere be constant along the internal function. However, since foreign capital is assumed sensitive to an increase in domestic interest rates, a downward movement along the internal function must imply a continuous improvement in the capital account – and thus in the overall balance of payments. If the external account always improves when moving down and along the internal function, it follows that the loci of points describing no change must trace out a steeper slope: i.e. for a given increase in the rate of interest a greater (more expansionary) budget change must occur to maintain external as opposed to internal balance. If this is the case, it follows that there is but one unique point, at Q, which reconciles both internal and external equilibrium. If exchange rates are assumed immutable, then the task of the policy-maker reduces to combining monetary and fiscal policy to achieve both objectives simultaneously.

The importance of Mundell's analysis relates to what he has previously termed the "Principle of Effective Market Classification" (17). This principle argues that efficient stabilization policy requires that policy instruments should be directed towards the policy objectives upon which they exert the most influence. Simply to assert the required equality between instruments and targets is by itself an insufficient condition for effective policy-making. Indeed, even though the number of instruments may equal the number of declared objectives the inappropriate use of the respective policy tools may be positively destabilizing. This may be easily demonstrated by considering the implications of a point such as Z in the previous figure. Such a combination of interest rates and budget surplus is perfectly consistent with the employment objective but at the same time implies a deficit upon the external account. Suppose the authorities decide to cope with the external deficit by the use of fiscal policy. An increase in the budget surplus will restore external equilibrium at point T but will simultaneously produce a departure from full employment. If monetary policy is now employed to restore the internal equilibrium it will require a decrease in the rate of interest to a position U but such a move generates an increase in the external deficit over its initial level. Thus, far from the combined instruments of monetary and fiscal policy being adequate to attain the dual objectives of internal and external stability, their inappropriate pairing with the policy objectives is positively destabilizing in its impact. At the same time, however, the use of monetary measures to correct the deficit and fiscal measures to meet the employment objective is perfectly consistent with the simultaneous achievement of both policy targets. This proposal has been attacked, most severely by Williamson (18) primarily upon the grounds that the long-term consequences are a higher rate of inflation and a lower rate of economic growth implying an intertemporal loss of welfare. However, this is to adopt a long-term view of what is essentially a short-term policy problem. If Mundell's policy prescription is taken to refer to a short-term balance of payments disequilibrium only, with the decision already taken to maintain the exchange rate, then the policy proposal seems appropriate enough. It should be emphasized that it does not obviate the need to correct the deficit upon the current account and it is essential that the policy-makers recognise that the use of a capital flow to offset a current account imbalance implies that the asset position will cumulatively change with long-run effects. Granted that this qualification is accepted then resort to such a policy mix would appear to be perfectly justified once the initial decision to maintain a specific fixed exchange rate has been taken. In addition, it would suggest that the repeated concern with the comparative efficacy of monetary versus fiscal policy is really misplaced (unless one is implicitly thinking of only one policy objective), and that more fruitful activity would lie in formulating the optimal policy mix to deal with any given situation.

Monetary Fiscal Policies for Economic Growth

In recent years, increasing attention has been directed towards the designing of monetary and fiscal policy mixes to raise the rate of growth. For the most part, such policy statements have concentrated upon raising the overall investment ratio at the expense of consumption. It has been widely assumed that fiscal policy can be utilized to reduce consumption whilst monetary policy can be adopted to stimulate investment. The correct policy mix therefore is able to transfer resources effectively from current consumption to investment activity with beneficial effects upon long-term growth rates.

In practice, this is to be achieved by specifically budgeting for a fiscal surplus which allows retirement of the debt from those classes having a propensity to invest. Providing interest rates are lowered to provide the necessary inducement, new investment will occur.* The great appeal of such a policy is that it is perfectly compatible with the maintenance of full employment since any offset in consumer expenditure will be compensated, if not more than compensated, by the ensuing rise in investment. Indeed, it is the case that Mundell's internal function summarises not only those combinations of budget surplus and interest rate consistent with full employment but also, implicitly, the scope of the policy change implied in the strict-fiscal easy-money prescription for enhanced growth. The internal function, referring as it does to a given income level, thus carries implications for the investment-consumption ratio which is obscured in the more familiar IS construct.

By linking such growth policy proposals directly to Mundell's analysis we specifically highlight their underlying weakness, namely their failure to consider the constraints imposed by the external sector. The essence of Mundell's analysis is that whilst there may be an infinite number of budget surplus-interest-rate combinations consistent with either internal or external balance there will be but one unique combination able to satisfy both simultaneously. It follows that since the force of an external deficit cannot be ignored for long, and likewise since there are strong political reasons limiting departures from full employment, the permissible monetary-fiscal policy mix for economic growth is effectively pre-determined (19). We may illustrate this dilemma by reference to Figure VII.7. Dividing the diagram into areas of high and low growth rates respectively we find that the joint internal and external equilibrium conditions dictate the latter. The only way in which the high growth region may be achieved would be by a successful devaluation of the currency which would be revealed by an inward shift of the external function (as indicated by the dotted line). This result should not surprise us unduly in view of our previous discussion of the need for equality between the number of objectives and instruments. The combined use of monetary and fiscal policy was able to secure the

* The reader will appreciate that a lowering of interest rates will normally accompany the process of debt retirement.

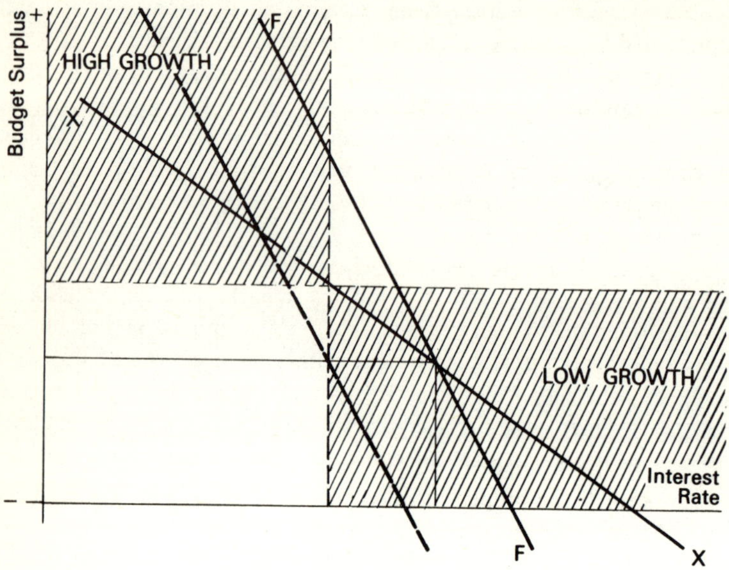

Figure VII.7

dual objectives of internal and external equilibrium when used efficiently; the additional objective requires an additional policy tool – in this case exchange-rate policy.

Monetary and Fiscal Policy Under Floating Exchange Rates

The foregoing analysis has explicitly assumed a regime of fixed exchange rates. For the sake of completeness it is necessary to enquire into the consequences of permitting the exchange rate to float freely. In general, adoption of a floating rate of exchange removes the force of the balance of payments constraint and thus makes the simultaneous attainment of internal and external goals easier to effect. In essence, a floating exchange rate provides a new automatic policy tool, an extra degree of freedom. The literature upon fixed versus floating exchange rates is now considerable,* with various conclusions springing from the model analysis according to the specific assumptions employed. In

* Amongst the more important contributions are Mundell (22, 16, 23), Johnson (24), Takayama (25) and Argy and Porter (26).

general, however, a concensus has emerged to the effect that a regime of floating exchange rates will enhance the effectiveness of both fiscal and monetary policy to pursue domestic stabilization goals.

Consider for example expansionary fiscal policy financed by bond sales. Conventionally, with the total money stock in circulation unchanged but with idle monetary holdings now transferred into active government spending, there is a rise in velocity which finances the income expansion. The expansion of income will be accompanied by a raising of interest rates, and indeed a rise in interest rates will be required to effect the initial sales of bonds. In turn, rising interest rates will curtail a certain degree of investment spending, thus countering if only partially the impact of the fiscal policy. When the exchange rate is fixed, the combined impact of expanding income and higher interest rates will impose two effects upon the overall balance of payments. On the one hand imports will rise, whilst on the other capital inflows are induced. If the propensity to import is high relative to the mobility of capital inflows, then the net effect will be a reduction in the effective money supply via the leakage through the payments deficit. The reduction in the money supply reinforces the limitations curbing the expansionary impact of the fiscal policy change. With a floating rate, however, depletion of the domestic money supply is prevented; instead the exchange rate takes the brunt of the adjustment by being permitted to depreciate. Hence, one offset to fiscal expansion is negated; fiscal policy is accordingly more effective with floating as opposed to fixed exchange rates – unless capital flows are highly mobile.*

Somewhat similar reasoning applies to monetary policy. When an increase in the money supply is brought about through the purchase of open market securities, raising their price and depressing interest yields, the fall in interest rates will normally exert an impact upon the demand for cash holdings by promoting a fall in velocity. The decline in velocity acts as an automatic stabilizer to the expansion of the money stock. In part it offsets the impact of monetary policy; in addition, however, if exchange rates are fixed, the expansion of income will generate additional restraints upon monetary policy, since the resultant payments deficit will itself imply a leakage of new money overseas. With floating exchange rates the current account drain is replaced by exchange rate

* If capital flows are highly mobile relative to the importing propensity, the exchange rate will appreciate under a floating regime and thus reduce the inflow of money that would otherwise occur on the current account under fixed rates.

depreciation and the velocity change remains the only offset. Various modifications around this basic theme are possible, depending upon the assumptions incorporated into the model analysis, particularly with respect to the interest rate sensitivity of venture capital. In general, however, the basic conclusion remains; floating exchange rates enhance the effectiveness of both fiscal and monetary policy to secure domestic stabilization goals, whilst simultaneously permitting the external objective to be discounted as an effective constraint. In principle, then, the case for fixed exchange rates rests essentially upon the belief that it is required to promote a sense of discipline upon democratically elected governments who would otherwise be inclined to pursue expansionary policies having potentially dangerous inflationary consequences.

Appendix – Positively Sloped IS Functions

Conventional portrayals of the IS/LM framework specifically relate investment expenditure solely to the rate of interest and consequently a negatively sloped IS curve results. If, however, investment is also a function of the income level, as suggested by accelerator type theories of investment, then a positively sloped IS function emerges as a distinct possibility. The condition for the IS curve to be positively sloped is simply that the marginal propensity to invest (the responsiveness of investment to income change), exceeds the marginal propensity to save (20). We illustrate this situation in Figure A.VII.1. Two implications may be noted. First, as indicated in the diagram, it implies that an increase in the money stock will be followed by a *raising* of the interest rate and not by a lowering as the conventional model predicts. This conclusion supports those monetarists who argue that movements in interest rates are a poor indicator of monetary ease or constraint and that prime consideration should be focussed on the volume of money in circulation. Secondly, it reverses the usual conclusion that monetary policy is less effective the greater the interest sensitivity of the demand for money (21). The conventional argument is that if the demand for money is highly interest elastic, then monetary expansion is accommodated by increased monetary holdings as interest rates fall, and the willingness of the public to hold money balances limits the fall in interest rates and the induced impact upon investment spending. If however, the IS function is positively sloped, the greater the interest

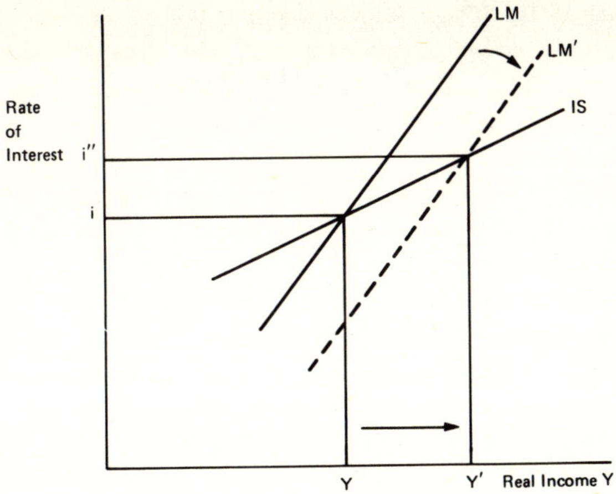

Figure A. VII.1

elasticity of the demand for money the less will be the rise in interest rates following monetary expansion. Diagrammatically, the greater the interest elasticity of the demand for money the less steep will be the slope of the LM function. If the IS curve is negative the lower slope of the LM function will reduce the impact of monetary policy; if the IS curve is positive the lower slope of the LM function will increase the effectiveness of monetary policy on the level of national income.

Chapter VIII The Economics of the Budget Constraint

Much of the earlier controversy stemming from the "Keynes versus the classics" debate was conducted within the confines of the simultaneous IS/LM framework outlined in the previous chapter. Indeed, IS/LM analysis became an extremely convenient pedagogical device able to lend itself equally to "classical" and "Keynesian" interpretations – all that was required was differing assumptions concerning the *slopes* of the IS and LM functions. Partly because attention was focused so firmly upon the respective slopes, initiating several sophisticated empirical and econometric studies, the issue of interdependence between IS and LM functions was never fully brought into question.

In sharp contrast, the recent monetarist revival of the quantity theory has raised this very issue by emphasizing the monetary–wealth effects of fiscal intervention. The link has been supplied by the concept of the government budget constraint and suggests that the conventional IS/LM functions are highly interdependent. Moreover, the interdependence may be such as to completely negate or "crowd out" the impact of fiscal policy intervention so as to render the long-run fiscal multiplier close to zero or even – in exceptional cases – negative.

The literature on the budget constraint is now extensive,* with the formal conclusions resting upon the particular assumptions involved – especially with respect to the existence and extent of any wealth effects. To indicate the issues and bring out some of the implications, consider the following statement of the budget constraint,

$$G + TP + IP - T = \Delta M + \frac{\Delta B}{i}$$

* Amongst the more important contributions are Blinder and Solow (1), Christ (2, 3), Hansen (4), Ott and Ott (5), Scarth (6), Silber (7) and Steindl (8).

where G represents government expenditure upon goods and services, TP represents government transfer payments in the form of pensions, unemployment benefits and so forth but excluding interest payments upon the national debt, IP the interest payments arising from such debt, T the total tax yield, ΔM the increase in the supply of high-powered money and $\Delta B/i$ is the monetary value of new bonds issued to the public. G + TP + IP is thus the sum of total government outlays, and if this exceeds tax receipts the constraint implies that the deficit must be matched by an increase in the supply of high-powered money, or in the issuance of additional bonds to the public. For simplicity, we assume that such bonds are non-redeemable; that they are consols. ΔB may then be interpreted as the additional interest paid on the issuance of new bonds where i is the market rate of interest. Now this constraint must be satisfied at all points in time whether government outlays fall short of tax receipts or vice versa. In the latter case, surplus taxes will be applied either to debt retirement or a curtailment of the high powered money supply.* Whilst the constraint must and will be satisfied at all points in time, however, it is only when government outlays are precisely matched by tax receipts – so that both ΔM and $\Delta B/i$ are zero – that the income level will be stabilized. In all other situations, the resulting monetary and/or wealth changes imposed upon the private sector will impinge upon the IS/LM functions and imply further income change.†

By way of illustration consider the analysis summarized with the aid of Figure VIII.1. We assume an equilibrium level Y^1, with government outlays precisely matched by taxes and with no change in the money supply or in the volume of bonds outstanding. In this situation suppose there occurs an autonomous increase in demand – let us say in export demand. The increase in demand is reflected in an outward shift of the IS curve and a new equilibrium income level is gained at Y^2. Such a conclusion is in keeping with the traditional Keynesian analysis. However, suppose, as seems likely, that taxes are endogenous and are positively related to income. The increase in the level of income will generate tax receipts in excess of government outlays. The excess will thus be applied either to retirement of the debt or to a reduction of the high-powered money supply, or, of course, to some combination of the two. This is the logic of the budget constraint. Let us assume,

* The actual course of action decided upon will generally be dictated by institutional considerations. Cf. Hansen (4)

† Note that it is insufficient for $\Delta M + \Delta B/i$ to equal zero.

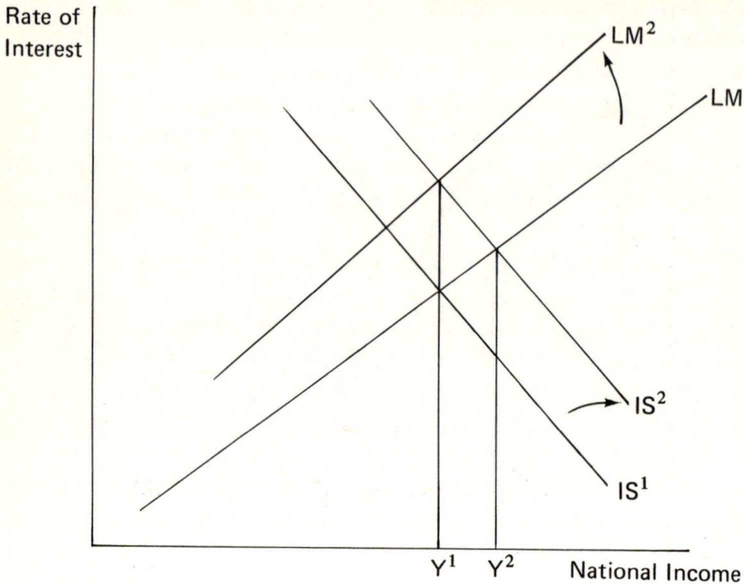

Figure VIII.1

first of all, that the additional induced taxes are applied to a reduction in the supply of high-powered money. The effect will be revealed in an inward shift of the LM curve.* Moreover, the inward shift of the LM curve will continue until the original income level Y^1 is reached; no other solution provides a stable equilibrium. As long as the income level exceeds Y^1, taxes are being generated in excess of current government outlays and thus additional surpluses are being created to curb the money supply still further. Consequently, the ultimate equilibrium will be as before; the long-run export expenditures multiplier in the present case is thus equal to zero and the conventional Keynesian analysis is completely negated by the assumed interdependence of the IS and LM functions.

Suppose however that, instead of the additional induced taxes being used to curb the money supply, they are used to effect retirement of the national debt. This situation we analyse with the aid of Figure VIII.2. Once again we assume that the increased export demand raises

* The LM curve, refers of course to the total money supply. Thus we tacitly assume, as seems reasonable, that the total money supply and the high-powered money supply move in the same direction.

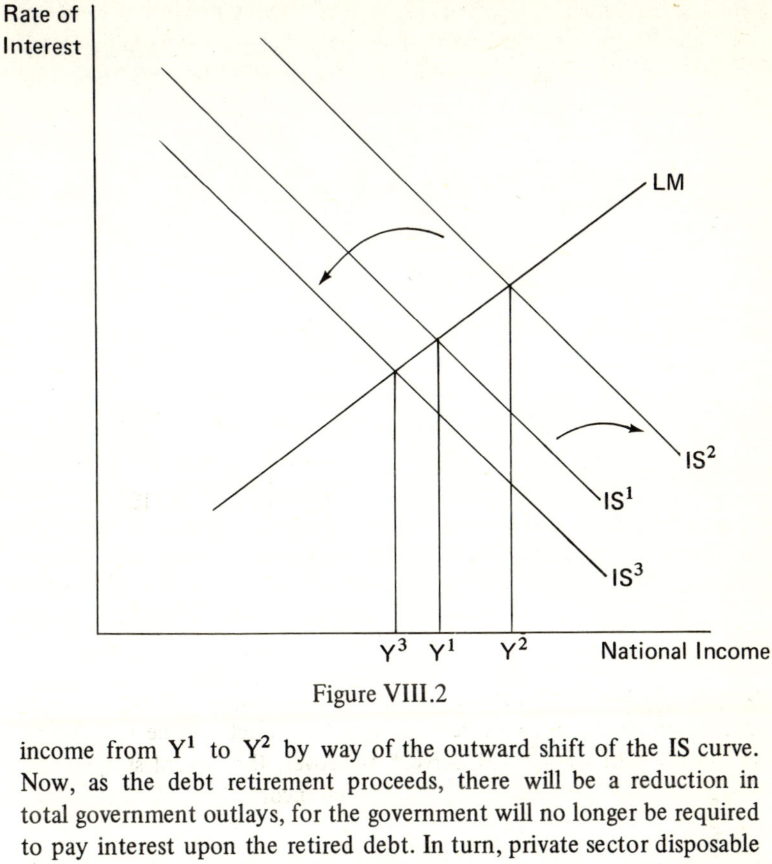

Figure VIII.2

income from Y^1 to Y^2 by way of the outward shift of the IS curve. Now, as the debt retirement proceeds, there will be a reduction in total government outlays, for the government will no longer be required to pay interest upon the retired debt. In turn, private sector disposable incomes fall, to the extent of the reduced interest payments, and consumption outlays will be reduced. This will be revealed in an inward shift of the IS curve which will continue as long as tax receipts exceed outlays. When the income level has been restored to Y^1, tax receipts will once again be as before, but they will still exceed government outlays in consequence of the reduced interest payments on the national debt. Hence, the inward shift of the IS curve will continue beyond Y^1 until some eventual equilibrium is regained – let us say at Y^3, where once again taxes precisely offset total government expenditures. Accordingly, in this instance the long-run export expenditures multiplier will be negative!

The preceding analysis indicates the logic of the budget constraint and suggests a considerable degree of interdependence between the IS and LM equations. It also implies, and this is very much the essence of the monetarist interpretation, that the standard Keynesian analysis is naive in focusing only upon the initial short-run or first-round impact. Moreover, it will be appreciated that the foregoing interaction derives from the logic of the budget constraint and the assumption of endogenous taxes; there is no need to invoke "wealth effects" to obtain these results.

Having indicated the nature of the budget constraint, let us now turn specifically to fiscal policy. Let us again assume an initial equilibrium situation, with government outlays exactly matched by fiscal receipts, and then allow for an increase in government purchases of goods and services. Again, the conventional analysis would reveal this as an outward shift of the IS curve raising the equilibrium income level from Y^1 to Y^2. The question that the conventional treatment ignores, however, is the manner in which such additional purchases are to be financed. As indicated by the constraint, the government possesses three possible alternatives. It may finance the additional purchases by increased taxation; it may expand the money supply; or it may sell additional bonds to the public.

These three methods are compared in the composite diagram of Figure VIII.3. In the first case, part (a), the additional taxes return the IS curve towards its original position. This is the method of balanced budget finance; the new equilibrium, Y^3, represents a situation whereby the increased government outlays are again matched by additional taxes – the latter arising from both a higher rate structure plus any induced element from the increase in income from Y^1 to Y^3. In part (b) of the composite figure we depict the method of new money creation. The outward shift of the IS curve is now reinforced by an outward shift of the LM curve. Equilibrium will be regained at Y^3 when income has risen sufficiently to generate additional fiscal revenues equal to the additional expenditures – with no change in the rate of taxation. Comparison of the income levels Y^3 in parts (a) and (b) of the figure form the basis of the monetarists' contention of the dominance of monetary over fiscal influences.*

* It will be appreciated that we are here comparing ultimate equilibrium situations. Initially the increase in government spending is financed by an equal amount of new money. If the new level of government spending is maintained over time, however, it will require an ever-increasing supply of high-powered money to finance the new constant level of expenditure. Ultimately, the continued outward shift of the LM curve will lead to an income level that generates the required taxes – rendering further monetary creation unnecessary.

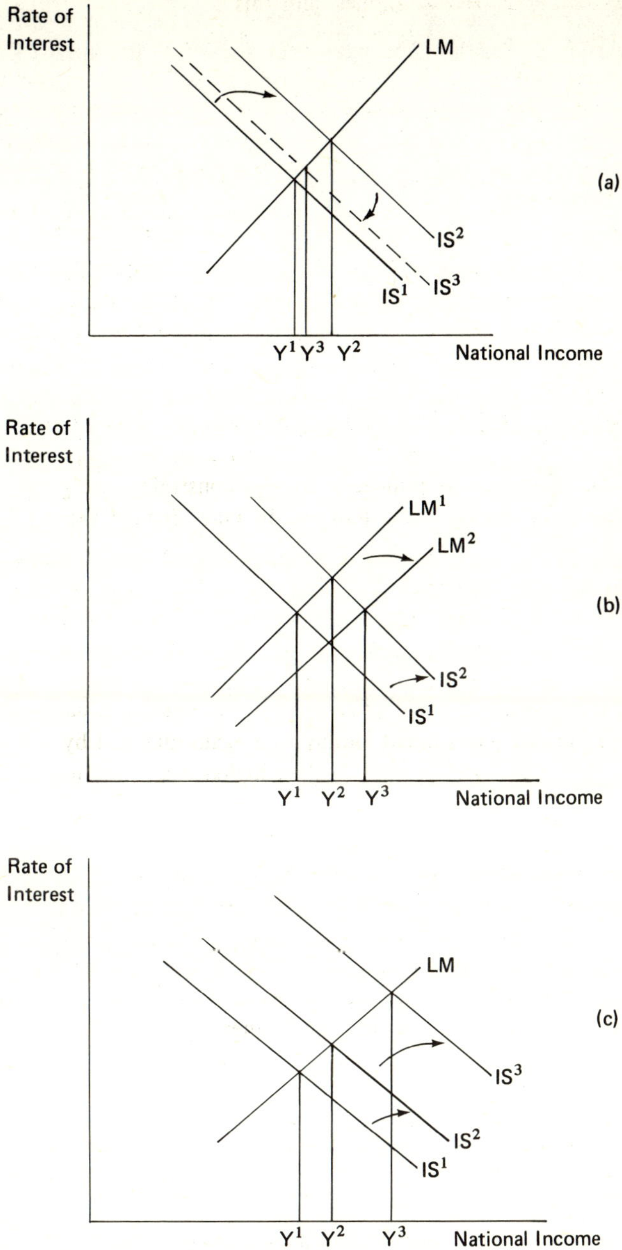

Figure VIII.3

Now consider the case of bond finance. Again there is no change in the rate of taxation; the government finances its outlays by persuading the public to purchase additional government securities. By issuing more securities the government raises its own outlays in the form of greater interest payments upon the expanded debt. Consequently, there is a further outward shift of the IS curve as private sector disposable incomes rise. Moreover, as long as the new level of government expenditure is maintained, additional securities will have to be issued at each successive time period, again creating further government interest payments. The outward shift of the IS curve is thus made continuous until that income level is reached which generates taxes equal to total outlays. In part (c) of the figure, this income level is indicated as Y^3. As long as tax receipts are assumed to be a positive function of income, the ultimate equilibrium income level in the case of bond finance must exceed that of monetary creation since total government outlays are greater by virtue of the additional interest payments upon the debt. Implicitly, it is on this point that Keynesians have rested their case for belief in the potency of fiscal intervention; increased government expenditure financed by debt can exert an expansionary impact upon the equilibrium level of national income.

However, this analysis explicitly ignores consideration of any wealth effects consequent upon the issue of new bonds. The introduction of wealth effects reinforces the monetarists' case against the potency of fiscal policy; their existence and/or strength thus constitutes a major issue between modern-day Keynesians and the adherents to the revised quantity theory.

At any point in time, private sector wealth can be thought of as comprising the holding of real capital assets, including claims to capital assets in the form of stocks and shares etc., plus the holding of debt issued by the government. The latter includes the money stock as well as interest-bearing bonds, whose nominal value varies with changes in the interest rate. Private sector wealth then can be represented as

$$W = K + \frac{M}{P} + \left(\frac{B}{i}\right)\Big/P$$

where K stands for real capital assets and P represents a general index of prices. How is private sector wealth influenced by the issue of new bonds? Clearly, the short-run value of *real* capital assets is unaffected by the manner in which the authorities choose to finance new expenditures. Equally, the total private holding of money balances will also remain unchanged when the government resorts to debt finance. This is because the government receives money balances from the public in exchange for bonds which it then puts back into circulation when financing its expenditures. The total of privately held money balances is unaltered, in aggregate, by the transaction, as long as prices remain stable. The only change then lies in the additional holding of private sector bonds by the public, and it is this element that constitutes the increment in private sector wealth. The increase in private sector wealth will generate an increased consumption demand reflected in a further outward shift of the IS curve. Equally, however, it will permit an increased demand for money balances reflected in an inward shift of the LM curve. *A priori*, it is not possible to determine which effect will dominate, but the monetarists' contention supports the case for "crowding out". In this view, consumption outlays are comparatively insensitive to wealth changes whereas the demand for money (being highly income-elastic) responds more positively. Accordingly, the inward shift of the LM curve is more marked than the additional outward shift of the IS curve so that the net effect is to counter the expansionary increase in government expenditures. This situation we summarize in Figure VIII.4. The initial income level is Y^1 determined by the intersection of IS^1 and LM^1. The increase in government spending shifts the IS curve to IS^2 and raises the income level to Y^2. Subsequent wealth effects generate a further increase in the IS curve to IS^3 but also impinge upon the LM curve moving it to LM^2. The ultimate equilibrium therefore implies the income level Y^3, which is less than the indicated Keynesian equilibrium Y^2. Indeed, theoretically, it is perfectly possible for Y^3 to lie below Y^1 implying that the long-run government expenditures multiplier may be negative when debt is the chosen means of finance.

The Keynesian counter-argument is to dismiss the alleged wealth effect as fallacious or to concede its existence but query its significance. The argument that the wealth effect is fallacious is logically correct. The fact that the government chooses to issue additional bonds cannot, of itself, raise the wealth of society. However, this is hardly the point at issue. Provided the private sector perceives its wealth as increasing and modifies its behaviour accordingly, a wealth effect is apparent whether or not the perception is justified. A more significant counter-argument revolves around the change in the interest rate. In order to persuade the public to purchase additional bonds the government will have to make the terms sufficiently attractive by raising the rate of

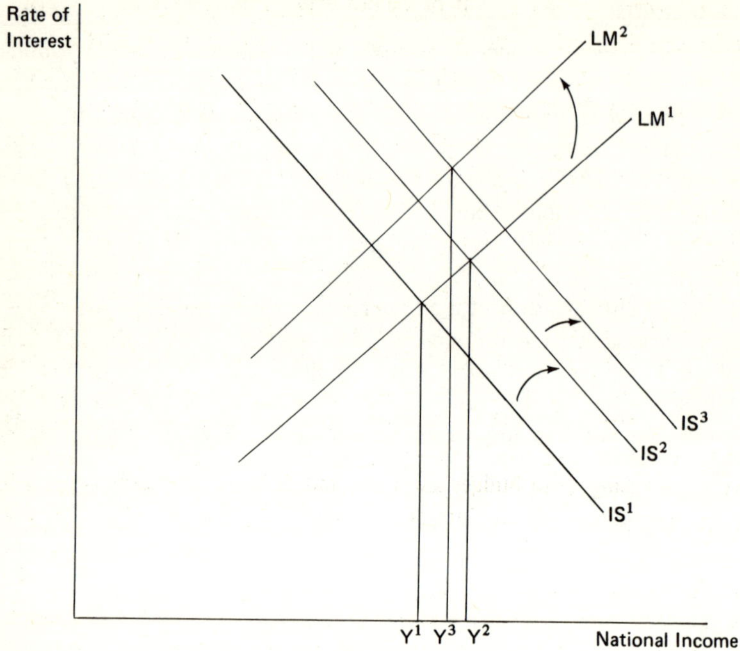

Figure VIII.4

interest. The raising of the interest rate will imply a negative wealth effect for all existing bond-holders, which to some extent will counter the increased volume of bond-holding. Secondly, it may be argued that increased national debt raises the prospect of future taxes to service and finance the debt. This depletion of permanent future income must offset, if only in part, the initial wealth effect.* Whether the current generation of bond-holders are sufficiently perceptive to take account of future tax burdens is difficult to resolve, but perhaps less questionable is the impact of the debt upon the quoted value of stocks and shares. As the interest yield on government bonds rises there will be a switch away from private sector securities implying a decrease in their nominal value. Finally, to the extent that the government expenditures are inflationary, the increase in the price level will reduce the real value of monetary holdings. The combination of all these reasons suggests limitations to the extent of wealth effects stemming from increased government debt.

* cf. Barro (9).

Regardless of the extent of wealth effects, their existence together with the concept of the budget constraint considerably extends the range for the potential crowding out of fiscal policy measures. Indeed, we may now distinguish three distinct cases of crowding out – cases where expansionary government spending is offset by the displacement of a similar volume of private sector spending. The first case, fully allowed for in Keynesian analysis and mentioned briefly previously, is where the increased income compels a rise in the rate of interest with adverse impacts upon private sector investment spending. This effect, which is consistent with independence between IS and LM functions, is greater the greater the interest elasticity of investment demand and the lesser the interest sensitivity of the demand for money. The Keynesian belief in the slopes of the IS and LM functions, as depicted in figures VII.1 and VII.2, thus minimizes the extent of such crowding out. Secondly, we have crowding out associated with the feedback impacts arising from budget surpluses and deficits; such effects specifically introduce formal interdependence between the IS and LM equations. Particularly where government expansionary policy leads to a deficit, the need to finance the deficit implies further changes. In the absence of new monetary creation, the additional sources of finance must be siphoned off from the private sector either by taxation or by inducing additional loans. In the former case, crowding out is obvious; expenditure declines by the amount of the tax multiplied by the marginal propensity to consume. In the latter case, the transfer of money to the government in exchange for bonds may also curtail consumption to some degree, but more probably it will imply a reordering of private sector portfolios, including a reduction in the amount of cash held idle. Indeed, this is the essence of the Keynesian position; bonds are purchased from the government sector by running down speculative cash holdings maintained solely for this purpose, and consequently no crowding out of alternative expenditure occurs. It is for this reason that the third case of crowding out – arising from the wealth effects accompanying fiscal intervention financed by debt – takes on renewed importance.

The analysis of crowding out suggests a much more limited role for fiscal policy than is implied in the earlier Keynesian literature. More important, however, is that, together with the concept of the budget constraint, it suggests a need for a much more sophisticated analysis of macro-economic policy incorporating all monetary, wealth and interest rate effects. In particular, it suggests that the traditional dichotomy of policy measures as "monetary" or "fiscal" may be outmoded and should be replaced by a more comprehensive and inclusive concept of "budgetary policy".

Chapter IX The Problem of Economic Growth

A widespread concensus exists as to the desirability of enhanced economic growth. Growth is seen as the key to raising *per capita* incomes, and in turn higher levels of income *per capita* are looked upon as an index of welfare. Whilst the identification of income *per capita* with economic welfare is admittedly *simpliste*, ignoring as it does the possible attendant costs of economic growth,* it is none the less the case that higher incomes *per capita* permit increased consumption of both goods and leisure. For the majority of people, the goods–leisure allocation together with some exercise of choice in making the allocation would provide an acceptable measure of their economic well-being. Moreover, economic growth is important in securing other goals of economic and social policy. With regard to the object of income redistribution, for example, policies to lessen the gap between the rich and poor will be more readily accepted by the former if their *absolute* living standards are not placed in jeopardy. Indeed, it is partly because the welfare implications of economic growth are so significant that government intervention in the economy has increased, in the form of social policies and transfers, to ensure that the benefits of the growth process are allocated in accordance with society's prevailing sense of equity.

Whilst a broad measure of agreement exists with regard to the desirability of economic growth, less concensus prevails with respect

* As emphasised by Mishan (1) in particular. Costs such as congestion and pollution are obvious enough but in reality stem from resource mis-allocation as opposed to economic growth *per se*. Less obvious, perhaps, is the fact that growth may diminish the freedom of choice mentioned previously (p. 9). In less advanced economies, it is particularly the case that growth promotes standardized products produced by more capital-intensive methods with which the far more varied output of handicraft industries cannot compete.

to the appropriate macro-economic policies to secure growth. This stems partly from disagreement amongst economists with respect to the ultimate causes of economic growth upon the one hand; but it also springs from the wide gulf that separates the *theory* of economic growth from the practical pursuit of economic growth upon the other. Much of existing growth theory focuses upon the stability of the growth path in long-run equilibria, or upon the time period for adjustment given some autonomous divergence from the growth path. In the main, therefore, growth theory has developed in a manner divorced from the practical short-run problems confronting policy-makers, and in large measure has ignored such run-of-the-mill considerations as the constraints imposed by balance of payments and inflation objectives. It is also the case that the pioneering formulations in growth theory, particularly the Harrod–Domar (2, 3) and one-sector neo-classical formulations (4, 5) either limited or restricted the rôle played by fiscal policy, whilst it is only comparatively recently that attempts have been made to incorporate the monetary variable in policy-oriented growth models (6).

The Cobb–Douglas Production Function

As a starting point to a consideration of the issues underlying economic growth, we will have recourse to one of the most well known and widely adopted concepts in economics, namely the Cobb–Douglas production function (7). As a purely theoretical statement the function relates output to factor inputs by an equation that takes the form

$$Q = AL^{\alpha}K^{\beta}$$

where Q is the measure of output in any given period, L the labour input and K the capital input whilst A and the exponents α and β are assumed constants. It follows that, with zero input, zero output is obtained; that is to say, diagrammatically, the production function passes through the origin. As an *empirical* assertion, the Cobb–Douglas production function claims that observed changes in output are best explained with values of α and β summing to 1 ($\alpha = 0.75$ and $\beta = 0.25$). A good deal of empirical work, largely associated with the name of Paul Douglas (8), has sought to reaffirm this fundamental, and mathematically very convenient, finding. Such a production function displays diminishing returns to the augmentation to any one factor input, but constant returns to scale, i.e. to the equal percentage augmentation of both inputs. It also asserts that, if both labour and capital receive payment in accordance with their marginal product, then total payment to both labour and capital will just be sufficient to exhaust the total output – a decidedly useful property for the function to display and possibly a reaffirmation of both the marginal productivity theory of distribution and the existence of competition in the modern economy. The empirical evidence is by no means conclusive and it may well be that the constant-returns Cobb–Douglas production function is invoked primarily on account of its mathematical versatility.*

For present purposes, however, and without specifically endorsing the constant-returns case, the formulation possesses the useful conceptual advantage of indicating the possible contributions to the growth process. Thus, for example, output can be raised by increasing the factor inputs directly, the actual combination of the factor increment being determined by their relative marginal products and relative money costs. Alternatively, any addition to output not explained in terms of factor augmentation must stem from changes in the value of A. The coefficient A may thus be regarded as a non-factor-augmenting source of growth and will include such important influences as innovation and technical change, cultural and social attitudes to work effort and so forth, which collectively may dominate changes in labour and capital inputs. It follows that, in assessing policies to promote growth, we may focus either upon policies geared to influencing the factor input or upon policies designed to influence the residual component, A. The policy conclusions arising from consideration of the more elementary growth models generally stress the role of factor inputs and minimize the importance of other influences. In part, this explains the wide gulf that exists between formal growth models emphasizing the long-term rate of population expansion and capital formation and the more pragmatic short-term policy measures which seek to promote greater productivity through improved resource allocation, innovation and technical change.

* For a lucid account of the mathematical properties together with certain reservations of the constant-return cases, see especially Archibald and Lipsey (9). It may be noted in passing that the assumption of constant returns to scale has a certain plausibility, in that the duplication of a given production process or plant might be expected to lead to a duplication of the output.

Policy Implications of the Harrod–Domar Model

The Harrod–Domar model of economic growth is basically at issue with the Cobb–Douglas formulation because it focuses attention primarily upon the degree of capital formation,* and moreover side-steps the question of diminishing returns by assuming the capital–output ratio a constant. In its simplest form, the Harrod–Domar model is but an extension of the Keynesian national income determination model that drops the assumption of fixed capital stock. Diagrammatically, the essence of the statement can be summarized in terms of the Keynesian closed economy income determination model. In Figure IX.1, the aggregate demand function intersects the 45° line at the full

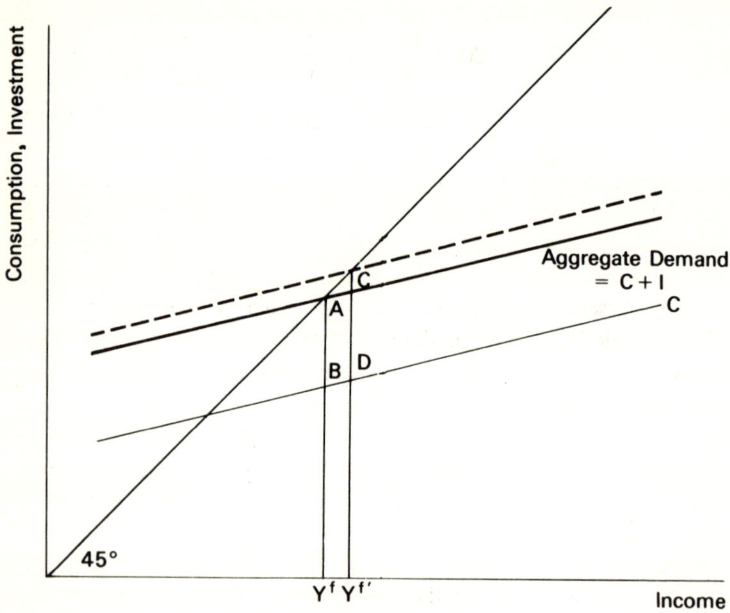

Figure IX.1

employment income level Y^f and net investment is equal to the vertical distance AB between the aggregate demand functions and the consumption function, C. Assuming a capital output ratio of 3:1, the full

* Although not entirely. In the Harrod formulation, the "natural" rate of population growth imposes an upper limit to the growth process.

employment income level will increase by $\frac{1}{3}$AB in the subsequent time period to the level $Y^{f'}$. Now if full employment is to be maintained, investment must increase to CD, generating a further increase in the full employment income level by the amount $\frac{1}{3}$CD in the following time period. The rate of increase of CD over AB thus provides a measure of the rate of increase in investment spending that is required to maintain the full employment income level, or more correctly to maintain full capacity working of the increasing capital stock. The increase in capacity income is accordingly equal to the increase in the capital stock divided by the capital output ratio or, alternatively, equal to the amount of net investment divided by the capital output ratio, V. Since, in the simple model, savings and investment are equal *ex post*, we have

$$\Delta Y = \frac{\Delta K}{V} = \frac{I}{V} = \frac{S}{V}.$$

The policy implications to be drawn from this analysis are obvious enough; measures that raise the overall savings ratio or the pace of capital formation will raise the rate of growth of productive capacity. Fiscal policy may thus be used to force down consumption, forcing savings upon the economy, whilst monetary policy can ensure low long-term rates of interest, thus providing the incentive to undertake investment. Essentially, the basic Harrod–Domar model provides the underlying logic in support of the strict-fiscal, easy-monetary prescription for advanced economic growth. Indeed, given the concept of the incremental capital–output ratio it becomes an almost self-evident proposition that the key to growth lies in a raising of the overall savings ratio. This approach may be perfectly permissible in the short run and is certainly relevant to the undertaking of specific development projects, but implicitly it rests upon the tacit assumption that the incremental capital–output ratio remains a constant. In a long-run analysis this is hardly likely to be the case; the very concept of diminishing returns would suggest that the incremental capital–output ratio would rise in response to capital formation. In this event, the attempt to use fiscal policy to generate forced savings may be self-defeating. A raising of the pace of capital formation in excess of profitable investment opportunities will be accompanied by a declining rate of profit and a sharply rising marginal capital–output ratio.

In many of the developing economies, such is the acute shortage of capital in relation to other co-operative inputs, and so meagre is the natural augmentation of real capital assets, that such considerations may justifiably be ignored from the practical policy point of view. Over the relatively short time horizon of the normal development plan, it may be reasonable to treat the incremental capital–output ratio as a constant and to budget accordingly when computing feasible rates of economic growth. Over the longer period, however, and when dealing with the more advanced and capital-abundant economies, such procedure is clearly unwarranted. The observed correlation between high growth rates and high investment ratios (10) is not in itself sufficient to support the policy implication of the Harrod–Domar model, for the high investment ratio may be the *consequence* of high growth rates raising the demand for increased capacity and thus persistently offsetting the onset of diminishing returns.

By focusing upon the aggregate investment or savings ratio, the Harrod–Domar analysis tends to overlook a policy recommendation that is really implicit in its basic formulation. The capital–output ratio adopted by the model is of course an aggregative one for the entire economy. In fact, however, incremental capital–output ratios may well differ, particularly in the short term, between competing sectors of the economy. Thus, even if we grant the plausibility of diminishing returns to capital investment, the overall growth rate can be improved by switching capital from sectors with relatively high capital–output ratios. In short, the efficient allocation of capital may be as important as its total quantity. From the long-term perspective it can probably be taken as granted that the normal workings of a competitive economy will ultimately secure the efficient allocation of even relatively immobile capital. From the more pragmatic short-run viewpoint of policy-making, however, this assumption may be unwarranted. Hence the concern for efficient allocation of investible resources revealed in government promotion of mergers, support for industrial reorganization, selective investment schemes and the like.

Policy Implications of The One-Sector Neo-Classical Model

In essence, the elementary neo-classical growth model renders the ultimate growth path of the economy dependent solely upon population expansion which is assumed autonomous. Hence, no positive role emerges for either fiscal or monetary policy as a determinant of long-run growth. Whilst such a conclusion rests upon the simplicity of the one-sector model employed and must be relaxed in more sophisticated treatments, none the less it imparts the flavour of the neo-classical construct; the idea of a self-regulating economy responding to inexorable economic laws leaving but a limited modifying role for policy-making.

In order to bring out some of the implications of the analysis consider the situation displayed with the aid of Figure IX.2.* Output *per capita* is shown to be a function of capital *per capita*. The function, however, is non-linear; increasing the amount of capital per worker leads to a raising of output per worker but at a diminishing rate owing to the assumption of diminishing returns to capital formation. Savings

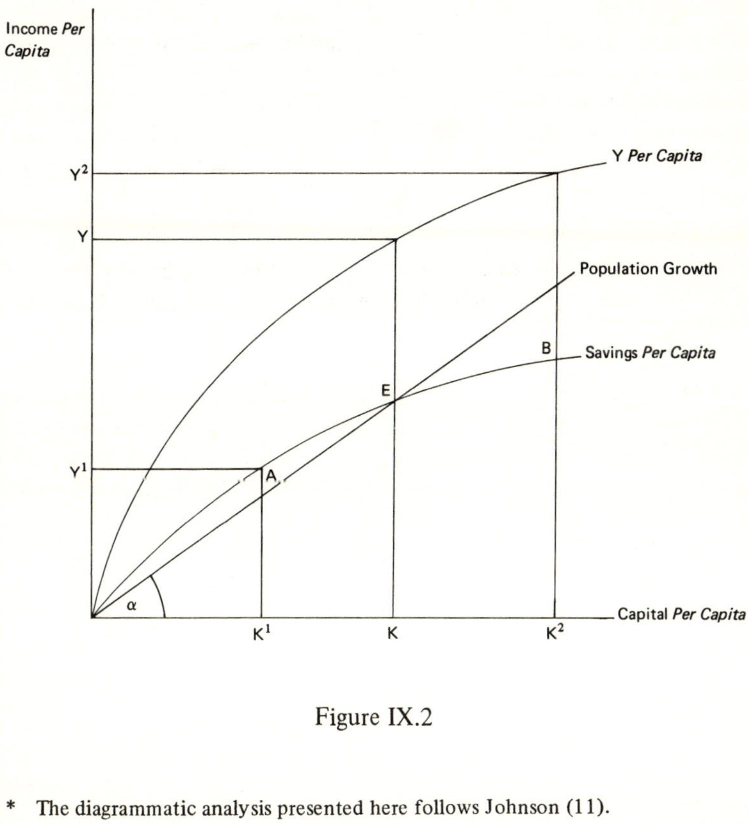

Figure IX.2

* The diagrammatic analysis presented here follows Johnson (11).

are assumed to be a constant proportion of national income. Thus the savings curve is drawn as a replica of the income *per capita* curve and is equally a function of capital *per capita*. Finally, we assume population growth to be autonomously determined at a rate indicated by the angle α; thus a raising of the growth rate of population would pivot the population curve to the left, increasing the size of α. We now have all the necessary ingredients of the neo-classical growth model.

The basic conclusion of the model is that equilibrium will ultimately be attained at point E, where capital *per capita* is equal to K and income *per capita* is equal to Y. That this point constitutes the only feasible stable equilibrium may be shown by considering other positions such as A or B. At A, the amount of capital per worker is K^1, consistent with the *per capita* income level Y^1. However, at this point the pace of capital formation, determined by the savings curve, exceeds the rate of population growth. Consequently, the amount of capital *per capita* is increasing implying a movement from K^1 in the direction of K. Similar reasoning applies to consideration of position B. Here, population expansion exceeds the degree of capital formation. The amount of capital per worker depicted by K^2 cannot therefore be maintained and the economy falls back towards position K. K constitutes a stable equilibrium in that the growth rates of both population and capital are here equated; accordingly, no change occurs in the amount of capital *per capita*, implying constancy in the amount of income *per capita*.

Since the income *per capita* curve is expressly assumed to be non-linear, the indicated adjustment process from K^1 or K^2 to K implies not only a change in the capital–labour ratio but equally a change in the capital–output ratio. The attainment of a long-run equilibrium implicit in the neo-classical construct, therefore, specifically assumes variations in the capital–output ratio. It should also be noted that important behavioural assumptions underly the adjustment process. Specifically, it is assumed that, if the pace of capital accumulation exceeds the growth rate of population, then the price of capital falls relatively to wage labour and entrepreneurs are provided with the incentive to adopt more capital-intensive techniques. Adjustments in the degree of capital intensity thus ensure the maintenance of full employment of both labour and the capital stock in long-run equilibria, regardless of their respective growth rates.

Since E is the indicated long-run equilibrium, it follows that the growth rate of the aggregate economy is equal to the growth rate of population, α. The conclusion follows since, if income *per capita* is constant, national income expands solely with population growth. The fundamental conclusion of the simple neo-classical model, then, is that population expansion is the ultimate determinant of economic growth. Fiscal policy, or indeed any other policy, is powerless to influence the long-run growth path as long as population expansion remains autonomous (12).

To demonstrate this point, consider Figure IX.3. We presume an initial equilibrium at E, determined by the intersection of the population growth curve with the savings curve. The initial *per capita* income level is accordingly Y. Now let us assume that the government forces an increase in the overall savings ratio by increasing taxes and using the proceeds for capital formation. The savings curve is shifted parametrically to the left and the new equilibrium is indicated at E^1. The amount of capital per worker must ultimately increase to K^1 implying a *per capita* income level Y^1. However, once Y^1 is obtained, the income *per capita* level is once again rendered constant and national income again grows in accordance with population expansion. Since the latter is unchanged the ultimate long-run growth path is also unchanged. Fiscal policy is able to effect a short-run increase in the amount of capital per worker, and is accordingly responsible for initiating an increase in *per capita* income but is powerless to influence the long-run growth path.

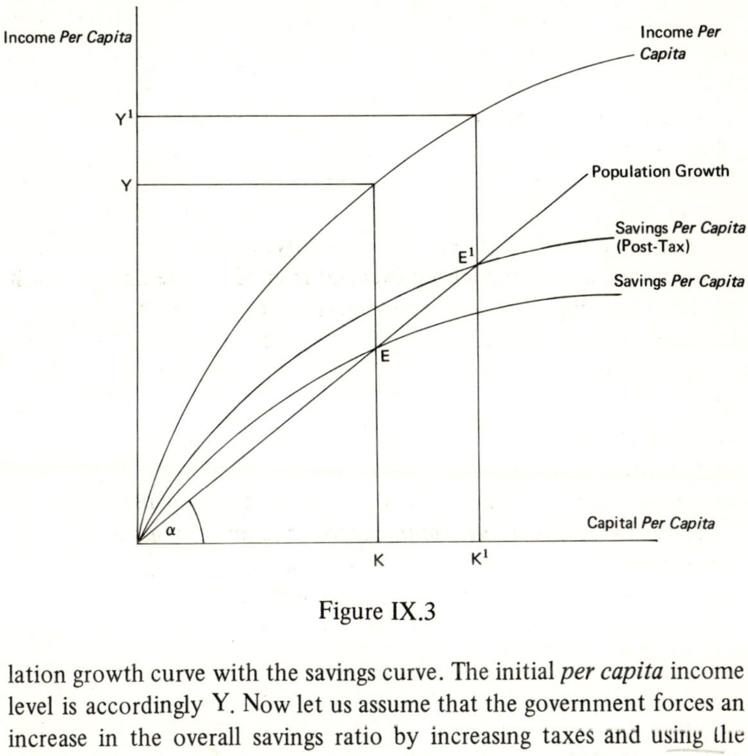

Figure IX.3

Although population growth is thus the principal determinant of economic growth in the neo-classical world, this need not necessarily imply the absence of any role for macro-economic policy. As we have seen, fiscal policy may influence the level of income *per capita* by altering the degree of capital intensity. This would suggest that the appropriate role for fiscal intervention would be to secure that degree of capital *per capita* consistent with the maximization of *per capita* consumption. The latter, equal to the difference between *per capita* income and *per capita* saving, may be adopted as a useful index of welfare. In the present case, where saving is assumed proportional to income, maximizing *per capita* consumption is akin to maximizing income. However, one can imagine other cases with more complex consumption functions where the welfare objective requires an actual decrease in the *per capita* income level. That rate of saving that maximizes consumption per capita, whether influenced by monetary/ fiscal variables or not, has been termed the Golden Rule of Capital Accumulation (13,14). Even if it is attained, however, the economy then continues to grow precisely as before at the predetermined rate α; policy measures do not disturb the long-term growth path.

Admittedly, the foregoing analysis has minimized the policy implications partly by the very simplicity of the model adopted. In particular, we have ignored the impact of technical change (indicated by a raising of the production function at all levels of capital *per capita*), which may in itself respond to policy variables. None the less, the analysis is conceptually useful in distinguishing alternative roles. Whereas, the Harrod–Domar model emphasized the importance of capital formation, the neo-classical model invokes the ultimate autonomous determinant of population growth. Both focus primarily upon factor augmentation. We now turn to consider other possible causes of economic growth, apart from factor inputs, which may reveal greater responsiveness to economic policy measures.

Other Influences upon Growth Rates

In addition to the augmentation of factor inputs emphasized in the conventional models, economists have stressed three other influences upon the overall growth rate. Principal amongst these has been the importance of technical change and innovation that reveals itself in increased output *per capita* at each level of capital *per capita* – that is, in terms of a parametric upward shift of the production function. In discussing this issue it is important, especially from the policy point of view, to distinguish between disembodied and embodied technical progress. Disembodied technical change implies increased productive efficiency of existing capital assets regardless of their age. Implicit in this concept is the notion of change occurring that allows existing assets to be used more efficiently. Embodied technical change in contrast implies increased productive efficiency stemming from the introduction of new capital assets that replace the old and that, owing to invention and innovation, are superior. A high rate of capital accumulation may thus be a prerequisite to significant embodied technical change taking place.

One consequence of the notion of embodied technical progress being dependent upon the act of investment was the development of the so-called "vintage growth model", where the capital stock is distinguished according to its age profile and where the more recent capital assets are the most productive. The pace at which existing capital assets are scrapped and replaced may depend in part upon the provision of depletion and accelerated depreciation allowances. To the extent that the latter are policy variables, therefore, it may be possible to influence the age profile of a nation's capital stock and hasten technological advance – or at least the pace at which innovating changes are incorporated into productive processes. By the same token, if there are factors weakening the incentive to replace existing assets, as for example the maintenance of an over-valued exchange rate which deters investment in the export sectors and which limits the inflow of external venture capital, then a nation's capital stock may possess an outdated age profile reflected in low productivity per head and limited technological advance.

The comparative importance of technical progress in the rate of economic growth is difficult to assess. In particular, in the case of embodied technical change, which is probably the more fundamental, it is by no means easy to distinguish the effects of technical change from the augmentation of the stock of capital per head. In principle, given time series data upon output per head and capital per head, all that is needed to separate the two is an estimate of the productivity of capital. But this in turn requires estimating the form of the production function in order to derive the marginal product of capital. It also assumes that capital does in fact receive payment equal to its marginal product and it is necessary to distinguish between the total capital stock and the percentage of capital actually utilised over the period in question. To bring out the implications involved consider the situation depicted in Figure IX.4. If at time t we observe the output per head–capital per

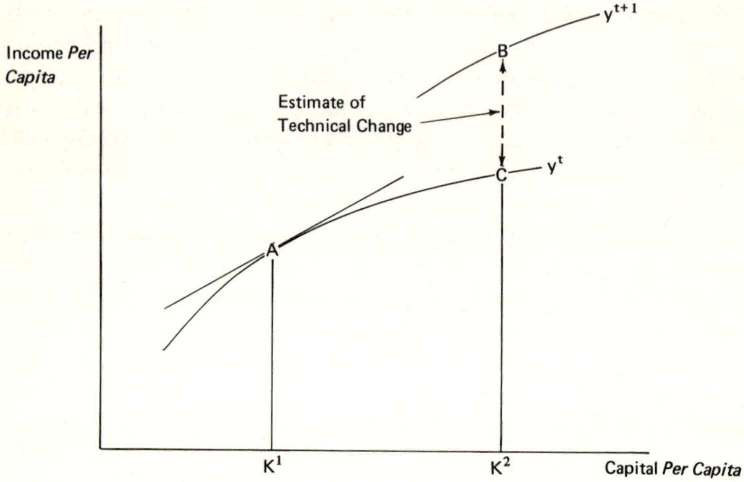

Figure IX.4

head combination denoted by point A, and if at time t + 1 the same relationship is denoted by point B, how can we estimate the increment in *per capita* income that stems solely from technical advance? If we are able to estimate a production function for the aggregate economy at time t (indicated by the income curve y^t), then a tangent drawn to the production function at time t will provide a measure of the marginal productivity of capital. The marginal productivity of capital multiplied by the increment in capital per head, $K^1 - K^2$, will then provide an estimate of the increment in income per head arising from capital accumulation, and this indicates that in the absence of any other co-operative influence income per head should be K^2C. The difference then between the observed income per head, K^2B, and the projected income level, K^2C, provides an estimate of the importance of technical change.

Quite apart from the difficulties involved in such a procedure and the assumptions upon which it rests to which we have already alluded, it will be appreciated that the term "technical change" is being used as a "catch-all" for any growth-augmenting factor other than capital accumulation. It includes, for example, improvements in the labour force which may arise from greater capital investment in education. Implicitly, therefore, such a procedure is likely to overstate the importance of technical change as commonly understood. None the less, and despite this qualification, pioneering attempts along these lines (15) indicated the overwhelming importance of technical progress in the overall rate of economic growth when compared with capital accumulation in itself. At the same time, if technical progress is primarily of the embodied variety as generally believed (16), then capital accumulation is important in being the vehicle of technological advance.

Before concluding that the appropriate policy recommendation should be more resources devoted to scientific education and research, it is necessary to distinguish between pure scientific advances and technological progress as actually applied in productive industrial investment. This is a point repeatedly emphasized by Cairncross (17); mere scientific progress and advances in knowledge and understanding are in themselves insufficient. It is the application of such scientific developments to actual productive processes that is the all-important factor. In turn, the application of new ideas to market processes will depend more upon social forces influencing the climate of innovation and the diffusion of knowledge and new ideas. Opposition to change stemming either from the side of conservative management or from restrictive trade union practices may limit the degree of technological progress even within a society where the degree of pure scientific research and achievement is remarkably high.* It is possible also that the attitude adopted by a government concerning the extent of its intervention and control – the degree of "red tape" and regulation and the extent and dependability of market demand conditions – will itself condition the speed of innovation and the adaptability to new techniques.

The measure of technical change discussed above includes general

* In many cases the fruits of scientific endeavour and research undertaken within one country are virtually a free good as far as other countries are concerned – such is the dissemination of ideas through publications, conferences, etc. A high rate of scientific research is thus not even a prerequisite for enhanced growth as long as the innovating spirit is present.

improvements in the labour force. Many economists would consider the betterment of the labour force as a prime factor in the growth process. Such improvement, whether stemming from better nutrition and well-being on the one hand (18) or education and training upon the other, is more correctly a consequence of investment in human capital and reinforces the claim for capital accumulation *per se*. In addition, however, there remains one source of increased labour productivity that in reality stems from neither investment in human capital nor technological progress but that is a consequence solely of job experience. This is reflected in a diminishing rate of labour input per unit of output over time as the total volume of output expands and has become known as the "learning process".

Finally, apart from the augmentation of factor inputs, technical advance and improvements in the efficiency of labour, superior growth performance will depend upon efficient resource utlization. When discussing the Harrod–Domar model of economic growth it was implicitly assumed that capital formation would be directed into the most productive sectors first. That is to say, investable funds would be allocated inversely in relation to incremental capital–output ratios. Equally similar reasoning applies to the allocation of labour. A transfer of labour from low productivity occupations to high will enhance the overall level of output without invoking any other co-operative factor. All that is involved is the allocation of labour to sectors having low labour–output ratios. This issue is closely identified to the alleged phenomena of "disguised unemployment" in less advanced economies, where labour is held to possess zero or near zero marginal productivity. A transfer of labour to more productive activities is then claimed to be an essential prerequisite for sustained economic growth (19). Similar reasoning has been applied to the more developed economies. Improvements in agricultural productivity, it is alleged, have permitted the transfer of agricultural labour into the more modern and more productive manufacturing sectors of the economy. Moreover, since it is the latter sectors that enjoy increasing returns to scale whilst the agricultural sector traditionally is confronted with diminishing returns, the overall change in output levels is compounded by induced productivity changes (20). The conclusion that emerges from this analysis is that the inability of the agricultural sector to undergo further contraction may impose a major constraint upon an important source of economic growth.

Growth Performance in the United Kingdom

The preceding analysis by no means exhausts the many-sided contributions to economic growth. Many influences interact, and some may be peculiar to any one country; it follows that simple inter-country comparisons of economic growth do not really take us very far and a country's growth performance should be weighed by reference to its own growth potential (21). None the less, by reference to almost any criteria, growth performance in the United Kingdom, particularly in the post-war years, has been sadly disappointing and has doubtless contributed to balance of payments difficulties and an excessive degree of price inflation.

Britain's poor growth performance has not only been of concern to successive British governments and United Kingdom-oriented policy-making analysts. It has also been subject to the scrutiny of those international agencies that have intervened to support sterling, and it has led to a major study sponsored by the Brookings Institute of Washington (22). Very broadly, it would be fair to conclude that the various studies that have been undertaken have not highlighted any one fundamental defect or weakness in the British economy. Instead, and possibly more disturbingly, they focus upon a number of interacting influences which have combined to limit both the growth performance and the potential of the United Kingdom economy. In concluding this chapter we will attempt to indicate the major findings of these studies and the policy conclusions that follow, in relation to the theoretical framework previously established.

1. Lack of Technological Progress

There appears to be a wide-ranging concensus that Britain's post-war growth performance has stemmed partly from a failure to exploit technical change. Especially in relation to the Common Market countries, an early study by Aukrust (23) indicated that the contribution to the growth of GDP rendered by technical progress was relatively low.* This conclusion emerges despite the fact that expen-

* The technique employed by Aukrust to estimate the contribution of technical change was similar to that analysed previously and is accordingly subject to the same qualifications. In particular, it assumed a constant-returns production function of the Cobb–Douglas variety with the exponents upon labour and capital, 0.7 and 0.3 respectively.

diture upon pure research and development has been comparatively high. Indeed, the Brookings study demonstrated that British expenditure upon research and development was some fifty per cent greater than the comparable expenditure in the United States when expressed as a percentage of GNP. It is not the lack of advances in knowledge, then, that is responsible for limited technical progress; rather, it is the failure to exploit such advances and apply them to investment and innovation in productive industry. In part, this failure or resistance to change springs from the conservature nature of British management and an alleged tendency to a general bias against the manager possessed of professional qualifications. Certainly, it appears to be the case that American-managed firms located in the United Kingdom, employing British labour belonging to British trade unions, earn a higher return upon their capital investment than do their British-owned competitors (24). Equally, there is evidence to suggest the converse; British-managed plants employing American labour in the United States also earn a lower rate of return upon capital than their immediate American-owned competitors. It is probably also the case that the restrictive practices of trade unions, reflected in overmanning in British industry, are conducive to a climate of opinion that resists innovation and change. Moreover, the pattern of wage negotiation and bargaining in Britain differs strikingly from the "key plant" bargaining characteristic of the United States. In the United Kingdom, wage and other negotiations are on an industry-wide basis which renders it more difficult for more progressive management to institute radical changes by striking a bargain with employees in return for higher wages.

Quite apart from the attitudes of labour and management, the degree of innovation and technical progress is doubtless linked to investment rates, which in turn probably respond to the pressure of demand. British industrial investment has been comparatively low in the post-war period, and one explanation commonly invoked is that management is unwilling to invest given uncertain demand conditions in the home market. The uncertainty of demand pressure, in this view, stems from the mistaken attempt (at least until 1967) to maintain an overvalued exchange rate for sterling, forcing the authorities to repeatedly invoke stop–go policies and deflate the economy in the face of an external payments crisis. At the same time, the overvaluation of the exchange rate has limited the incentive to move resources into the export sector which reinforces the underlying reason for the lack of investment – namely the external payments deficit at full-employment income levels. If this analysis is correct, it would suggest that the termination of sterling's role as a reserve currency would enhance the prospects of raising Britain's future growth rate.

2. Misallocation of Capital Investment

Although the investment record of British industry in the post-war period has been comparatively low, the overall investment – GNP ratio has not been unduly out of line with the experience of other relatively advanced economies such as the United States and Western Europe. There has been substantial investment in the public sector, especially in the nationalized industries. It is thus not the lack of capital formation that is responsible for Britain's comparatively disappointing performance. Consequently, the question is raised as to whether existing capital assets are used efficiently and whether new investment is being directed into the appropriate sectors. With regard to the first question, there are several studies (25) that point to the low productivity of capital employed in certain sectors of the economy when compared with overseas companies using virtually the identical equipment. Again, this would appear to spring from restrictive practices imposed by trade unions and condoned by management, as revealed in overmanning, but it also results from the fact that a good many capital assets are allowed to stand idle for considerable periods of times. Considerable opposition, upon the side of both labour and management, appears to exist with regard to multi-shift operations.

Turning to the issue of public sector investment, it is a fact that many of the nationalized industries were taken into public ownership essentially because they were experiencing secular decline in the wake of competition from newer products and services. They have been maintained for a host of reasons, partly out of consideration of the social costs associated with regional unemployment. Whilst a strong case can be made for their continued existence, it remains a fact that in many cases they possess relatively high capital–output ratios. Precisely the same point can be made in relation to public investment in newer industries such as aerospace industry. Whilst there may be some technological spin-offs that ultimately benefit other sectors of the economy, it none the less remains the case that the capital–output ratio is extraordinarily high. Few advocates of Concorde, for example, can be found who would base their case upon the potential earnings in relation to investment costs. Similar arguments can be applied to investment in education, health and the social services; it is not that these activities are undesired, but the fact remains that a large part of such total investment is possessed of relatively high capital–output ratios carrying implications for the overall growth rate.

The Allocation of Labour – Too Few Producers?

We have already indicated the importance of allocating labour to its most productive sector and have suggested that one source of economic growth is the transfer of labour from agriculture, characterized by diminishing returns, to the manufacturing sector, which enjoys increasing returns. This is the argument propounded by Kaldor (20); the force of it lies not just in a once-and-for-all increase in output per head but also in the associated productivity changes stemming from the raising of total output. It is beyond question that the ratio of agricultural income to total income is inversely correlated with the level of income *per capita*, and indeed such a ratio has been suggested as a possible index of economic development. It is then but a short step to Kaldor's pessimistic conclusion. Britain's comparative poor growth performance in recent years is a natural consequence of having exhausted the surplus reservoir of agricultural labour to draw upon. The British economy has "matured" and, having eliminated excess agricultural labour, has exhausted the potential for accelerated growth. Moreover, Britain must pay the penalty for being the first industrial nation, the potential for fast growth having been exhausted before it could attain exceptionally high levels of productivity *per capita* and hence real income *per capita*. If this thesis is accepted, and it has been the subject of some considerable dispute (26), then the policy conclusion that follows is obvious enough. The surplus labour required for expansion in the more productive manufacturing sector must be siphoned off from the service sectors. The latter, broadly characterized by relatively constant returns, must substitute for the traditional agricultural role. Hence the rationale for the former selective employment tax, imposed at positive rates upon services and applied negatively to manufacturing. The SET levy was thus an attempt to effect a shake-out of excess labour from the service sectors of the economy to provide the required manpower needed by the all-important growth (and export) manufacturing sectors.

More recently, a not too dissimilar argument has been advanced by Bacon and Eltis (27, 28, 25). In their view, Britain's current economic problems spring not from the lack of surplus agricultural labour, but rather from the transfer of industrial labour into the expansion of the public sector. The slow growth rate is a direct consequence of the process of de-industrialization. Adapting a distinction originally made by Johnston (29), they argue that the British economy is now structurally unbalanced with the industrial sectors producing marketable output suffering a relative decline *vis à vis* those sectors producing non-marketable goods and services. The comparative growth of the public sector is not of course unexpected or even undesired; indeed, to the extent that the public sector supplies goods that are fairly income-elastic – as for example educational services – then one might expect the public sector to grow fairly predictably in the course of economic development. Bacon and Eltis's argument is that this relative expansion of the public sector has proceeded at an unprecedented pace in Britain's case and has now reached a critical level of inbalance. In part, the blame lies in the relative ease of moving out of recession by stimulating central and local government employment. The labour thereby absorbed into the public sector was thus no longer available to British industry during the resulting upswing of the cycle, and this was contributing to the premature curbing of the boom. The rapid acceleration of public sector wages that occurred during the mid-1960s served to intensify the impact by increasing the tax burden generally but – in real terms – relatively upon the industrial sectors.

Fundamentally, it is the output of those sectors producing marketable commodities and services that has to provide a surplus – over and above the needs of those sectors – to finance the consumption and investment needs of the non-marketable sectors and also to provide the supply of net exports. If expansion of the public sector proceeds too far, the inevitable consequence is a fall either in the volume of exports or in the level of investment in the productive manufacturing sector. The force of the argument is compounded when productivity changes are taken into account because these will normally be more significant for those sectors producing marketable output. The evidence produced in support of this thesis is impressive. Bacon and Eltis contend that over the period 1961–73 the percentage growth rate of the non-industrial sector (excluding agriculture) in Britain was of the order of 32 per cent – approximately twice that of France and Germany and roughly three times that of Italy and the United States. Moreover, whilst the service sector can be productive and can generate export earnings, the bulk of the increase in services over this period was dominated by the public sector; local government employment increased by some 53.8 per cent, central government by 14.4 per cent, whilst other service sector employment experienced but a 7 per cent growth.

Although differences of opinion inevitably emerge as to the underlying reasons for Britain's slow growth rate, there appears to be a growing concensus that it does not lie in the rate of augmentation of factor inputs alone but rather in the manner in which such inputs are combined and allocated. This does not imply that an improved performance is relatively easy to effect; resistance to change, especially in the question of job reallocation, is extremely difficult to overcome. In addition, if the Bacon–Eltis thesis is correct, opposition to fundamental resource reallocation is likely to be strongest in those sectors most able to effect the required transfer – namely the upper echelons of central and local government service. Finally, the extent to which fundamental change can be affected depends in part upon the social history and attitudes of society and its institutions. For reasons that are deep-seated and long-standing, Britain has maintained a sense of class division more appropriate to the days of pre-war unemployment; capital and labour are viewed as competing forces in their claims upon national output rather than as co-operative inputs in the augmentation of that output.

Two final points may be noted. It would appear that Britain's growth prospects and performance have been virtually unaffected by Common Market membership. Whilst there were political arguments in favour of joining the EEC, the economic case was never very compelling (30). In particular, it would appear that the "growth through market size" argument, emphasizing the importance of economies of large-scale operation has been overstated. Secondly, the evidence of the post-war period does indicate a certain correlation between the increase in productivity and the increase in exports; in Britain's case, the comparative slow growth of productivity has been matched by the failure to significantly expand exports (31). One explanation for this phenomenon is simply that in the absence of export expansion significant growth of incomes is revealed in an increase of imports and eventual external payments deficit, forcing the adoption of deflationary policies. The repeated application of "stop–go" remedies must reduce the growth rate of income and presumably the incentive to invest. In terms of this analysis, therefore, perhaps the ultimate cause of slow growth in the United Kingdom has been an attempt to maintain an overvalued exchange rate for sterling and to preserve sterling as an international reserve currency. An overvalued exchange rate reduces the incentive to invest in the export sector and also minimizes the inflow of foreign capital seeking to invest in the economy generally. In consequence, and in terms of the vintage growth model, the export sector becomes relatively antiquated and inefficient, unable to compete in export markets, thus intensifying the overvaluation of the currency. The comparative experience of the United Kingdom, where the pound has most probably been overvalued in the post-war period, and that of Germany, where the Deutschmark has most probably been undervalued, is frequently invoked in support of this thesis. An interesting conclusion emerges from this analysis. Devaluation should not be looked upon as something able to effect a short-term improvement in the current account, for it does nothing to transform the underlying inefficiency of the export sector. Rather, the benefits of devaluation reveal themselves very gradually over time, and primarily upon the capital account of the balance of payments, as foreign investment in productive assets becomes relatively cheaper.

References

Chapter I

1 Kenneth J. Arrow *Social Choice and Individual Values* Wiley, New York, 1951

2 William S. Vickrey *Micro-Statics* Harcourt Brace & World, New York, 1964 pp. 272 ff.

3 Joan Robinson "Disguised Unemployment" *Economic Journal* June 1936

4 James Tobin "Inflation and Unemployment" *American Economic Review* March 1972

5 E. J. Mishan *The Costs of Economic Growth* Staples Press, London, 1967

6 Michael Lipton *Assessing Economic Performance* Staples Press, London, 1968

7 Cf. Francesco Forte and Harold M. Hochman "Monetary and Fiscal Policy: Ambiguities and Definitions" in Haller and Recktenwald (eds.), *Finanz- und Geld- Politik im Umbruch* Von Hase & Koehler, Mainz, 1969

8 A. W. Phillips "The Relation between Unemployment and the Rate of Change of Money Wage Rates in the United Kingdom, 1861-1957" *Economica* November 1958; reprinted in M. G. Mueller (ed.) *Readings in Macroeconomics* Holt, Rinehart & Winston Inc., New York, 1966 and in R. J. Ball and Peter Doyle (eds.) *Inflation – Selected Readings* Penguin Modern Economics, London, 1969

9 Ann Romanis Braun "Wages in the United Kingdom: Has There Been a Shift in the Phillips Curve?" *International Monetary Fund Staff Papers* March 1971

10 Charles L. Schultze "Has the Phillips Curve Shifted? Some Additional Evidence" *Brookings Papers on Economic Activity* No. 2, 1971

11 David E. W. Laidler "The Phillips Curve, Expectations and Incomes Policy" in *The Current Inflation* H. G. Johnson and A. R. Nobay (eds.) Macmillan, London, 1971

12 Sidney Weintraub *A General Theory of the Price Level* Chilton, Philadelphia, 1969

13 Henri Theil "On the Theory of Economic Policy" *American Economic Review* May 1956; *Economic Forecasts and Policy* North-Holland Publishing Co., Amsterdam, 1961; and "Linear Decision Rules for Macro-Dynamic Policy" in B. Hickman (ed.) *Quantitative Planning of Economic Policy* Brookings Institution, Washington, 1965

14 Jan Tinbergen *On the Theory of Economic Policy* North-Holland Publishing Co., Amsterdam, 1952

15 Cf. D. A. L. Auld "A Measure of Australian Fiscal Policy Performance, 1948-9 to 1963-4" *Economic Record* September 1967; and "Fiscal Policy Performance in Canada 1957-67" *Public Finance* No. 3, 1969

16 Cf. D. J. Smyth "The Measurement of Fiscal Performance" *Economic Record*, December 1968

17 R. G. Lipsey and J. M. Parkin "Incomes Policy: A Re-Appraisal" *Economica* May 1970

18 Kenneth F. Wallis "Wages, Prices and Incomes Policies: Some Comments" *Economica* August 1971

19 Leslie Godfrey "The Phillips Curve, Incomes Policy and Trade Union Effects" in *The Current Inflation* Harry G. Johnson and A. R. Nobay (eds.) Macmillan, London, 1971

Chapter II

1 Edmund S. Phelps *et al Microeconomic Foundations of Employment and Inflation Theory* W. W. Norton & Co., New York, 1970
2 R. W. Clower "The Keynesian Counterrevolution: A Theoretical Appraisal" in F. H. Hahn and F. P. R. Brechling (eds.) *The Theory of Interest Rates* I.E.A. London, 1965
3 Axel Leijonhufvud *On Keynesian Economics and the Economics of Keynes* Oxford University Press, London, 1968
4 R. L. Crouch *Macroeconomics* Harcourt Brace Jovanovich Inc., New York, 1972
5 Maurice Peston "The Micro-economics of the Phillips Curve" in Harry G. Johnson & A. R. Nobay (eds.) *The Current Inflation* Macmillan, London, 1971
6 M. L. Truu "On the Micro-Economics of 'Stagflation' " *South African Journal of Economics* September 1971
7 Gosta Edgren, Karl-Olaf Faxen & Clas Erik Odhner "Wages Growth and Distribution of Income" *Swedish Journal of Economics* 1969, pp. 133-160
8 T. Balogh *Labour and Inflation* Fabian Tract 403, London, 1970

Chapter III

1 Milton Friedman and Walter W. Heller *Monetary versus Fiscal Policy: A Dialogue* Norton & Co., New York, 1969, pp. 46 and 50
2 E. Cannan (ed.) "The Report of the Bullion Committee 1810" in *The Paper Pound* London, 1920
3 Irving Fisher *The Purchasing Power of Money* revised edition 1922, Augustus M. Kelly, New York, 1963
4 J. M. Keynes *A Tract on Monetary Reform* Macmillan, London, 1923
5 Don Patinkin *Money, Interest and Prices* second edition, Harper & Row, New York, 1965
6 D. H. Robertson *Money* Pitman & Co., London, 1922
7 G. C. Archibald and R. G. Lipsey "Monetary and Value Theory" *Review of Economic Studies* October 1958
8 Milton Friedman "The Optimum Quantity of Money" in *The Optimum Quantity of Money and Other Essays* Macmillan, London, 1969
9 Warren L. Smith "On Some Current Issues in Monetary Economics: An Interpretation" *Journal of Economic Literature* September 1970
10 J. M. Keynes *A Treatise on Money* Macmillan, London, 1930
11 J. M. Keynes *The General Theory of Employment, Interest and Money* Macmillan, London, 1936
12 Milton Friedman "The Quantity Theory of Money: A Restatement" in Friedman (ed.) *Studies in the Quantity Theory of Money* University of Chicago Press, Chicago, 1956
13 Don Patinkin "The Chicago Tradition, the Quantity Theory and Friedman" *Journal of Money, Credit and Banking* February, 1969
14 Milton Friedman (ed.) *Studies in the Quantity Theory of Money* University of Chicago Press, Chicago, 1956
15 Cf. Stephanie K. Edge "The Relative Stability of Monetary Velocity and the Investment Multiplier" *Australian Economic Papers* December 1967

16 Milton Friedman "Money: Quantity Theory" *The International Encyclopaedia of the Social Sciences* Vol. 10, 1968, p. 434
17 David E. W. Laidler *The Demand for Money: Theories and Evidence* International Text Book Co., Scranton, Pennsylvania, 1969
18 Nicholas Kaldor "The New Monetarism" *Lloyds Bank Review*, July 1970
19 C. A. E. Goodhart "The Importance of Money" *Bank of England Quarterly Bulletin* June 1970
20 A. A. Walters *Money in Boom and Slump* Hobart Paper 44, Institute of Economic Affairs, London, 1969
21 A. D. Bain *The Control of the Money Supply* Penguin Modern Economics, London, 1970
22 C. A. Sims "Money, Income and Causality" *American Economic Review* September 1972
23 W. Baumol "The Transactions Demand for Cash: An Inventory Theoretic Approach." *Quarterly Journal of Economics* Vol. 66 No. 4, 1952
24 J. Tobin "Liquidity Preference as Behaviour Towards Risk" *Review of Economic Studies* February 1958
25 J. Tobin "Money, Capital and other Stores of Value" *American Economic Review* Vol. 51, 1961; reprinted in J. Tobin *Essays in Economics* Vol. I, North Holland, Amsterdam, 1971
26 J. Tobin "An Essay on the Principles of Debt Management" in *Fiscal and Debt Management Policies* Commission on Money and Credit, Prentice-Hall, Englewood Cliffs, N. J.; reprinted in J. Tobin *Essays in Economics* Vol. II, North Holland, Amsterdam, 1971

Chapter IV

1 Axel Leijonhufvud *On Keynesian Economics and the Economics of Keynes* Oxford University Press, London 1968
2 Milton Friedman "A Theoretical Framework for Monetary Analysis" *Journal of Political Economy* March/April 1970
3 Milton Friedman and Anna Schwartz "Money and Business Cycles," *Review of Economics and Statistics* Supplement, February 1963
4 Nicholas Kaldor "The New Monetarism" *Lloyds Bank Review*, July 1970
5 Leonall C. Andersen and Jerry L. Jordan "Monetary and Fiscal Actions: A Test of their Relative Importance in Economic Stabilization" *Review of the Federal Reserve Bank of St. Louis*, November 1968
6 Frank De Leeuw and John Kalchbrenner "Monetary and Fiscal Actions: A Test of their Relative Importance in Economic Stabilization – Comment" *Review of the Federal Reserve Bank of St. Louis* April 1969. This issue also contains a reply by Andersen and Jordan.
7 J. Helliwell, H. Shapiro, G. Sparks and A. Walters "The Money Supply is Alive and Well and Living in St. Louis" mimeo, Bank of Canada, Research Department Branch
8 M. J. Artis and A. R. Nobay "Two Aspects of the Monetary Debate" *National Institute Economic Review*, August 1969
9 Committee on the Working of the Monetary System *Report* Cmnd 827, H.M.S.O., London, 1959: The Radcliffe Report
10 Milton Friedman "The Role of Monetary Policy" *American Economic Review*, March 1968

11 R. M. Solow *Price Expectations and the Behaviour of the Price Level* Manchester University Press, Manchester, 1969
12 David Laidler Discussion Paper on H. G. Johnson's "Recent Developments in Monetary Theory" in David R. Croome and Harry G. Johnson (eds.) *Money in Britain 1959-1969* Oxford University Press, London, 1970
13 David E. W. Laidler "The Phillips Curve, Expectations and Incomes Policy" in *The Current Inflation* H. G. Johnson and A. R. Nobay (eds.) Macmillan, London, 1971
14 Council of Economic Advisers *Economic Report of the President 1972* U.S. Government Printing Office, Washington, 1972
15 P. G. Cox "The Identification of Money" *Journal of Economic Studies* December 1968
16 R. S. Sayers "Monetary Thought and Monetary Policy in England" *Economic Journal* December 1960
17 W. T. Newlyn "The Supply of Money and its Control" *Economic Journal* June 1964
18 Central Statistical Office "A Note on Definitions of the Money Supply" *Economic Trends*, August 1970
19 H.M. Treasury "Money Supply and Domestic Credit" *Economic Trends*, May 1969
20 "Domestic Credit Expansion" *Bank of England Quarterly Bulletin* Supplement to September Issue 1969
21 J. J. Polak "Monetary Analysis of Income Formation and Payments Problems" *International Monetary Fund Staff Papers* November 1957
22 J. J. Polak and L. Boissoneault "Monetary Analysis of Income and Imports and its Statistical Operation" *International Monetary Fund Staff Papers*, April 1960
23 H. G. Johnson "The Monetary Approach to Balance of Payments Theory" in H. G. Johnson, *Further Essays in Monetary Economics* George Allen & Unwin, London, 1972
24 H. G. Johnson "Money and the Balance of Payments" *Banca Nazionale del Lavoro Quarterly Review*, March 1976

Chapter V

1 J. M. Keynes *The General Theory of Employment, Interest and Money* Macmillan, London, 1936, pp. 242-243
2 G. L. S. Shackle *The Years of High Theory: Invention and Tradition in Economic Thought 1926–1939* Cambridge University Press, 1967, Chap. 13
3 T. Wilson and P. W. S. Andrews (eds.) *Oxford Studies in the Price Mechanism* Oxford University Press, London, 1951
4 J. F. Ebersole "The Influence of Interest Rates upon Entrepreneurial Decisions in Business – A Case Study" *Harvard Business Review*, Autumn 1938
5 W. H. White "Interest Inelasticity of Investment Demand: The Case from Business Attitude Surveys Re-examined" *American Economic Review*, September 1956
6 Committee on the Working of the Monetary System *Report* Cmnd 827, H.M.S.O., London 1959: The Radcliffe Report
7 J. M. Keynes *How to Pay for the War* Macmillan, London and Harcourt Brace, New York 1940

8 Eugene A. Birnbaum "The Growth of Financial Intermediaries as a Factor in the Effectiveness of Monetary Policy" *International Monetary Fund Staff Papers*, November 1957
9 Warren L. Smith "On the Effectiveness of Monetary Policy" *American Economic Review*, September 1956
10 J. G. Gurley "The Radcliffe Report and Evidence" *American Economic Review*, September 1960
11 A. A. Walters "The Radcliffe Report – Ten Years After; a Survey of Empirical Evidence" in Croome and Johnson (eds.) *Money in Britain 1959–1969* Oxford University Press, London, 1970
12 J. G. Gurley and E. S. Shaw "Financial Aspects of Economic Development" *American Economic Review*, September 1955
13 H. P. Minsky "Central Banking and Money Market Changes" *Quarterly Journal of Economics*, May 1957
14 Warren L. Smith "Financial Intermediaries and Monetary Controls" *Quarterly Journal of Economics*, November 1959
15 N. J. Gibson *Financial Intermediaries and Monetary Policy* Hobart Paper No. 39, Institute of Economic Affairs, London, 2nd Edition 1970
16 A. D. Bain *The Control of the Money Supply* Penguin Modern Economics, London, 1970, pp. 129-136
17 J. K. Galbraith "Market Structure and Stabilization Policy" *Review of Economics and Statistics*, May 1957
18 Victor Argy "The Impact of Monetary Policy on Expenditure with Particular Reference to the United Kingdom", *International Monetary Fund Staff Papers*, November 1969, p. 463
19 Michael J. Hamburger "Interest Rates and the Demand for Consumer Durables" *American Economic Review*, December 1967
20 Colin Wright "Some Evidence on the Interest Elasticity of Consumption" *American Economic Review*, September 1967
21 Thomas Mayer *Monetary Policy in the United States* Random House, New York 1968, p. 119
22 John Kareken and R. M. Solow "Lags in Monetary Policy" in *Stabilization Policies* published for the Commission of Money and Credit, Prentice-Hall, New York, 1963
23 Milton Friedman "The Lag in Effect of Monetary Policy" *Journal of Political Economy*, October 1961
24 Milton Friedman "Note on the Lag in Effect of Monetary Policy" *American Economic Review*, September 1964
25 Victor Argy "The Lags in Monetary Policy: An Assessment of Alternative Approaches" *Banca Nazionale del Lavoro Quarterly Review*, Rome 1965
26 Thomas Mayer "The Lag in the Effect of Monetary Policy: Some Criticisms" *Western Economic Journal* September 1965
27 W. H. White "The Timelessness of the Effects of Monetary Policy. The New Evidence from Econometric Models" *Banca Nazionale del Lavoro Quarterly Review*, September 1968
28 J. Ernest Tanner "Lags in the Effects of Monetary Policy: A Statistical Investigation" *American Economic Review*, December 1969
29 Victoria Chick *The Theory of Monetary Policy* Gray-Mills, London, 1973
30 R. G. Davis "How Much Does Money Matter?" *Federal Reserve Bank of New York Monthly Review*, April 1969
31 J. Tobin "An Essay on the Principles of Debt Management" in *Fiscal and Debt Management Policies* Commission on Money and Credit, Prentice-Hall, Englewood Cliffs, N.J., reprinted in J. Tobin *Essays in Economics* Vol. II, North Holland Amsterdam, 1971

Chapter VI

1 D. J. Smyth "Can Automatic Stabilizers be Destabilizing?" *Public Finance* Nos. 3–4, 1963
2 G. C. Archibald and Richard G. Lipsey *An Introduction to a Mathematical Treatment of Economics* Weidenfeld & Nicolson, London, 1967, pp. 140ff
3 E. Cary Brown "The Static Theory of Automatic Fiscal Stabilization" *Journal of Political Economy*, October 1955
4 Wilfred Lewis Jnr. *Federal Fiscal Policy in the Post War Recessions* The Brookings Institution, Washington, 1962
5 G. Hauser and P. Burrows *The Economics of Unemployment Insurance* Allen and Unwin, London, 1969
6 A. P. Thirwell "Unemployment Compensation as an Automatic Stabilizer" *Bulletin of the Oxford University Institute of Economics and Statistics*, Oxford, February 1969
7 R. A. Musgrave and M. H. Miller "Built in Flexibility" *American Economic Review* March 1948; reprinted in *American Economic Association Readings in Fiscal Policy* Richard D. Irwin Inc., Homewood Illinois, 1955
8 R. A. Musgrave *The Theory of Public Finance* McGraw-Hill, New York, 1959, pp. 520 ff.
9 M. J. Bailey *National Income and the Price Level* McGraw-Hill, New York, 1962
10 Carl S. Shoup *Public Finance* Weidenfeld & Nicolson, London, 1969, Chap. 22 and Appendix A.
11 A. T. Peacock "The Multiplier and the Valuation of Government Expenditures" in *Finanzarchiv*, Band 30, Heft 3, 1972
12 Milton Friedman *A Theory of the Consumption Function* Princeton University Press, New Jersey, 1957
13 A. T. Peacock & G. K. Shaw *The Economic Theory of Fiscal Policy* Allen and Unwin, London, 1971, Ch. 2
14 G. K. Shaw *Fiscal Policy* Macmillan Studies in Economics, Macmillan, London, 1972, pp. 63 ff
15 R. Eisner "Fiscal and Monetary Policy Reconsidered" *American Economic Review* December 1969
16 W. L. Smith "Monetary-Fiscal Policy and Economic Growth" *Quarterly Journal of Economics* February 1957
17 E. Cary Brown "Analysis of Consumption Taxes in Terms of the Theory of Income Determination" *American Economic Review* March 1950
18 A. T. Peacock and J. Williamson "Consumption Taxes and Compensatory Finance" *Economic Journal*, March 1967
19 B. A. Forster and G. K. Shaw "The Tax Mix and Aggregate Demand: A Respecification" *Public Finance* No. 2 1976.
20 Carl S. Shoup *Public Finance* Weidenfeld and Nicolson, London, 1969, Chaps. 9 and 16
21 Marian Krzyaniak and R. A. Musgrave *The Shifting of Corporate Income Tax* John Hopkins, Baltimore, 1963
22 J. C. R. Dow *Management of the British Economy* Cambridge University Press, 1964, published for the National Institute of Economic and Social Research
23 W. J. Baumol "Pitfalls in Contracyclical Policies: Some Tools and Results" *Review of Economics and Statistics* February 1961
24 Paul A. Samuelson "Interactions Between the Multiplier Analysis and the Principle of Acceleration" *Review of Economic Statistics* May 1939
25 A. T. Peacock and G. K. Shaw *The Economic Theory of Fiscal Policy* Allen and Unwin, London, 1971, pp. 119-125

26 A. R. Prest "Sense and Nonesense in Budgetary Policy" *Economic Journal* March 1968
27 R. A. Musgrave and P. Musgrave "Short-Run Aspects of Fiscal Policy" in R. E. Caves *et al.*, *Britain's Economic Prospects* Brookings Institution, Washington, 1965
28 G. D. N. Worswick "Fiscal Policy and Stabilization in Britain" *Journal of Money Credit and Banking* August 1969
29 J. A. Bristow "Taxation and Income Stabilization" *Economic Journal* June 1968
30 B. Hansen (assisted by W. W. Snyder) *Fiscal Policies in Seven Countries* 1955-65 O.E.C.D. Paris, 1969
31 W. W. Snyder "Measuring Economic Stabilization 1955-65" *American Economic Review* December 1968
32 E. Morss and A. T. Peacock "Measuring the Economic Impact of the Budget in Developing Countries" in A. T. Peacock (ed.) *Quantitative Analysis in Public Finance* Praeger, New York, 1969
33 J. Lotz "Techniques of Measuring the Effects of Fiscal Policy" in O.E.C.D. *Economic Outlook Occasional Studies* July 1971
34 R. C. O. Matthews "Why has Britain had Full Employment Since the War?" *Economic Journal*, September 1968
35 Walter Eltis "The Failure of the Keynesian Conventional Wisdom" *Lloyds Bank Review*, October 1976
36 Wynne Godley "What Britain Needs is Growth – but it must be the right kind" *The Times*, 1 November 1976
37 R. G. Lipsey "The Foundations of the Theory of National Income: An Analysis of some Fundamental Errors" in Maurice Peston and Bernard Corry (eds). *Essays in Honour of Lord Robbins* Weidenfeld and Nicolson, London, 1972.

Chapter VII

1 D. M. McDougall and T. E. Dernburg *Macro-Economics* McGraw-Hill, New York, 4th Ed. 1972 Part II
2 Joseph P. McKenna *Aggregate Economic Analysis* Holt, Rinehart & Winston, New York, 3rd Edition 1969, Chap. 9 ff
3 Edward Shapiro *Macro-Economic Analysis* Harcourt, Brace and World, New York 2nd Edition 1970, Chap. 19 ff.
4 David E. W. Laidler *The Demand for Money: Theories and Evidence*, International Textbook Co., Scranton, Pennsylvania, 1969, Chap. 1
5 Milton Friedman "Comments on The Critics" *Journal of Political Economy* Sept./Oct. 1972
6 Milton Friedman "A Monetary Theory of Nominal Income" *Journal of Political Economy* March/April 1971
7 Milton Friedman "A Theoretical Framework for Monetary Analysis" *Journal of Political Economy* March/April 1970
8 Karl Brunner & Allan H. Metzler "Friedman's Monetary Theory" *Journal of Political Economy* Sept./Oct. 1972
9 James Tobin "Friedman's Theoretical Framework" *ibid.*
10 Paul Davidson "A Keynesian View of Friedman's Theoretical Framework for Monetary Analysis" *ibid.*
11 Don Patinkin "Friedman on The Quantity Theory and Keynesian Economics" *ibid.*

12 J. M. Holmes & D. J. Smyth "The Specification of The Demand for Money and the Tax Multiplier" *Journal of Political Economy* Jan./Feb. 1972
13 Alan Peacock and G. K. Shaw *The Economic Theory of Fiscal Policy* Allen and Unwin, London, 1971, Chap. 3
14 Dwayne Wrightsman "IS, LM, and External Equilibrium: A Graphical Analysis" *American Economic Review*, March 1970
15 Francesco Forte "Towards a European Currency" *Sir Ellis Hunter Memorial Lecture No. 5*, University of York, 1970
16 R. A. Mundell "The Appropriate Use of Monetary and Fiscal Policy for Internal and External Stability" *International Monetary Fund Staff Papers*, March 1962; reprinted in Lindauer (ed.) *Macroeconomic Readings* The Free Press, New York, 1968
17 R. A. Mundell "The Monetary Dynamics of International Adjustment under Fixed and Flexible Exchange Rates" *Quarterly Journal of Economics* 1960
18 J. H. Williamson "On The Normative Theory of Balance-of-Payments Adjustment" in *Monetary Theory and Monetary Policy in the 1970's* G. Clayton, J. C. Gilbert & R. Sedwick (eds.) Oxford University Press, London, 1971
19 G. K. Shaw "Monetary-Fiscal Policy for Growth and the Balance-of-Payments Constraint" *Economica* May 1967; reprinted in N. F. Keiser (ed.) *Readings in Macroeconomics* Prentice-Hall, New York, 1970
20 Thomas, F. Dernburg & Duncan M. McDougall *Macroeconomics* 4th Edition McGraw-Hill, New York, 1972, p. 302ff
21 William L. Silber "Monetary Policy Effectiveness: The Case of A Positively Sloped IS Curve" *Journal of Finance* December 1971
22 R. A. Mundell "The Monetary Dynamics of International Adjustment Under Fixed and Flexible Exchange Rates" *Quarterly Journal of Economics*, May 1960
23 R. A. Mundell "Capital Mobility and Stabilization Policy Under Fixed and Flexible Exchange Rates" *Canadian Journal of Economics*, November 1963
24 H. G. Johnson "Some Aspects of a Theory of Economic Policy in a World of Capital Mobility" in T. Bagiotti (ed.) *Essays in Honour of Marco Fanno* CEDAM, Padova, 1966; reprinted in *Further Essays in Monetary Economics* George Allen & Unwin, London, 1972
25 Akira Takayama "The Effects of Fiscal and Monetary Policies under Flexible and Fixed Exchange Rates" *Canadian Journal of Economics*, May 1969
26 Victor Argy and M. G. Porter "The Forward Exchange Market and the Effects of Domestic and External Disturbance under Alternative Exchange Rate Systems" *IMF Staff Papers*, November 1972

Chapter VIII

1 A. Blinder and R. M. Solow "Does Fiscal Policy Matter?" *Journal of Public Economics* November 1973
2 C. F. Christ "A Simple Macro-economic Model with a Government Budget Constraint" *Journal of Political Economy* January/February 1968
3 C. F. Christ 'A Model of Monetary and Fiscal Policy Effects on the Money Stock, Price Level and Real Output" *Journal of Money Credit and Banking*, November 1969
4 B. Hansen "On the Effects of Fiscal and Monetary Policy: A Taxonomic Discussion" *American Economic Review*, September 1973

5 D. J. Ott and A. F. Ott "Budget Balance and Equilibrium Income" *Journal of Finance*, March 1965

6 W. M. Scarth "Fiscal Policy and the Government Budget Restraint under Alternative Exchange-Rate Systems" *Oxford Economic Papers*, March 1975

7 W. L. Silber "Fiscal Policy in IS–LM Analysis: A Correction" *Journal of Money, Credit and Banking*, November 1970

8 F. G. Steindl "Money and Income: The View from the Government Budget Restraint" *Journal of Finance*, September 1974

9 R. J. Barro "Are Government Bonds Net Wealth?" *Journal of Political Economy*, November/December 1974

Chapter IX

1 E. J. Mishan *The Costs of Economic Growth* Staples Press, London, 1967

2 R. F. Harrod "An Essay in Dynamic Theory" *Economic Journal*, March 1939

3 E. D. Domar "Capital Expansion, Rate of Growth and Employment" *American Economic Review*, March 1947

4 R. S. Solow "A Contribution to the Theory of Economic Growth", *Quarterly Journal of Economics*, February 1956

5 T. Swan "Economic Growth and Capital Accumulation" *Economic Record*, November 1956

6 D. Levhari and D. Patinkin "The Role of Money in a Simple Growth Model" *American Economic Review*, September 1968

7 C. W. Cobb and P. H. Douglas "A Theory of Production" *American Economic Review*, March 1928

8 P. H. Douglas "The Cobb–Douglas Production Function Once Again: Its History, Its Testing and Some Empirical Values" *Journal of Political Economy*, October 1976

9 G. C. Archibald and R. G. Lipsey *An Introduction to a Mathematical Treatment of Economics* 2nd edn, Weidenfeld and Nicolson London, 1973

10 T. P. Hill "Growth and Investment According to International Comparisons" *Economic Journal*, June 1964

11 H. G. Johnson "The Neoclassical One-Sector Growth Model: A Geometrical Exposition and Extension to a Monetary Economy" *Economica*, August 1966

12 A. T. Peacock and G. K. Shaw *The Economic Theory of Fiscal Policy* 2nd edn, Allen & Unwin, London, 1976, Ch. V

13 E. S. Phelps "The Golden Rule of Accumulation" *American Economic Review*, September 1961

14 E. S. Phelps "Second Essay on the Golden Rule of Accumulation" *American Economic Review*, February 1965

15 R. M. Solow "Technical Change and the Aggregate Production Function" *Review of Economics and Statistics*, August 1957

16 R. M. Solow "Technical Progress, Capital Formation and Economic Growth" *American Economic Review*, May 1962

17 A. Cairncross *Inflation, Growth and International Finance* George Allen & Unwin, London, 1975

18 C. S. Shoup "Production from Consumption" *Public Finance*, Nos. 3–4, 1965

19 W. A. Lewis "Economic Development with Unlimited Supplies of Labour" *The Manchester School*, May 1954

20 N. Kaldor *Causes of the Slow Rate of Economic Growth of the United Kingdom* Cambridge University Press, 1966
21 E. F. Denison *Why Growth Rates Differ: Postwar Experience In Nine Western Countries* Brookings Institution, Washington, 1967
22 R. E. Caves *Britains Economic Prospects* Brookings Institution, Washington, 1968; George Allen & Unwin, London, 1968
23 O. Aukrust "Factors in Economic Development: A Review of Recent Research" *Weltwirtschaftliches Archiv*, Band 93, No. 1, 1964
24 J. H. Dunning "U.S. Subsidiaries in Britain and their U.K. Competitors" *Business Ratios*, Autumn 1966
25 R. Bacon and W. Eltis *Britain's Economic Problems: Too Few Producers* Macmillan, London, 1976
26 R. E. Rowthorn "What remains of Kaldor's Law?" *Economic Journal*, March 1975
27 R. Bacon and W. Eltis "How We Went Wrong" *Sunday Times*, 2 November 1975
28 R. Bacon and W. Eltis "The Chances We Missed" *Sunday Times*, 9 November 1975
29 J. Johnston "A Macro-Model of Inflation" *Economic Journal*, June 1975
30 D. MacDougall *Studies in Political Economy* Vol. I, Macmillan, London, 1975
31 W. Beckerman *et al.*, *The British Economy in 1975* Cambridge University Press 1965.

Suggestions for Further Reading

The following additional references and sources not specifically mentioned in the text may serve as suggestions for further reading. The numbers in parentheses indicate the chapters to which they have the most relevance.

Anderson, Leonall & Carlson, Keith, "A Monetarist Model for Economic Stabilization", *Federal Reserve Bank of Saint Louis Review*, April 1970 (3, 4, 5)

Argy, Victor, "The Role of Money in Economic Activity: Some Results for 17 Developed Countries", *IMF Staff Papers*, Nov. 1970 (3, 4, 5)

Auld, D.A.L., "Wages, Prices and a Progressive Personal Income Tax", *Economic Studies*, Dec. 1970 (2, 6)

Bacon, R.W., & Eltis, W.A., "Stop-Go and De-Industrialization", *National Westminster Bank Review*, Nov. 1975 (9)

Bailey, Martin J., "The Optimal Full Employment Surplus", *Journal of Political Economy*, July/Aug. 1972 (6)

Ball, R.J., & Burns, T., "The Inflationary Mechanism in the U.K. Economy", *American Economic Review*, Sept. 1976 (4, 5)

Ball, R.J., Burns, T., & Laury, J.S.E., "The Role of Exchange Rate Changes in Balance of Payments Adjustment: The United Kingdom Case", *Economic Journal*, March 1977 (7, 9)

Barro, R.J., & Fischer, S., "Recent Developments in Monetary Theory", *Journal of Monetary Economics*, April 1976 (3, 4, 5, 8)

Blinder, A.S., & Goldfeld, S.M., "New Measures of Fiscal and Monetary Policy 1958–1973", *American Economic Review*, Dec. 1976 (6, 7, 8)

Blinder, A.S., & Solow, R.M., "Does Fiscal Policy Still Matter? Reply", *Journal of Monetary Economics*, Nov. 1976 (6, 7, 8)

Blomqvist, A.G., "Monetary and Fiscal Policy Under Fixed Exchange Rates: Reply and some Further Results", *The Scandinavian Journal of Economics*, Vol. 78, No. 4. 1976 (7)

Brittain, Samuel & Lilley, Peter, *The Delusion of Incomes Policy*, M. Temple Smith, London 1977 (1, 4)

Brothwell, J.F., "A Simple Keynesian's Response to Leijonhufvud", *Bulletin of Economic Research*, May 1975 (2)

Brunner, Karl & Meltzer, A.H., "Mr. Hicks and the Monetarists", *Economica*, Feb. 1973 (2, 3, 8)

Burrows, P., "The Upward Sloping IS Curve and the Control of Income and the Balance of Payments", *Journal of Finance*, March 1974 (7)

Cagan, P., & Schwartz, Anna J., "Has the Growth of Money Substitutes Hindered Monetary Policy?", *Journal of Money, Credit and Banking*, May 1975 (5)

Carlson, K.M., & Spencer, R.W., "Crowding Out and Its Critics", *Federal Reserve Bulletin of St. Louis*, Dec. 1975 (8)

Chang, Winston & Smyth, David J., "Stability and Instability of IS-LM Equilibrium", *Oxford Economic Papers*, Nov. 1972 (7)

Cobham, D.P., "The Debate Over the Letter of Intent", *The Banker*, Feb. 1977 (5)

Coddington, Alan, "The Keynesian Economics: The Search for First Principles", *Journal of Economic Literature*, Dec. 1976 (2)

Cramp, A.B., "Does Money Matter?", *Lloyds Bank Review*, Oct. 1970 (3, 4, 5)

Cripps, Francis & Godley, Wynne, "A Formal Analysis of the Cambridge Economic Policy Group Model", *Economica*, Nov. 1976 (6)

Crouch, R.L., "Special Deposits and the British Monetary Mechanism", *Journal of Economic Studies*, Dec. 1970 (5)

Currie, D.A., "Optimal Stabilization Policies and the Government Budget Constraint", *Economica*, May 1976 (7, 8)

S. Weintraub & P. Davidson, "Money as Cause and Effect", *Economic Journal*, Dec. 1973

Eckstein, Otto & Feldstein, Martin, "The Fundamental Determinants of Interest Rates", *Review of Economics and Statistics*, Nov. 1970 (5)

Eilbott, P., "The Effectiveness of Automatic Stabilizers", *American Economic Review*, June 1966 (6)

Eisner, R., "What Went Wrong?", *Journal of Political Economy*, May/June 1971 (5, 6, 7)

Eltis, Walter, "The Keynesian Conventional Wisdom", *Lloyds Bank Review*, July 1977 (5, 6, 7, 8)

Fand, David I., "CROS Theory of Inflation", *Financial Analsts Journal*, July-August 1969 (6, 7)

Fleming, M., *Monetary Theory*, The Macmillan Press Ltd., London 1972 (3)

Fried, Joel, "Inflation–Unemployment Trade-Offs Under Fixed and Floating Exchange Rates", *Journal of Political Economy*, Jan/Feb 1973 (7)

Friedlaender, Ann F., "Macro-Policy Goals in the Post-War Period: A Study in Revealed Preference", *Quarterly Journal of Economics*, Feb. 1973 (1)

Friedman, Benjamin M., "Even the St. Louis Model Now Believes in Fiscal Policy", *Journal of Money, Credit and Banking*, May 1977 (4)

Friedman, Milton, "Inflation and Unemployment", (Nobel Lecture), *Journal of Political Economy*, June 1977 (3, 4)

Friedman, Milton, *The Counter Revolution in Monetary Theory*. Occasional Paper No. 33, IEA London 1970 (3)

Goldstein, Morris, "The Trade-Off Between Inflation and Unemployment: A Survey of the Econometric Evidence of Selected Countries", *IMF Staff Fund Papers*, Nov. 1972 (1, 4)

Gordon, R.J., "Recent Developments in the Theory of Inflation and Unemployment", *Journal of Monetary Economics*, April 1976 (3, 4, 5)

Gramlich, Edward M., "The Usefulness of Monetary and Fiscal Policy as Discretionary Stabilization Tools", *Journal of Money, Credit and Banking*, May 1971 (5, 6, 7, 8)

Grossman, Herschel I., "Aggregate Demand, Job Search and Employment", *Journal of Political Economy*, Nov./Dec. 1973 (2)

Grossman, Herschel I., "Tobin on Macro-Economics: A Review Article", *Journal of Political Economy*, Aug. 1975 (3)

Grossman, H.G., "Was Keynes a Keynesian?", *Journal of Economic Literature*, Sept. 1972 (2)

Hahn, F.H., "Professor Friedman's Views on Money", *Economica*, Feb. 1971 (3)

Hall, Robert E., "Prospects for Shifting the Phillips Curve Through Manpower Policy", *Brookings Papers on Economic Activity*, No. 3 1971 (1, 4)

Helliwell, J.F., "Monetary and Fiscal Policies for an Open Economy", *Oxford Economic Papers*, March 1961 (7)

Hicks, John, "Must Stimulating Demand Stimulate Inflation?", *Economic Record*, Dec. 1976 (4, 8)

Hicks, John, "The Mainspring of Economic Growth", (Nobel Lecture) *Swedish Journal of Economics*, Vol. 75. 1973 (9)

Hindley, B., & Perlman, M., "The Pigou Effect: An Elaboration", *Journal of Monetary Economics*, July 1976 (2)

Hines, A.G., *On the Reappraisal of Keynesian Economics*, Martin Robertson and Co. Ltd., London 1971 (2)

Howitt, P.W., "Stability and the Quantity Theory", *Journal of Political Economy*, Jan/Feb. 1974 (3)

Hynes, J. Allan, "On the Theory of Real Balance Effects", *Journal of Money Credit and Banking*, Feb. 1974 (3)

Infante, E.F., & Stein, J.L., "Does Fiscal Policy Matter?", *Journal of Monetary Economics*, Nov. 1976 (8)

Jackman, R., "Keynes and Leijonhufvud", *Oxford Economic Papers*, July 1974 (2)

Johnson, Harry G., "The Keynesian Revolution and the Monetarist Counter-Revolution", *American Economic Review*, May 1971 (3, 4)

Johnson, Harry G., "A Monetary Approach to Balance of Payments Theory: A Diagrammatic Analysis", *The Manchester School*, Sept. 1975 (4)

Kahn, R., "Mr. Eltis and the Keynesians", *Lloyds Bank Review*, April 1976 (6)

Kaldor, N., "Conflicts in National Economic Objectives", *Economic Journal*, March 1971 (1)

Kaldor, N., "Inflation and Recession in the World Economy", *Economic Journal*, Dec. 1976 (1, 9)

Kenen, Peter, B., "The Balance of Payments and Policy Mix Simulations Based on a U.S. Model", *Journal of Finance*, May 1974 (7)

Keran, Michael, "Monetary and Fiscal Influences on Economic Activity–The Historical Evidence", *Federal Reserve Bank of St. Louis Review*, Nov. 1969 (4)

Kern, D., "The Implications of D.C.E.", *National Westminster Bank Quarterly Review*, Nov. 1970 (5)

Laidler, David, "Simultaneous Fluctuations in Prices and Output: A Business Cycle Approach", *Economica*, Feb. 1973 (3, 4)

Laidler, David, "Inflation in Britain: A Monetarist Perspective", *American Economic Review*, Sept. 1976 (3, 4, 5)

Laidler, David & Parkin, J.M., "Inflation–A Survey", *Economic Journal* December 1975 (3, 4, 5, 8)

Leijonhufvud, Axel, *Keynes and the Classics*, Occasional Paper No. 30 IEA, London 1969 (2)

Levi, M.D., "Effectiveness of Monetary vs. Fiscal Policy as Revealed by the Behaviour of Inventory Stocks: An Empirical Investigation", *Journal of Monetary Economics*, April 1975 (4, 8)

Malinvaud, Edmond, *The Theory of Unemployment Reconsidered*, Basil Blackwell, Oxford, 1977 (2)

McGrath, Brian, "Implications of the Government Budget Constraint", *Journal of Money, Credit and Banking*, May 1977 (8)

Meyer, L.H., "Wealth Effects and the Effectiveness of Monetary and Fiscal Policies", *Journal of Money, Credit and Banking*, Nov. 1974 (8)

Meyer, L.H., "The Balance Sheet Identity, The Government Financing Constraint and the Crowding-Out Effect", *Journal of Monetary Economics*, Jan. 1975 (8)

Meyer, L.H., & Hart, W.R., "On the Effects of Fiscal and Monetary Policy: Completing the Taxonomy", *American Economic Review*, Sept. 1975 (8)

Miller, M.H., "Can A Rise in Import Prices be Inflationary and Deflationary?", *American Economic Review*, Sept. 1976 (4)

Millward, R., "Price Restraint, Anti-Inflation Policy and Public and Private Industry in the United Kingdom, 1949–73", *Economic Journal*, June 1976 (1, 4)

Modigliani, F., "The Monetarist Controversy or Should We Forsake Stabilization Policies?", *American Economic Review*, March 1977 (3, 4, 8)

Mundell, R.A., "The Nature of Policy Choices", Ch. 14 of R.A. Mundell, *International Economics*, Macmillan, New York, 1968 (1, 7)

Musgrave, R.A., "On Measuring Fiscal Performance", *Review of Economics and Statistics*, May 1964 (6)

Noe, Nicholas N., & Furstenberg, George M., "The Upward Bias in the Consumer Price Index Due to Substitution", *Journal of Political Economy*, Nov./Dec. 1972 (1)

Norton, W.E., "Debt Management and Monetary Policy in the United Kingdom", *Economic Journal*, Sept. 1969 (5)

Okun, Arthur M., & Teeters, Nancy H., "The Full Employment Surplus Revisited", *The Brookings Papers on Economic Activity*, No. 1 1970 (6)

Paish, F.W., *Rise and Fall of Incomes Policy*, 2nd Edition. IEA London 1971 (1, 4)

Park, Yung Chul, "Some Current Issues on the Transmission Process of Monetary Policy", *IMF Staff Papers*, March 1972 (3, 4, 5)

Parkin, M., "A 'Monetarist' Analysis of the Generation and Transmission of World Inflation: 1958–71", *American Economic Review*, Feb. 1977 (4, 7)

Patinkin, Don., "Money and Wealth: A Review Article", *Journal of Economic Literature*, Dec. 1969 (3, 4, 5)

Patinkin, Don., "John Maynard Keynes: From the *Tract* to the *General Theory*", *Economic Journal*, June 1975 (3)

Peacock, Alan T., "Giving Advice in Difficult Times", *Three Banks Review*, March 1977 (1)

Peel, D.A., "On the Case for Indexation of Wages and Salaries", *Kyklos*, Vol. 3, Fasc. 2. 1977 (1, 4)

Pepper, G.T., & Wood, G.E., *Too Much Money. . .?* Hobart Paper No. 68. IEA London 1976 (3, 4, 5)

Peston, M.H., "The Tax Mix and Effective Demand", *Public Finance No. 3*, 1971 (6)

Peston, M.H., "The Correlation Between Targets and Instruments", *Economica*, Nov. 1972 (1, 7)

Peston, M.H., *Theory of Macroeconomic Policy*, Philip Allan, Oxford 1974 (1, 6, 7)

Porter, Michael J., "Capital Flows as an Offset to Monetary Policy: The German Experience", *IMF Staff Papers*, July 1972 (5, 7)

Powell, J. Enoch, "Inflation and the Money Supply", *The Banker*, Jan. 1973 (4, 5)

Pratten, C.F., "The Reasons for the Slow Economic Progress of the British Economy", *Oxford Economic Papers*, July 1972 (1, 9)

Pratten, C.F., "The Efficiency of British Industry", *Lloyds Bank Review*, Jan. 1977 (9)

Romans, J.T., "Moral Suasion as an Instrument", *American Economic Review*, Dec. 1966 (1)

Rowan, P.C., "Godley's Law, Godley's Rule and the 'New Cambridge' Macroeconomics", *Banca Nazionale Del Lavoro Quarterly Review*, June 1966 (6)

Schwartz, Anna J., "Why Money Matters", *Lloyds Bank Review*, Oct. 1969 (3)

Shaw, G.K., "Economic Growth: Policies and Constraints" in R.M. Grant and G.K. Shaw (eds) *Current Issues in Economic Policy*, Philip Allen, Oxford, 1975 (9)

Silber, William L., "Fiscal Policy, Tax Structure and the Permanent-Income Hypothesis", *Kyklos*, Vol. XXIV, Fasc. 1. 1971 (5, 6)

Silber, William L., & Polakoff, Murray E., "The Differential Effects of Tight Money: An Econometric Study", *Journal of Finance*, March 1970 (5)

Smith, David, "A Monetary Model of the British Economy 1880–1975", *National Westminster Bank Quarterly Review*, Feb. 1977 (4, 5)

Stein, Jerome L., "Unemployment, Inflation and Monetarism", *American Economic Review*, Dec. 1974 (4)

Stein, Jerome L. (ed), *Monetarism*, North Holland, Amsterdam 1976 (3, 4, 5, 7, 8)

Stewart, S., "The International Competitiveness of the U.K. Economy and The Sterling Exchange Rate: A Note", *Journal of Economic Studies*, Nov. 1976 (9)

Streit, M.E., "The Phillips Curve: Fact or Fancy? – The Example of West Germany", *Weltwirtschaftliches*, No. 4. 1972 (1, 4)

Sumner, M.T., "Fiscal Policy and the Permanent Income Hypothesis", *The Manchester School*, Dec. 1974 (6)

Swoboda, Alexander K., "Monetary Policy under Fixed Exchange Rates: Effectiveness, the Speed of Adjustment and Proper Use", *Economica*, May 1973 (7)

Tobin, James, "Money and Income: Post Hoc Ergo Propter Hoc", *Quarterly Journal of Economics*, May 1970 (3)

Tobin, James, "Inflation and Unemployment", *American Economic Review*, March 1972 (4)

Tsiang, S.C., "The Dynamics of International Capital Flows and Internal and External Balance", *Quarterly Journal of Economics*, May 1975 (7)

Tullock, Gordon, "Can you fool all the people all the time?", *Journal of Money, Credit and Banking*, May 1972 (1, 4)

Tussing, A. Dale, "Can Monetary Policy Influence the Availability of Credit?", *Journal of Finance*, March 1966 (5)

Tylecote, Andrew B., "The Effect of Monetary Policy on Wage Inflation", *Oxford Economic Papers*, July 1975 (4, 5)

Vanderkamp, J., "Inflation: A Simple Friedman Theory with a Phillips Twist", *Journal of Monetary Economics*, Jan. 1976 (4)

Veron, Jack., "The Multiplier Concept and Monetary Restraint", *Quarterly Journal of Economics*, May 1975 (5, 8)

Wagner, John R., "Mr. Burrows and Mr. Silber: A Suggested Interpretation", *Journal of Finance*, Dec. 1975 (7)

Weintraub, E. Roy, "The Microfoundations of Macroeconomics: A Critical Survey", *Journal of Economic Literature*, March 1977 (2)

Wiles, P., "Cost Inflation and the State of Economic Theory", *Economic Journal*, June 1973 (4)

Williams, D., Goodhart, C.A.E., & Gowland, D.H., "Money, Income and Causality: The U.K. Experience", *American Economic Review*, June 1975 (3, 4)

Williamson, J., & Wood, G.E., "The British Inflation: Indigenous or Imported?", *American Economic Review*, Sept. 1976 (4)

Zwick, Burton, "The Adjustment of the Economy to Monetary Changes", *Journal of Political Economy*, Jan./Feb. 1971 (3, 5, 8)

Index